THE SMART GUIDE TO

Bachelorette Parties

By Sharon Naylor

Author of *The Smart Guide to Wedding Weekend Events*

The Smart Guide To Bachelorette Parties

Published by
Smart Guide Publications, Inc.
2517 Deer Chase Drive
Norman, OK 73071
www.smartguidepublications.com

For information, address: Smart Guide Publications, Inc. 2517 Deer Creek Drive, Norman, OK 73071

SMART GUIDE and Design are registered trademarks licensed to Smart Guide Publications, Inc.

International Standard Book Number: 978-0-9785341-0-3

Library of Congress Catalog Card Number: 2011924539
11 12 13 14 15   10 9 8 7 6 5 4 3 2 1

Printed in the United States of America

Cover design: Lorna Llewellyn
Copy Editor: Ruth Strother
Back cover design: Joel Friedlander, Eric Gelb, Deon Seifert
Back cover copy: Eric Gelb, Deon Seifert
Illustrations: Lorna Llewellyn
Indexer: Cory Emberson
Sharon Naylor Photograph: Rich Penrose
V.P./Business Manager: Cathy Barker

For Jen, Pam, Jill, and Madison

ACKNOWLEDGMENTS

A wonderful circle of amazing people helped bring this book to you, and I adore them! First, I must thank my fabulous agent Meredith Hays for leading me into the Smart Guide family with this and future books. I'm thrilled to write for the series. Shane McMurray of TheWeddingReport.com granted access to the latest statistics in the wedding world, and the teams at Caneel Bay, Tao Las Vegas, and so many other gorgeous destinations shared their newest getaway bachelorette party packages with us.

Thanks and hugs to the thousands of brides, bridesmaids, and moms who wrote in with fabulous and funny stories of their own real-life bashes—many of your suggestions, and warnings, are here in these pages.

And, of course, thank you to the Smart Guide team for creating a fantastic series of helpful guides. I'm proud to work with you all.

TABLE OF CONTENTS

INTRODUCTION

The bride is going to *love* the Bachelorette Party you plan for her! And everyone who's lucky enough to get an invitation to this party of yours is going to rave about your party-planning perfection for a long, long time.

You have in your hands the Smart Guide to planning a unique, personalized party the bride is never going to forget. So many websites out there are filled with cliché, been-there-done-that lists and tired themes and games, and that's why so many other parties seem like the same thing over and over again. Your party is going to stand out! And the bride gets the best bachelorette bash anyone's been to in their lives. All thanks to you, when you pick and choose from the collection of inspirations and brand-new offerings found in this book.

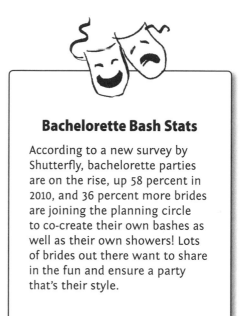

Bachelorette Bash Stats

According to a new survey by Shutterfly, bachelorette parties are on the rise, up 58 percent in 2010, and 36 percent more brides are joining the planning circle to co-create their own bashes as well as their own showers! Lots of brides out there want to share in the fun and ensure a party that's their style.

The very first step toward making this party unforgettable is involving the bride. That's right, she gets a say in the style and theme, and this can be the greatest gift of all. After all, she might have a lot of people—from her parents to her future in-laws to her groom to her vendors—involved with her wedding plans, "suggesting" what they want, overriding what she wants. When you call her up and say, "What do you want?" that can make her very, very happy. She's going to get lots of things her way! What more could a bride want? Of course, you can reserve a few topics as top secret so that she's surprised by some of the plans you pull off, giving her the best of both worlds. You become the best bachelorette bash planner ever!

Her Style Is Key

You have to match the bachelorette party style and theme to the bride. It's a must. If she's not a partier, that bar crawl drink fest isn't going to make her happy. She's going to think you planned that kind of party because it's what *you* wanted—the number one complaint of brides whose friends meant well but didn't match the style to the bride. They didn't know they had options.

This Smart Guide saves you from that party-planning disaster, offering you a collection of different party styles and themes that veer away from the alcohol-fueled, wild, and raunchy party. Here, you'll find spa parties where your guests can get mani/pedis poolside just like celebrities do at their parties, private VIP fashion shows at boutiques that close down just for your group, five-star dinners at the best restaurant in town, surprise tickets to the hottest concert tour of the season, and even girls' getaway bachelorette party trips to Vegas, ski resort towns during celeb-filled film festivals, winery tours, and exotic tropical island resorts for four days in the sun.

And, yes, if the bride wants that shots-and-stripper party with the phallic-shaped cake and raunchy, let-loose wildness, that's in here too!

So before you go any further, do the smart thing and call the bride right now to ask her which kind of party she really and truly wants. Does she want to stay local or get away from it all? Does she want a dress-up night on the town or does she want a more laid-back party? Take notes and let her guide the party's style.

I'm Not Made of Money

Smart party planning is not just all about style, theme, and impressive décor, food, drinks, and dessert. Those are the outward impressions that make the final product a soaring success. Smart planning involves accomplishing that for less money. And this book is your saving grace, with lots of Money Mastery tips scattered throughout the pages, saving you 40–75 percent on different elements of your party and even giving you the inside scoop on how to arrange for some party elements for free.

Bachelorette Bash Stats

According to TheWeddingReport.com, a national bridal industry survey site, the average bachelorette party planner will spend $152 as her share of the party expenses.

If you're a maid of honor or bridesmaid, you're already spending a nice chunk of change for your dress, shoes, the shower, gifts, and so many other required responsibilities in your role as part of the bride's honored inner circle. So you're likely very interested in how to plan a hot party on a budget. It's true that some brides, worried about their bridesmaids' mounting bills, said they didn't want a bachelorette party at all, but they regretted it months later. They really wished they had given the green light to the bash.

The Smart Guide to Bachelorette Parties gets rid of the guilt and saves the bride's dream of sharing a fabulous celebration with her friends.

And it saves you money guilt as well. Not just with money-saving tips, but also by keeping your planning tasks organized within your team so that no one is wasting money. That's one of the top budget-busters out there, and it can stop here.

You may be the planner in charge—the maid of honor, the sister, the local best friend—or you may be part of an equal-power planning group. Whichever your role, you bring a priceless resource to the table in the form of this book, and you *all* get to have more fun, plan smartly and swiftly, and save a nice bit of money. In the end, you're hosting a fantastic, fun, photo-worthy, friend-filled bachelorette party bash that puts all others in the shadows.

Here are some of the tip highlights you're going to find throughout this book:

> ➤ Style Savvy: Tips for making your party elements stylish and sophisticated rather than buying props that look cheap
>
> ➤ Money Mastery: Tips for getting more for less money, without the savings showing to anyone
>
> ➤ No More Drama: Tips for co-planning with bridesmaids and others who might be slow to pay and who are bossy, gossipy, or who have other drama queen qualities and are quick to steamroll their ideas
>
> ➤ Shop Here!: Suggestions on great deals at unexpected websites and store chains
>
> ➤ Steal My Party Idea: Real-life bachelorette party hosts share their celebration inspirations for you to steal or tweak
>
> ➤ Bachelorette Bash Stats: A look at national trends in bachelorette party expenses and ideas

Smart planning equals fun planning! Remember to keep your eyes on the ultimate goal—to make the bride happy—but don't get uptight and anxious about the planning process. Stay calm, keep your sense of humor, and use the tips in this book to help everyone else enjoy the process too; the planning part can be as much fun as the actual party. "We auditioned five male dancers for my sister's party," says one maid of honor, "and one of them was so incredibly cheesy with his orange tan and awkward gyrations! I was dying laughing, but all the other bridesmaids just had these blank looks on their faces. How could they not see the humor in this?!"

Throughout this book, you'll be reminded to dial down the stress factor and not take party planning so seriously. And you'll be able to laugh about the orange, awkward male stripper and the supposed phallic cake that turns out looking more like a palm tree or the Eiffel Tower. That's the priceless stuff behind the scenes, the stories the bride will love hearing about—and seeing photos and videos of—later.

Now let's start planning the party!

PART ONE

Party Planning Basics

CHAPTER 1

Who's Involved

In This Chapter

➤ Choosing a team leader

➤ Including the moms

➤ Assigning planning tasks

➤ Making the guest list

In this chapter, you'll name the members of your party-planning team and decide on which roles they will play, which tasks they will take on, and how you'll work together on the large and small details of the celebration. Once the team is established, the next part of the *Who's Involved* question is creating a guest list, and here is where you'll make that all-important list of names that determines the party's size and cost.

Who's the Leader

Traditionally, the maid of honor headed up the bachelorette party planning group, and the bridesmaids were her "supporting staff." Now, since we live in a global society with many friends and relatives living in different cities, states, and countries, it might not be the maid of honor leading the team. Perhaps she lives far, far away and is wildly busy with her career, her kids, studying for professional exams, and any number of other important responsibilities. So the party plans might fall to a bridesmaid, a sister, or a friend who's not even in the bridal party.

Without the traditional model to rely on, it's now a very important step to decide who's going to lead the way and be the chief organizer of the party-planning circle. And that circle might include both bridesmaids and non-bridesmaids, friends and family members who have never met before and who live in different cities, states, and countries.

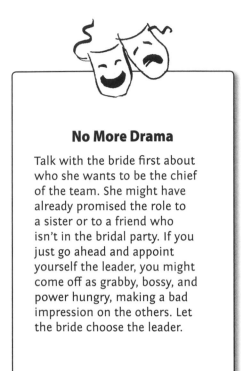

No More Drama

Talk with the bride first about who she wants to be the chief of the team. She might have already promised the role to a sister or to a friend who isn't in the bridal party. If you just go ahead and appoint yourself the leader, you might come off as grabby, bossy, and power hungry, making a bad impression on the others. Let the bride choose the leader.

So it's going to take a little bit of work to make sure that your group has a structure, a leader, and a team that can operate under a great system of communication. This is where you begin your smart planning by setting the roles in motion and letting the other ladies know that you're taking the lead with the planning, that is if you want to be the leader.

Bear in mind that every successful team needs a leader, or else everyone's conflicting ideas and demands turn quickly into chaos. When that kind of jockeying for position begins, plans get added, prices soar, and work efforts may double. So if the well-meaning bride who just wants peace says you should all plan together, just show her this book and let her know that a leader is essential.

Traits and Duties of a Good Leader

The leader brings ideas to the bride, organizes the plans, makes sure deadlines are met, and ensures other crucial tasks that keep the party-planning wheels moving are being completed. The leader doesn't make all the decisions; she monitors and motivates so that planning this bash is truly a team effort.

That said, your elected leader has to have great diplomatic skills, organizational prowess, and the time to devote to planning a party. Be honest now. Are you the best person for that top position? If you're crushed for time, you might wish to tell the bride you're 100 percent on board as a supporting member of the group, and you'd like to take the lead on tasks *a, b,* and *c.* But perhaps that friend of hers who's really great with people would be better for the lead position.

Here's a little secret for smart planning: it can be better if the other co-planners don't know the leader all that well; that they're not related, they haven't grown up together, gone to school together, or worked together. Why is this? Sometimes people feel more comfortable walking all over those they're used to overriding. They know who's nice, who's a pushover, and who's going to take their side in a debate. If you're a satellite friend who no one knows that well, the other co-planners won't know how to "work you," and that could be the perfect formula for being the leader. So don't automatically assume that the leader has to be someone who's everyone's best friend. Your outsider status could be a brilliant perk.

Moms On Board?

Yes, it's true. Since many moms may be bumped from the wedding plans when brides and grooms choose to work on their plans as a team, today's moms often love to join in the fun and excitement of planning additional wedding events. The bride, not knowing how to appease a demanding mom-in-law who wants to turn her Tuscan-inspired outdoor wedding into a crystal-dripping country club affair, might offer her mother-in-law the chance to plan a breakfast or the rehearsal dinner. And some brides who don't choose the racier bachelorette party think it's a fine idea for their groom's mom, their mom, or a stepmom to help plan their spa-party bachelorette bash.

The challenge here is authority. You can probably handle a bossy bridesmaid who's constantly e-mailing with her ideas, but you might feel a bit jittery about shooting down the groom's mom's country club dreams. Now not all moms are steamrollers. Most recognize that they're a part of the team, not the automatic team captain, and they're all too happy to work on any projects you send their way. But if the mom in question thinks she's automatically in charge, it's going to take a gentle reminder in the form of a phone call—so that she can hear the friendliness in your voice—introducing yourself as the person in charge of the party and asking her what interests she has and which tasks she would like to work on. She'll get the picture. If she tries to claim choosing the location or setting the menu, all you have to do is let her know that you'll be working on those things as a committee.

Let the Bride Announce It

When the bride decides who's going to be the leader of the team, it works best, and avoids most drama and conflict, if she sends out an e-mail introducing everyone to the person—perhaps you—who will be in charge of the bachelorette party plans. She'll tell everyone to expect an e-mail from that person soon, and she'll tell everyone how excited she is to join the planning group and have a great time at the party.

If you're the leader, you'll then reach out to all your co-planners via e-mail as well, say hello, assure everyone that you're looking forward to working with them, invite them to e-mail you with what they want to work on or to suggest any vendors they've worked with on their own weddings. And you'll let them know you have this book, so you're well-armed with lots of planning ideas and budget savers. If you know the date and style of the party the bride wants, now's when you let everyone know what she has chosen.

If you're able to meet in person with local co-planners, now's a good time to ask for dates that work for everyone in the following two weeks. You're showing consideration for their schedules, which is always a smart start for the team's leader.

No More Drama

You might have a few skittish co-planners in your group, those who have been a part of a chaotic, "mean girls" circle of bridesmaids or co-planners, so this introductory e-mail from you can put them at ease. When they see that you're not going to be a tyrant like the last maid of honor, bridesmaid, or sister they worked under, they'll relax, defenses will go down, and work will be able to begin on the party in smooth comfort with one another.

Money Mastery

Entertainment agencies are companies that offer a variety of entertainment options for various events. Besides male dancers, an entertainment agency may do bookings for musicians, comedians, magicians, and other acts. Many wedding coordinators are familiar with these agencies and can direct you to one that is reputable.

What Do You Want to Do?

It's wise to let the co-planners know that you want to know what they want to work on. Some may wish to scout locations for the party. Some may know of a great entertainment agency where they have booked male dancers for other bachelorette parties. Some may be crafty and will make the invitations or favors. And some may wish to cook, bake, run the games, or handle all manner of additional tasks.

Rather than pitch an open question of "What would you like to do?" it's far more efficient to e-mail out a list that looks like this one: *"Hello! As we get started on the party plans, I'd love to know which tasks you'd like to work on:*

➤ Make invitations

➤ Address and send invitations

➤ Shop for décor

➤ Research party locations

➤ Talk to caterers

➤ Create menu

➤ Research cake bakers

➤ Attend cake tasting

➤ Research entertainers

➤ Create bar menu

➤ Shop for liquor

➤ Choose games

➤ Make game cards

➤ Set up for the party

➤ Run the games

➤ Clean up

Thanks so much!"

The ladies can simply e-mail you back with their choices, and you then have instantly-created teams of people who will work on each task. Tell those who live far away that they can participate in research tasks by searching online, if they'd like. And they can make and ship any crafts they'd like to work on. It's always a great sign to them when you take the long-distance co-planners into consideration.

Creating the Guest List

Guest lists for bachelorette parties are best kept on the small side. Not everyone who's invited to the wedding needs to be invited to this party, which is traditionally kept to just a VIP list of the bride's closest friends, sisters, and bridesmaids. This keeps costs down, obviously, but it also makes important issues like transportation easier. Think about the fact that twelve people can fit in a stretch limo comfortably; twenty people would require two limos. If your guest list totals thirty or so people, your transportation will almost certainly need to be a pricier party bus.

Now if your location doesn't require transportation, your guest list can be larger, according to your budget. For instance, an at-home party might welcome twenty to forty guests. There's plenty of room at your place for a buffet spread and cocktails for forty!

Again, this decision is up to the bride, and many party planners wait to get the guest list first before making any decisions about where the party will be held or what the menu will be. The bride hands over her list, you see the fifteen names on it, and you can then search for a restaurant that would be perfect for your smaller group. It doesn't work as well the other way around, because restaurant and caterer bookings require a head count.

Money Mastery

Before you assign tasks, tell each planner that she needs to let everyone know the prices of the items and services she's looking at before she makes any purchases, so that the group has some say in the expenses they're splitting. If a notoriously monied planner wants to spend hundreds on a cake, the more budget-crunched will surely vote for a less ornate version. Tell the group that they agree to others' veto power if they want to split all costs evenly, or the group can decide to pay for their own purchases...and then the entire group still splits the bigger costs of catering, the bar tabs and transportation. Open a dialogue to see if they all like having the freedom to foot the bills for their own tasks—still with group approval regarding style—or if they prefer to split everything evenly. We'll get deeper into the money issue in Chapter 3. This is simply an important rule to set for planners choosing their tasks.

No More Drama

The bride is the one who gets to wade through the tricky diplomacy of "if I invite this friend, then I have to invite those friends." She knows best who has the sensitive soul and would be offended by being left off the list, and you might not be aware that her best friend/cousin will be in town that weekend. So leave the guest list creation up to her.

Who Makes the Cut?

The bride undoubtedly has a collection of close friends she would never dream of leaving off the list. She may then have some B-list friends who can be added to the list if the plans and budget allow. She's used to the tier system of listing guest names according to musts and maybes, since she used the very same system for creating her wedding guest list.

One important consideration when it comes to the guest list is the style of the party. If the raunchy factor is going to be high—with male dancers, lots of drinking, phallic-shaped necklaces and props, and off-color T-shirt slogans—some care needs to be taken with regard to the bride's more conservative friends— and her fifteen-year-old sister and her mom and the groom's mom. Some brides say they want that wild party, but they wouldn't be comfortable if the groom's sisters saw her throwing back hard drinks and taking a twirl on a stripper pole, dancing with the stripper, and accepting drinks from guys in a bar.

Steal My Party Idea

"I didn't want his sisters to see how hard my friends can party, so I requested that the group dinner be one night, with them all invited. Then, we planned the wilder party for a different night," says Tracy, a recent bride. "We completely avoided that awkward departing for the second phase of the night that I'd experienced before, when the people who weren't included in the clubbing could tell that the rest of us were off to someplace amazing. This way, no one's feelings were hurt, and I wasn't worried at all. The moms and my groom's little sister were at the dinner, as were our grandmothers who got a kick out of being invited to a bachelorette party. And the next weekend, my friends and I hit the town and went a little bit crazy. It was perfect." Lila, bridesmaid

So here's the solution: a two-part celebration. For phase one of the evening, all those on the guest list—including moms and underage sisters—join the group for a lovely dinner out. They feast on a fine meal and have a spectacular time. After the meal, with full understanding that the racier part of the evening is ahead of the group, the moms and kids head home while everyone else departs for phase two: the hotel suite where the X-rated décor is set up and where the male dancer will perform.

Tame Party Guest Lists

Of course, if there's no stripper pole, male dancer, or phallic-shaped cakes, then the entire issue of guest sensitivity is eliminated, and the bride may have a fabulously easy time of creating her guest list without worry.

For a spa party, brunch, ski trip, winery tour, or other exciting outing, the only consideration for the bride is the etiquette of sending invitations to those who live far away. When sending out wedding invitations, she may have chosen to send courtesy invitations to those who live far away, even though they'd never be able to attend, thus avoiding the diplomatic nightmare of leaving out extended family. For this party, though, she is released from the must-invite pressures and can send invitations to faraway friends and relatives she most wants to come. If they can make it—great. Many people miss their long-distance friends terribly if they've moved away for work or love, and they see these events as a great reason to plan a trip to get together with old friends. Some people use their vacation days to do so!

If they cannot attend, the bride has done them the honor of including them, which is very much appreciated. Again, this one is for the bride to decide.

And if the party centers around an activity like skiing, the bride can even include guests who do not ski. They can tour the area, go shopping, enjoy the spa, and otherwise have a wonderful time while the rest of the group is on the slopes. So remind the bride that activity-centered parties can welcome all of her guests, so that she doesn't turn her back on her wished-for ski weekend just because her future sisters-in-law aren't skiers.

Destination Party Guest Lists

If the bride wishes to plan a getaway party in which all of her friends fly with her to Vegas or to a spa in Arizona, a tropical beach on St. John, or even to Disney World (which is a wildly popular bachelorette party locale for those who wish to go young rather than go wild), she'll test the waters to see if her friends would be able to attend a getaway party considering the cost of airfare and hotel reservations. It can be quite pleasantly surprising how few have . . . reservations about the plan.

Money Mastery

As you discuss a getaway party with the bride, remind her that many airlines and hotels grant special event discount fares if you have more than ten people in your group. Many throw in discount rental cars as well. So she doesn't need to keep the invitation list ultrasmall unless she wishes to. There may be a great financial incentive to invite twenty friends along.

Guest List Troubleshooting

You can solve the most common bachelorette party guest list dilemmas by following some troubleshooting steps.

The Add-On

Problem: One of the bride's close friends e-mails to ask if she can bring a friend to the party, someone who doesn't know the bride, so that she will know someone there. You don't have room in the budget, and the dinner reservations are already set.

Solution: Use the same diplomacy the bride uses when she gets a pushy response card saying, "I'm bringing a date" when no such option was given on the invitation. Just call the person to say, "I'm so sorry to say that I can't allow any extra guests, since we're already at full capacity and everything's set. Don't worry about not knowing anyone there! We're a friendly bunch, and of course the bride is going to love having time to spend with you."

Problem: That pushy friend responds that she can only attend if you let her invite that guest since she is her ride.

Solution: Talk to the bride. Not in a gossipy or complaining way, but just to find out what the bride suggests as a smart solution. Allow the additional guest or confirm your previous response with the explanation that you can't allow one person to bring a friend, or everyone else will get angry that they couldn't bring someone along. If she can't come, sorry.

Problem: The bride's mother has invited her friends along without permission, and now she says she can't uninvite them because that would be rude.

Solution: Handle her rudeness yourself and spare the bride the frustration of this one. Call the bride's mother to explain that the plans have already been made to accommodate the guest list the bride created, and that the bride has her heart set on this being a party just for her own closest friends. Explain that there were many friends the bride didn't invite, and you'd hate for her to be upset that people she doesn't know are at her party. Suggest that the mother invite her friends to the morning-after breakfast or other event for which she is the host, so that they can enjoy her fabulous party-planning style.

Problem: You haven't heard back from someone you sent an invitation to, and the party is just a few days away.

Solution: Call that person directly to ask if she's coming to the party. Sometimes e-mail responses get lost in the ether or go into your

No More Drama

Make it a rule that no one on your planning team will post anything about the party on Facebook, Twitter, or any other social site where the bride's other friends could see details of the party preparations, much less figure out where the party will take place. It's a smarter move to keep the plans quiet for the sake of a manageable guest list.

spam file, and sometimes people just get distracted and forget to respond. Make a friendly call to each and every nonresponder and finalize the guest head count.

Problem: Word got out about the party, and now the bride's friends are contacting you to ask if they can come.

Solution: Explain that this is just one private party that you've arranged for the bride. Its style and location require the small guest list that you have, and you are unable to open a can of worms by allowing extra guests when you're sharing planning responsibilities and expenses with the other hosts. Encourage those other friends to plan something special that they can do with the bride as their own celebration. There's no rule saying the bride can celebrate only once!

CHAPTER 2

The Perfect Timing

Timing is everything, right? In this chapter, you're going to tackle the two most important issues when it comes to picking the right date and time for your party. The first is choosing a day that works for the bride. If she's booked on the day you've chosen, it would be a disaster. If she's ultra-busy with wedding plans, exhausted, or even out of town for work, that too would be disastrous. So the first element of your smart planning is getting the date right.

The second element is choosing the right time for your chosen style of party, and while it might seem obvious that dinners at night and daytime is right for a spa party by the pool, there are some tricky issues when it comes to time of day and what guests expect—and you'll get the solutions here.

Check in with the Bride

Bachelorette parties are most often not planned as a surprise for the bride. After all, the weeks prior to her wedding are usually the most hectic of all. She may have booked appointments with her caterer, or she may have the final fitting on her gown planned for that day. She may have a thousand things to do for the big day, and she may also be working triple-time to complete all of her work projects so that she can take time off for her honeymoon. You wouldn't want the frazzled bride to show up at your house thinking she's just popping in to pick something up with plenty of time to race to her fitting, only to discover all of her best friends wearing hot pink boas and handing her a strong martini, ready to party until the sun comes up. That's going to put her into a sweat.

Steal My Party Idea

"I let my bridesmaids know that I would be studying for the bar exam the month before my wedding, and I wasn't going to have one spare minute during that time. I didn't even want phone calls from anyone, that's how busy I would be. But we set the party for the weekend *after* my test when I could relax."
—Felicia, bride

No, the best course of action is to let *her* choose the day for her bachelorette party. She knows her schedule and with lots of advance notice can block off two days for the celebration—one for the party and one for the day after to recover from the party! The day after is a big deal. The bride may have appointments in the morning with her wedding vendors, and she may even have Sunday morning breakfast with her in-laws already planned. She will not enjoy going to her future mother-in-law's house with a pounding headache and feeling nauseated. The bride can steer her breakfast plans and all other obligations clear of her bachelorette bash.

Others' Big Days

You'll also want to make sure you're steering clear of other people's big days . . . their weddings, their own bridal showers, or the tests they're studying for. Take the lead and e-mail all of your co-planners right away to ask them for their blocked-off days *before* you and the bride plan the party date.

Speaking of big days, you don't want to plan your bachelorette party during the same weekend as the bridal shower. The bride might know when her shower is, but she might not. So if you're not in the wedding party, take the time to reach out to the maid of honor or a bridesmaid you know to be sure you get the all clear on the date the bride has chosen for her bachelorette party. It would be war if you were to snag the day and wreck the shower.

How Far in Advance

In addition to choosing the right day for the party, you need to determine how far in advance of the wedding you need to start planning. Bachelorette parties may best be planned for different lengths of time before the wedding. Take into account, for instance, that a getaway bachelorette party—that weekend on an island—may be far more affordable during the off-peak season. If the wedding is in June, you and the other co-planners may save thousands of dollars if you plan a trip during the first weeks of May before prices double. A spa party, on the other hand, may be a welcome diversion for the bride the weekend before the wedding when she most needs to de-stress and spend quality time with her friends.

Here's a primer on the most common prewedding timing of the top styles of parties:

➤ The Girls' Getaway to a resort destination: One to three months prior to the wedding

➤ The Spa Party: One to two weeks prior to the wedding, unless the bride requests a date that is a month or so earlier to accommodate her schedule

➤ The Dinner Party: Two weeks prior to the wedding is the most common date chosen for this style of party, again to give the bride that fun night out with her friends so she can de-stress before the wedding

➤ The Dinner Party, Weekday-Style: If the bride and all of her closest friends live in the same hometown, it may work out beautifully for you to plan this dinner event for a Thursday night or other non-busy weekday

Money Mastery

Holiday weekends may be when everyone's in town and able to attend a party for the bride. But for travel- and restaurant-based parties, prices may be elevated due to the special calendar day. So perhaps it would be better to host your dinner party at your place—and show off your fabulous home—rather than spend 30 percent more for your party plans at a restaurant that just raised its menu and bar pricing.

➤ The "We've Got Tickets!" Party: If your party will center around the biggest concert of the year, a Broadway play, or other big event, then your event happens whenever *that* happens. Let's say that Michael Bublé, the bride's favorite singer, will be in town three months before the wedding. You can grab group tickets for the show, and her party will take place then! There's no rule saying this bash has to happen within a month before the big day

➤ The Wild and Racy Bar Crawl: Again, the bride needs to pick this day out for her two-day block of available time, but this type of party most often happens two to four weeks before the wedding day

The Right Time of Day

There's an etiquette to the timing of parties, and it has to do with what guests expect as far as whether or not they'll get a meal. Brides navigate this issue too when it comes to planning their reception styles—dinner, cocktail party, etc.—so here are the smart rules for planning your party's start time:

➤ Brunches start at 11 am

➤ Luncheons start at noon

➤ Tea parties and high tea start at 3 pm or 4 pm

➤ Dinner parties start anywhere from 6 pm to 9 pm, depending on your crowd's style

➤ Cocktail parties start anywhere from 7 pm to 9 pm

➤ Dinner first, then club-hopping events start at 6 pm

➤ Spa parties by the pool start at 3 pm, after peak daytime sun

If your party plans include tickets to see a concert, play, or other performance, set your preshow dinner for two hours prior to the show so that you all have plenty of time to eat, drink, and relax together. If your dinner location is close to the theater or stadium where the show will take place, you can expect the crush of the show crowd to slow down service. So set your dinner start time for two and a half hours prior to the show.

Where's the drama in the timing of your party? It all has to do with dinnertime. Let's say you've planned a cocktail party at your place starting at 6 pm You have lots of pretty platters of light appetizers and finger foods as the perfect cocktail party fare. The problem occurs when guests show up hungry, expecting dinner. To them, 6 pm is dinnertime. You might be one who eats dinner at 7 pm, but they don't know that. With the liquor flowing, those hungry guests are going to get tipsy fast. When your party starts at 7 pm, and you include in your invitation that light cocktail party fare will be provided, everyone knows to eat dinner beforehand.

Always provide information on what to expect as far as food whenever you plan your party for the late afternoon to evening hours. Cocktail parties are the most confusing for party guests, and it's a smart move by any host to spread the word that there will not be a sit-down meal at your soiree.

How Long Do Parties Last?

You don't have to put an end time on your invitations for most styles of parties. A fabulous dinner party at your home can stretch on until midnight when everyone's sated and socializing. That night-clubbing crawl doesn't have to end when the limo drops you all off back at your place or the bride's house; everyone can keep the party going until dawn there, snacking on late-night fare and hitting the liquor cabinet, or

Steal My Party Idea

"Several of the bride's friends drove for hours to attend the party, and I wanted to make sure they could hang out and talk after the official party closed down and others went home. So I stocked up on the kinds of snacks we all used to enjoy in college—a pizza (this time, organic), nachos, a cheese ring from Entenmann's. And it was the most fabulous after-party! Even if all the girls had stayed, I would have had enough fun late-night snacks." —Lauren, bridesmaid

firing up the espresso maker instead. And who knows how long Michael Bublé is going to sing at his concert?

You can certainly put an end time for brunch and tea parties as a thoughtful service to guests who have busy schedules and things to do after the party. Indicating on the invitation that the party will be from 2 pm to 4 pm lets them know they can still get all of their weekend To-Do's done.

It is important for you to think about the ending hours of the party and decide what you wish to have on hand in case guests want to extend the celebration.

CHAPTER 3

 # What's Your Budget?

In This Chapter

> Decide on your priorities

> Decide how you'll split the costs

> Create a budget chart

> Offer money-crunched planners free alternatives

> Say no to wildy expensive ideas

Everyone may have big ideas for the party, but your budget is going to make many of the decisions for you. If any of your co-planners are bridesmaids, they already have big expenses ahead of them, and everyone else has money issues of their own. Some may have more expendable cash and others are hoping to pull off a great party for pennies.

Your planning group needs to talk about money right up front. What you'll spend, what you'll spend it on, and how you'll divide the costs. This chapter will start you off with smart strategies to tackle the cash topic from the very beginning, so money dilemmas don't pop up along the way.

Create Your Money Priority List

As a group, decide which elements of the party are the most important for the bride's happiness and the success of the celebration. Will it be a gourmet meal? A top-shelf bar? A stay at a great resort? A fabulous cake? These items will get the largest portion of your budget, such as a full 50 percent of the money devoted to the catering and cake, and 50 percent covering everything else.

If you're communicating with the rest of the group via e-mail, here's the smartest way to organize this essential first step: You explain that a priority list will help you all choose the top three items that will get the biggest cash investment, and then you provide a starter list, which might include catering, cake, and drinks. You'll then ask the others if they agree, and invite them to submit their choices. Some may send in a vote for a stripper or a limo, and those will be added to the priority list. Nothing's ranked yet, but you know what's to be discussed at the next stage.

Next is deciding what's not going to be on your must list, the things that can be minimized or made on the cheap, or that can be eliminated from the plans altogether. Some items that often end up on the chopping block are décor balloons, extra desserts beyond the cake, and those X-rated décor items that many guests find amusing for a minute and are then forgotten. Your co-planners will feel much better about this no-buy list, giving their wallets a breather.

How to Divide Expenses

This next step is that awkward one that the loaded issue of money presents—especially when you're not close friends with the other party hosts. It's time to choose your payment plan. To help you decide on the smartest plan for your group, here are the most common payment scenarios:

Everyone splits the entire totaled cost of the party equally.

This is actually quite tricky, since the friend who books the entertainer might wind up spending $200 more to get the better plan, another friend might book the party bus without first checking in with the group, and then everyone else is stuck absorbing one-sixth of a much bigger total than they expected—or have the money for.

This plan works best if one chief planner is doing the actual shopping and booking, always with the mind-set of keeping costs as low as possible. She'll work off of the priority list to invest more in that catering, cake, and drinks, and take the inexpensive road with the decorations.

Everyone agrees to split the costs of the high-priority items, and then each pays for her own detail.

This is the plan that often works best when co-planners have differing financial situations. Everyone agrees to divide the costs of the catering, cake, and spa professionals, and then those who volunteered to make invitations, favors, and décor pay for their own responsibilities.

Money Mastery

Keep these solo expenses under a set amount of money, such as $30, as a point of fairness for all volunteers. You'd be surprised at the number of party planners who take on the décor task, then pout and complain that they spent $200. When you set a cap, you keep expenses down for all.

Here's another smart party-planning secret: as a group, decide on plan B options for each and every expense category. Let's say the friend in charge of the cake discovers that the tiered cake shaped like a Tiffany ring box costs $300. Rather than overspend, she knows to go to the plan B you've all agreed on: a simple circular cake with white chocolate filling and smooth icing, with a faux Tiffany box placed on top and blue icing "pearls" piped around the edges of the cake. It's elegant and inexpensive, fitting into the budget at a sweet $40.

Making a Budget

You'll find a budget chart in the back of this book with all of the party-planning categories listed alongside space for recording your estimated and actual expenses. At the start of your plans, you'll all agree on a price range for each item from the catering to the cake to the spa party manicurist. This range serves to keep planners' spending controlled, with each seeing that only $100 to $200 is budgeted for liquor, so forget about those bottles of Dom Pérignon.

It's a smart move to pre-research some of these expenses, so ask everyone to start checking out the prices of the services you're considering, such as spa experts, bartenders for your at-home party, limos, party buses, restaurants. Everyone can simply e-mail you the sites that they've found, or forward expert quotes to

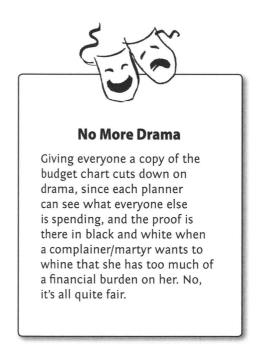

No More Drama

Giving everyone a copy of the budget chart cuts down on drama, since each planner can see what everyone else is spending, and the proof is there in black and white when a complainer/martyr wants to whine that she has too much of a financial burden on her. No, it's all quite fair.

you. With a team of researchers handling one or two elements apiece, this task gets done quickly—in as short as a week. For the sake of efficiency, give them a deadline for giving you the numbers.

You then fill out the budget chart in the back of this book with those estimate ranges, and e-mail scanned copies of it to each of your co-planners. Now, everyone knows what's being spent where.

For further organization of your budget chart, highlight the expenses that the group will split, and let everyone know that you will send an updated chart once you start booking sites and pros, and placing orders.

An important consideration is whose credit card goes on file at each of the bars and restaurants you'll be visiting. Talk to the group to find out who wants to be the one who has her card charged at each place, then arrange for each co-planner to pay back her share of the balance. This *has* to be agreed upon right at the beginning. Leaving this important detail forgotten is one of the biggest party-planning don'ts and can spell disaster when you're all out at the clubs and your card gets declined, or when everyone else claims poverty and your card gets abused all night. Talk about it. It's the smart thing to do, so that everyone can start clearing room on their cards before the party.

The No-Money List

Money-crunched co-planners love the no-money list! Since time is as precious a commodity as money these days, a co-planner who doesn't have $50 to contribute to the bar expenses can "work off" her financial share by taking on several labor-based tasks, doing that research legwork, and taking on time-consuming tasks that the others might be too busy to handle. When this co-planner volunteers to complete any number of the busy-work tasks, her contribution is worth more than money.

"People pay wedding coordinators to do these extra time-consuming tasks," says maid of honor Talia. "So when one of the girls offered to do all of the shopping, crafting, and calling guests for their RSVPs, it was a fantastic freedom for all of us, and a smart way for her to contribute. It was perfect."

Here are some of the top no-money contributions that anyone in your planning group—including you—can claim as her free share of the responsibilities:

➤ Researching sites and touring restaurants, gardens, spas, and all other locales

➤ Researching caterers and attending tastings to report back on menu ideas

➤ Researching vendors on bridal website reviews

➤ Researching rental agencies and figuring out what items are needed for rentals

➤ Calling contacts to get first-person recommendations of who to hire for this party

➤ Researching transportation companies and arranging the limo or party bus rides with copies of the itinerary (provided in the back of this book)

➤ Researching destination girls' getaway resorts and flight deals

➤ Talking with resort event planners to organize the details of your group's visit

➤ Shopping for DIY project supplies

➤ Making décor items

➤ Making party favors

➤ Making the invitations

➤ Sending the invitations

➤ Being in charge of RSVPs and calling nonresponders

➤ Shopping for all menu, cake, and bar supplies

➤ Cooking and baking for the party

➤ Arranging fun games to play at the party and being the game leader

➤ Overseeing rentals deliveries and setup

➤ Set up for the party

➤ Clean for the party

➤ Overseeing rentals pickup

Money Mastery

You'll find lots of budget-saving tips throughout this book for the entire group's smart spending in every category.

Saying No to a Wildly Expensive Proposed Plan

Just about every bachelorette party-planning group faces at least one suggestion for a wildly expensive idea proposed by a co-planner, a mom, or even a party vendor. Some members of your planning group may have more expendable money and more expensive tastes, so it may be up to you to reject that pricy plan without creating a new world war among your co-planners.

A smart way to say no when a pricy idea about a location is e-mailed to the group is to write right back—even if you're not the planning captain—with this message: "That sounds great, but I think it's a bit above the budget we have! How about we talk about going to X, Y, or Z instead? They're a lot closer to us, and I've heard from friends that they throw in a lot of free stuff for bachelorette party groups."

It's not enough just to say no to an idea; you have to send out two or three alternatives, the reason you're suggesting them, and what the benefits are, including freebies. If you just say, "That's too expensive," the group is left with nothing concrete to discuss.

So put that office diplomacy to work with a compliment opener, suggest additional ideas that may work better for everyone's budget, timing, and travel comfort, and many of the other planners will be grateful that you took the lead in getting the group to a more affordable, yet still fantastic, plan.

CHAPTER 4

What's Your Location?

> ## In This Chapter
>
> ➤ Your party site's musts
> ➤ Choosing a site on the town
> ➤ Choosing a location for your spa party
> ➤ Hosting at home
> ➤ Choosing a destination party site
> ➤ Making the bride's dream come true

The location you choose for your party will determine many of its greatest moments. For instance, if you're all in Las Vegas, you might find yourselves in a celebrity-packed VIP room at one of the hottest nightclubs in town. A beachfront restaurant could place your party in front of a stunning, colorful sunset with dolphins playing out in the ocean. A party at your home allows you the privacy and freedom to get wild.

In this section, you'll explore the perks and pitfalls of various locations, and you'll learn the smartest steps to booking your ideal party place.

First, consider what style you'd like for your party venue. Use a checklist like this one to help you search for your setting:

> ➤ ____ Privacy
> ➤ ____ Enough time (a five-hour time limit, unlimited access to your space)
> ➤ ____ Beautiful scenery (outdoor views, oceanfront, city lights, gardens)
> ➤ ____ Wait staff and servers
> ➤ ____ Tables, chairs, banquet tables

➤ _____ Modern décor (such as an elite day spa with a water wall and great lighting)

➤ _____ In-house catering

➤ _____ No age restrictions if you'll have guests under age twenty-one (they won't be allowed into bars and casinos)

➤ _____ Easy access (public transportation means out-of-town guests won't need to rent cars to get around)

➤ _____ Other:

➤ _____ Other:

➤ _____ Other:

You're looking for an attractive party space that is clean and inviting. Since privacy is the first item on this list, consider if this is one of your top priorities. Will you be happy with your party being one of five that a hotel has going on at the same time? Will you require a private party room at a restaurant, or would your group enjoy sitting at a long table in the midst of all other diners, attracting attention with each of your toasts and cheers for the bride? (Single party guests say they like to be out in the open, where they get to scope the room for attractive men!) Will your wild bunch be best kept to a private suite at a hotel, or would your home be the ideal setting for either a quiet, cozy dinner or a crazier, liquor-fueled bash?

Compare your party group's personality to the locations you're considering for the party and choose wisely so that no one winds up in trouble or thrown out onto the street for disturbing other patrons.

Out on the Town

Parties out on the town might stay in one place, such as at a fine restaurant or jazz club, or they might be a succession of stops at eateries and bars. Your task as party host or co-planner is to ensure that the location or locations you choose meet your group's needs.

At a restaurant, a group of twenty or more might not be seated in the main dining area. You might have to book a private dining room, and if you haven't done so weeks before the party, you may be turned away at the door. So your search begins with making phone calls about each establishment's dining group size.

Your circle of party planners becomes invaluable when they can suggest the best bars and clubs, knowing as they do which nightspots are hot on a Friday night and which are hotter on Saturday. They may also provide an inside scoop on which restaurants treat their special party groups well, as opposed to restaurants that are snootier and less welcoming to larger parties.

Style Savvy

A private party room gets you a dedicated team of servers who may be better able to time your meal courses, provide you smoother service, give you VIP treatment, and many restaurants will throw in a complimentary treat. At a jazz club, for instance, your group may be presented with after-dinner shots of dessert plum wine, gratis. Yes, big groups get that auto-tip added in, but the privacy and elevated service make it more special for the bride. Far better than waiting an hour for hectic servers in a crowded restaurant dining room and sharing space with another bachelorette party!

Barhopping

Ideally, your barhopping route will be located in a town that has multiple bars and clubs within walking distance. Your group dances and drinks at one club, and then when the scene starts to fizzle, you walk down the block to the next happening club and continue the party there.

One thing may slow you down, though: the velvet rope. Some clubs are so popular that fire codes require them to limit their patrons. Lines form outside the club, and burly bouncers determine who gets to step inside. Bachelorette party planners may pre-empt the buzz kill wait in line by visiting the club ahead of time to acquire or purchase VIP access passes that some clubs hand out for group parties. Bar managers will want to see the invitation to make sure you're truly a party group, so bring one along, or print out your Evite, as proof.

Transportation is an issue for this style of party, so decide if your location will require the constant service of a limo that waits outside of each stop and brings you to the next one miles away. That's included in a three- to five-hour limo package, so you are free to have the driver take you in style to each stop. Or, your location of clubs clustered within walking distance might allow the more affordable plan of a limo drop-off at the first stop, then a separate limo pick up at the last stop. That can cost hundreds less.

Special-Event Outing

If your group will attend a concert or show, you'll be primarily in one place for most of the evening, but dinner is usually a key part of the preshow activities. Your limo or ride can drop you off at a restaurant that's clear across town to keep you clear of the preshow dinner crowd close to the theater—again, you'll assess the restaurant for its private dining area requirements, a fabulous and varied menu, attractive décor, and fine service to make this a fabulous dining experience for the bride and her guests.

Later in this book, you'll delve more into the selection of a fabulous restaurant for that party style; for now, your concern is the location itself. Can your guests get to the restaurant on their own? Is the restaurant accessible by public transportation, affordable taxi (as opposed to a twenty-minute, pricy taxi ride from the train station), or by car? Will everyone need to come to your place and hop into that limo?

Chapter 5 will help you master the money angle of booking a limousine or party bus, so don't fear that your party will be stuck in a two-block radius! You're simply considering the logistics of where you'd like to take the party during this special celebration. It's often not advisable to dine right next door to the theater, since hundreds of other show goers may pack the place, leading to frustrating service and increased prices.

Spa Party Site

Will you choose an on-site spa party, with your group taking over the entire salon or spa? Or will you invite spa experts to work their magic at your home, or at another party host's home, which has been transformed into a calming oasis of soothing décor and soft music, with green tea spritzers and fresh, fruity smoothies on the menu?

Here is where you'll begin and complete your search for the perfect pampering party location.

Go Where You Know

Never choose a spa or salon that you haven't experienced personally, or that isn't on a co-planner's speed dial. Any establishment can create an attractive image on its website, with photos that are several years old, or styled, or perhaps not even of that particular branch. Bachelorette party groups have been hoodwinked in the past by misleading advertising, and they show up to a dilapidated, less-than-clean salon filled with less-than-professional professionals.

Due to the importance of this party, you'll want to select the newest, cleanest, most indulgent spa with the greatest number of pampering services. And that's another factor of choosing the location of this spa party. At the salon, your guests will have access to the spa's equipped rooms. So that means they can enjoy hot stone massages, steam or sauna room visits, or pedicures in rooms with a full water wall and sound system. A spa party held at your house means the experts simply bring their pedicure kits and massage tables to your place. The treatments will be indulgent, yes, but the environment at the spa could make your group feel like they've taken a trip to a five-star spa on a tropical island.

The Party's at Your Place

Hosting your party at home allows you to control every factor of the environment, from décor to music to where you'll set up your bar and the buffet. Speaking of which, you have to have room for a bar and the buffet. So before you plan the party at your home, be sure that your place has the ideal layout for entertaining. A small, cramped apartment kitchen will make for a tight squeeze when guests try to access the bar you've set up there. And if you only have two couches, guests will be standing all night.

If your home doesn't have space for a dedicated food area, bar, and sitting areas, check to see if any of your co-planners would allow for the party to take place at their more spacious houses.

Steal My Party Idea

"This is where the bride's mother became an important part of the team. *Her* house is huge, with a great big terrace out back, a pool area, a dining room and a big-screen television. Not to mention a long driveway that would allow for plenty of parking for our guests. If the party was at my place, they'd have to park in a parking garage blocks away. So we asked if she'd allow us to host at her house, and she was thrilled." —Lainie, maid of honor

Who's Doing the Work?

You won't be stuck doing all the cooking and serving at an at-home party. Many catering companies provide not just an array of amazing edibles, but also kitchen staff to heat up, prepare, plate, and serve the food. Their uniformed servers take over the kitchen area, making sure platters come out to the guests piping hot, and timing the courses perfectly. Waiters circulate with trays of hors d'oeuvres, and a bartender mixes the drinks. Hiring a party staff for your at-home party means you get the perks of one-location hosting without slaving over the stove or blending drinks all night.

If you don't have the budget for a staffed at-home party, you can still host at your place. Your menu will just need to be prep-friendly and easy to set out on one pleasing buffet table. Setup and cleanup are up to you and your helpers, a task that can be enjoyable when everyone has a glass of wine in hand and organized teamwork is in action.

What Do You Need?

Hosting a party at home often requires you to rent a number of essential items. You may have enough wine glasses and party dishes if you entertain often, and your co-planners may be willing to bring over their platters, punch bowl, coffee maker, and other vital items.

You may still need to rent circular tables, quality chairs, even couches to set out by the pool like celebrities have at their parties. You'll explore more about what to rent later in this book. It's mentioned here to alert you that this location may require a sizeable rental budget.

Party Freedom

Your party can get loud and wild into the nighttime hours. Noise is a big concern for bachelorette bashes where the music is turned up and thirty women are screaming over the gyrations of a male dancer. That kind of scene may not please the neighbors in your apartment or condo complex, so keep in mind the noise factor when you choose your location.

Another factor of party freedom involves who else resides at the home. Will the home-owner's spouse, boyfriend, or kids spend the evening elsewhere, or will they be downstairs watching television? Many a bachelorette party group has been stunned and disappointed to find out that the host's four kids were right downstairs, and, of course, they didn't stay downstairs for long. Or that the host's 150-pound dog who doesn't like his crate would be mingling with guests, grabbing food from the coffee table, jumping up on people, and otherwise being an unwelcome party crasher.

Another perk of a party held at home is that you have the space for as long as you need it. Your fabulous party doesn't come to a close when bars are flickering lights at last call. If your guests wish to stay until sunrise, they can! This location doesn't make you feel pressured that anyone's waiting for your space, like you might encounter at a restaurant or spa.

Is Your Décor Party-Ready?

If you have white carpets or new white couches, priceless artwork, a glass coffee table, or newly painted walls, your place might not be the best environment for a wild party at which drunken guests wielding glasses of red wine and berry margaritas are likely to wreck your pricy décor. If the adage "It's not a party until something gets broken" is the party cry of your circle of friends, your home is definitely *not* the place for a bash—even if you have the largest space.

And don't fool yourself into thinking that your home will be fine if you plan an outdoor party on your deck

No More Drama

If a co-planner volunteers her house, you need to have a delicate yet essential conversation with her to ask that her spouse, kids, dog, cats, and mother-in-law steer clear of the party. If she cannot promise total clearance of others, her place is not the right place to be. Tell her that you're assessing locations right now, and while she may wish to host, the adult elements of the party are unsuitable for her kids to witness.

or near your pool. All it takes is one rainy night and everyone's inside with their staining drinks and food—and you'll be a wreck. Particularly if you have roommates or live with your boyfriend or husband who would be irate if his space was damaged by your party guests.

Destination Bachelorette Parties

Everyone might wish to take a vacation together, bringing the bachelorette party to the shores of a tropical island resort or to the nonstop action of Vegas or to a quaint ski town or to wine country. Your job as the planner, then, is to choose the destination and the resort, and make the arrangements for the group. Again, more details on this style of party come later in the book. You're thinking right now about the perks and pitfalls of planning a party that requires travel.

Some groups of friends always do destination bachelorette bashes, with each new bride choosing a fabulous new location, or with the group going to Vegas every time. It becomes the group's "thing."

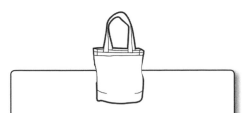

Shop Here!

If you'll host the party at your place, call your home or apartment insurance provider to request an extra insurance rider that covers any damage or injury occurring during your party. It's inexpensive, protects you, gives you peace of mind, and can pay to replace those carpets as well as cover the emergency room visit of the guest who falls and bangs her head on that glass coffee table. Choose the right insurance plan to cover injuries as well as belongings, regardless of whether or not liquor will be flowing. Someone with a fresh pedicure can easily trip and hit that coffee table, too!

Flights Required?

Unless you all live on an island or just off the Vegas strip, chances are that most if not all of you will need to fly to the destination. Is that within everyone's budget, even with a group discount on airfare or great prices through an online discount travel agency?

The timing of the party may impact travel plans and prices if your chosen date is within peak season or on a holiday weekend, so prohibitive prices may render this location off the possibility list.

Resort Packages

Resorts and casinos welcome bachelorette parties with open arms, offering affordable packages and shining suites often reserved for high rollers and celebrities. So you might find that a getaway plan is actually far more affordable than you and your guests expect.

Money Mastery

The competitive world of tourism has given birth to the fabulous bachelorette party group package that you'll find at many top-name resorts and even on cruise lines. Package pricing may include airfare and transfers; an all-inclusive meal and drinks plan with a free cake, entertainment, photos, and welcome gift baskets thrown in could mean your group gets more than its money's worth. The end result is a three-day party at the price you might have spent for one indulgent night on the town.

Speak with the special events team at top-rated resorts to find out what's in their celebrations packages. Resorts create these packed offerings for all kinds of groups, not just ones associated with destination weddings. The perks may include free cocktail parties, scuba outings, tickets to concerts taking place at the casino, and room upgrades. Breakfasts may be free. And you might just get your own concierge assigned to your group, delivering anything you request.

As for the drawbacks of the destination bachelorette bash, not all of the bride's friends and family members have the time to get away for multiple days, so they might be unable to attend. If they're busy with work or school, a vacation may be just a dream for them, and this more extensive plan could be more than they can handle. Keep in mind that who she shares her celebration with means more to the bride than the colors of the drinks and the pecs on the stripper. If some guests say they're averse to a getaway bash, it may be best to save the girls' vacation for another time in the future and plan a different style of party or a different location.

Destination Perks

Use this checklist to keep track of the perks you'd like to see at the destination location you choose for the bachelorette party:

➤ _____ A pool

➤ _____ A beach

➤ _____ Spa treatments

➤ _____ 5-star dining

➤ _____ Shopping

➤ ____ Adventure (kayaking, hiking, etc.)

➤ ____ Swimming with dolphins

➤ ____ Skiing and winter sports

➤ ____ An outdoor hot tub

➤ ____ Big-name entertainment

➤ ____ Dancing

➤ ____ Different culture

➤ ____ Eco-friendly travel and amenities

➤ ____ Other:

➤ ____ Other:

➤ ____ Other:

The Bride's Dream Destination

The bride might want to select more than just the date of the party. If it works with your budget and with the guests' ability to make it, the party destination could be the bride's choice. If she's always wanted to go to wine country, but her fiancé never wanted to use a vacation weekend for that kind of getaway, this could be her big chance—and to spend that adventure with her girls would be priceless. She might have wanted St. John for her honeymoon, but her groom went there on his last honeymoon with his ex. Now, she gets to go with you.

And she might choose a fun childhood favorite destination such as Disneyland or Universal's Wizarding World of Harry Potter™ theme park as a playful location for the party. If you all went to camp together when you were kids, she might want to go camping—only this time at a more upscale camp with well-appointed cabins and working plumbing. If you went to Miami for your first spring break together, she might wish to revisit the partying scene with her best friends again, only this time as the soon-to-be bride.

Does your bride have a dream destination? She might not be aware that she gets to choose, so find out now if she'd love a getaway for her party.

Steal My Party Idea

"We wanted to take everyone to Vegas, but a few of the girls said they didn't have the time or the money to get away. So we cut out the flight and the three-day stay and just had the party at the Hilton in the bride's hometown! It was still phenomenal and we still got the presidential suite overlooking the city, the free champagne waiting for us, the fabulous dinner. All that was missing was the flight and the extra expenses! Everyone was able to come, and the bride had a great time!" —Laura, bridesmaid

Steal My Party Idea

"We knew the bride was a big Johnny Depp fan, and we wanted to see if we could make her dream of meeting him come true. So we checked On Location Vacations (OnLocationVacations.com) to see where Johnny was currently filming his latest movie, booked our trip to the city where he'd be shooting for the next six months, and turned the bachelorette weekend into an adventure of scouting for him! We got a glimpse of him, too, from a distance! The bride said that was a dream come true for her, and this was the best bachelorette party trip anyone could ever want." —Lila, bridesmaid

CHAPTER 5

Transportation

> **In This Chapter**
>
> ➤ Elegant limousine
>
> ➤ Look-at-me party bus
>
> ➤ Exotic car considerations
>
> ➤ Your car, the free alternative
>
> ➤ Walking distance destinations

The next essential to tackle is the very important issue of transportation. If your party's style will be that club-hopping outing with alcohol flowing, you need a safe ride from place to place with no risk of drunk driving or accidents. A limousine or party bus is then a high priority, both for its protection of your guests and for the immensely fun atmosphere and experience you provide for the bride and her circle of celebrating friends.

In this chapter, you'll explore the many options of arranging your rides, from classic stretch limousine to the attention-getting Escalade Stretch to a nightclub-on-wheels party bus with strobe lights, satellite television, a bar, and a restroom. You'll choose the perfect-sized vehicle for your guest list and discover the inside secrets to booking your ride wisely and for less money.

If your party plans don't call for a party on wheels, you'll find out how to arrange safe rides using your own cars, decorated and stocked for the bride's delight. And of course with a single-locale party, you may not need transportation at all. Here is where you and your team arrange your transportation plan.

How Big Should It Be?

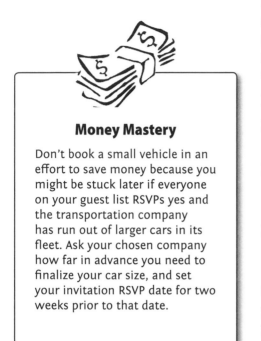

Money Mastery

Don't book a small vehicle in an effort to save money because you might be stuck later if everyone on your guest list RSVPs yes and the transportation company has run out of larger cars in its fleet. Ask your chosen company how far in advance you need to finalize your car size, and set your invitation RSVP date for two weeks prior to that date.

Size does matter, especially when it comes to planning a comfortable ride for all. You don't want twenty party guests crammed into a car meant for twelve, unable to move, veritable sardines. So here is your primer for which types of cars are best for your guest head count:

➤ A nonstretch limousine seats between four and six

➤ A mid-sized stretch limousine seats between six and ten

➤ A larger stretch vehicle, such as a Cadillac Escalade Stretch, Lincoln Navigator Stretch, or other specialty vehicle seats between fifteen and twenty

➤ A party bus seats up to fifty people and is recommended for parties with guest lists over twenty

Prices vary depending upon the style of vehicle you book, so in addition to spacious comfort for your guests, there is a very important budget issue connected to your transportation plans. You have to get the numbers right. How do you do this when you have to book your ride before your guests have RSVP'd? Talk to the transportation agency about your unknown total head count, and create an agreement in your contract that allows you to downsize your booked vehicle in case your thirty-person head count turns into a ten-person guest list. Most transportation agencies will be happy to oblige, since they depend upon word-of-mouth referrals for their survival. If you tell your other party-planning friends that this transportation agency was pleasantly helpful in downsizing your vehicle reservation, your friends may hire that agency too.

Limousine

Did you know that limousines and party buses are the only vehicles allowed on the road with open containers of alcohol inside? If your party group will enjoy cocktails or champagne toasts during the rides to and from your planned stops, these types of vehicle bookings are a must. Open containers of alcohol in any other type of vehicle could send you all to jail.

Before we get into the smart steps to finding and booking your limousine for the party, think first about the esthetics of the limo you want. While reputable limousine agencies will only let gleaming new models off their lots, some hang on to older models of limos, those boxier limos that impress no one and announce that you saved money. Insist upon seeing the limo you're renting, and reserve it by license plate number in your contract. Step inside to check that everything is new, in good order, and functional. Never book a limo over the phone without checking it out. That's a party space. It sets the tone for your party from the moment you all climb aboard. So take the time to inspect it well.

Next up is color. A white limousine is traditionally bridal and is in demand during wedding season. You may see online that white limos cost less than black limos, but that is not always the case these days. Yes, five years ago, brides considered the white limo to be *the* color of choice, but a growing number of wedding couples prefer the color contrast of the black limousine that shows off the bride's white dress far more attractively. What does this have to do with you? The price sheet for white or black cars may state the same prices for any special event, particularly bachelorette parties that count as wedding packages.

Money Mastery

Forget about the advice you may see on sketchy websites recommending that you call yourselves a "party group" rather than a "bachelorette party group" when you book your professionals as a way to avoid automatic higher pricing related to wedding event bookings. Drivers are not dumb, and lying about your party's true nature will not earn you points with the transportation company. Limo rental pros tell me that when a bachelorette party group books under a faux ID, saving themselves $100, transportation companies are far more likely to charge them for extra cleanup if the car requires it—even for cigarette smoke scents and drink spills. They may not charge the more honest groups for the air freshening treatment needed and the easy stain remover sprays to the carpets. You anger the management, you pay the price. You won't read that on a message board, so be honest with the transportation company, and enjoy your good karma.

Finding It

If anyone in your circle of planners has planned a wedding before, she may have a direct line to the best-priced, highest-quality transportation company in town. As might the bride if she's using a limo in her wedding plans, and it's okay to ask her. She spent hours researching and interviewing, or her wedding coordinator pointed out the winner in the crowd. If she or others have input for you, you're steps ahead in the process.

If you're searching without the benefit of a co-planner's intimate knowledge of the limousine rental realm, here are the smart steps to locating the reputable companies out there:

➤ Ask your parents if they or their contacts hire limousine companies for rides to the airport—first-hand experience is always best, and well-to-do corporate types work with the best agencies in town

➤ Contact the high-end hotel chains in your area to ask which limousine companies they hire to transport their VIP guests. They too only work with the best

➤ Visit WeddingMapper.com to get direct access to local brides and grooms who not only post reviews of the limo companies they'd hired for their big days, but also welcome your e-mailed questions

➤ Ask coworkers if they have hired limousines for their social and corporate needs, and it can't hurt to ask the boss as well. Your company's event planner likely has leads on reputable companies

➤ Look beyond reviews on bridal websites. While many may be objective and honest, transportation companies do post positive reviews on themselves, and negative reviews on their competitors, as a marketing ploy. If, however, you see dozens of negative reviews on a particular agency, with photos of ancient limos and rickety drivers, then that input should count

➤ Talk to the professionals you are hiring for the party. Your caterer, existing in the bubble of wedding and special event professionals, knows all of the vendors in town extremely well—the good, the bad, the lawsuit-worthy. He or she may be able to point you to a fine company

Choosing the Right One

Size and color aside, you're looking at inner perks such as satellite radio and television; mood lighting, including colorful pinlights in the ceiling that change color; a great sound system; that rack of champagne flutes along the wall with ice compartments; and comfy, clean, unscathed seats.

If these perks are pleasing to you, ask vital questions about the car's functionality using the following list for any type of vehicle you rent (party bus, classic car, convertible, etc.):

➤ How old is the vehicle? Ideally, it will be from a fleet that's less than five years old. Some companies trade out cars annually to always have the newest and best models

➤ Will the vehicle be washed and waxed before our event?

➤ Do you keep a vehicle available in case this particular vehicle has engine trouble? Most agencies reserve several backup cars to speed out to you if your car gets stuck

➤ Do you have a no-smoking policy for inside the vehicle? The most attractive limousine might come to you a few hours after a cigar smoker or a group of chain-smokers had occupied it, which makes for an unpleasant environment

➤ Does the driver have experience driving a vehicle of this size? Limo drivers have to pass tests to be allowed to operate stretch vehicles, and you want a driver who has expertise in maneuvering a large car, especially if your chosen party locale has lots of one-way streets and tight passages

➤ Does the driver use a GPS system in the car? This can be essential for him to get you smoothly to and from your locations

➤ What will the driver wear? Most reputable companies require drivers to wear suits for professional appearance. You don't want your driver in a sweatshirt and track pants

➤ What's your overtime policy? You booked the car for five hours, but that time starts when the car leaves the lot, and ends when the car returns "home." If you lose track of time during the party, will you be slapped with a huge overtime fee?

➤ What's your cancellation policy? If the party must be postponed, or if for any reason you must cancel, will you get your deposit back? Will you have to pay the entire bill?

➤ What's your gratuity policy? Many companies add an automatic 18 percent or more to your bill to be sure the driver receives a tip, so this is one element you must be aware of so that you don't double tip at the end of the night

Booking It

When a contract is presented to you, you must ensure that it contains all of your party's details: time and location of pickup, the expected number of stops, the end time, and all of the extras you've requested such as ice and snacks in the limo. Take the time to read the contract well, and ask for any changes to the boilerplate contract wording you deem necessary. Most companies will work with you to make the contract fair.

When you sign on the dotted line, you will be asked to pay a deposit to reserve the limo. Always pay with a credit card to prove and protect your payment. You must request, receive, and keep track of your contract copy. You don't want to get stuck with a company that insists you never paid. Administrative errors do happen, especially in busy companies, so keep this paper in your files for reference and for your smart week-before confirmation of your reservation.

Fun Extras

You don't need the red carpet that some limousine companies will roll out for you, like they do for some weddings. But it can be fun to have the limousine stocked with the bride's favorite snacks and drinks. The company can often provide these items for you, but that order usually comes at a higher price than you could arrange on your own.

Another essential to have in the limousine or any party vehicle: a box of small-sized trash bags, the kind you would use to line a bathroom trash can, just in case anyone overdoes it with the alcohol. An easy-to-grab trash bag saves everyone's shoes, the inside of the car, and the outside of the car for those hang-your-head-out-the-window moments.

Steal My Party Idea

"We stocked the limo with the bride's favorite champagne and the veggie chips she loves, along with plenty of bottles of water so that we could all last a lot longer throughout the night. We had one drink compartment loaded with champagne, and the other drink compartment filled with water bottles and orange soda, her favorite. We also brought along a box of her favorite cupcakes iced in her wedding colors—orange and red." —Dina, bridesmaid

Party Bus

When a party bus pulls up in front of a nightclub, everyone scrambles to see who's about to emerge. That makes your group the center of attention, with celebrity-worthy arrival style. Full-sized buses feature nightclub-like décor, leather seats, mood lighting, a great sound system, satellite television on big-screen TVs, and some even have poles for dancing.

This fun group ride is ideal for a larger party group, and also for a party plan that involves an hour-long ride into a major metropolitan area where dinner and dancing are scheduled. The party then begins at the moment of pickup and continues as you're in transit.

These buses are pricy to book, and some party hosts say they grappled with the idea of asking party guests to chip in for the cost of the ride. "I asked around and found out that our extended group of friends had a precedent already set by prior bachelorette party hosts—they asked guests to 'contribute what you can' to a party bus fund, and their guests happily chipped in. So we all felt much better about asking our thirty guests to give $10 each. Not a full share of what the bus cost, but it helped," says Alice, a maid of honor and chief planner for her bride's bash. Now, etiquette rules of old say that you never ask your guests to pay for anything during a party you've invited them to, but some groups are comfortable enough sharing expenses for parties within their circle. Ask the bride first, though. She might be mortified that you asked the guests for money. If she says no, it's a no.

Finding It

Party buses are often on display at bridal shows, so if the bride has asked you to attend a bridal expo with her, exploring the party bus may be on your To-Do list. If that time has passed, and the bride has already gone to bridal shows with or without you, you can still attend several of the many free bridal expos that take place every weekend. Just log onto the website for your area's regional bridal magazine and click on Wedding Shows or Events. You'll discover a lineup of shows you're welcome to attend as your research expedition.

Choosing the Right One

Obviously, you'll want to book the party bus that you toured. Write down that bus's license plate number to be sure you reserve that exact party bus, not an older or different model the company also has on its lot. You can request that exact vehicle on your order form and contract.

Money Mastery

At bridal shows, step into each party bus to see what amenities it has to offer. Be sure to look into the restrooms to be sure they're clean and functional. If the bus passes muster, ask for details on the party packages for that vehicle's rental, and ask if the company has a different, lower-priced package for bachelorette parties.

What's fun about party buses is they are available now in fabulous outer colors and styles. There's the sleek, all-black bus with silver swirls, and the fun hot-pink party bus designed

Style Savvy

Before you invest in any signage or soap pens to decorate the party bus—or limo, for that matter—check with the company to find out their rules about decorating the vehicle. Some forbid it, wishing to protect the finish of their valuable vehicles. Signs attached to the rear bumper can scratch the paint when they swivel in the wind, and the company may also forbid the placement of your large sign in the back window of the vehicle since it obstructs the driver's view. There are some companies, though, that recognize your group's enjoyment in personalizing and decorating the party vehicle, so they may provide their own, tested, safe soap pens for your use in decorating the side windows only, or they may okay cling décor for the windows as well. It's best to ask before you buy, though.

especially for girls' nights out. Improved lighting effects may feature a strip of silver or hot-pink pin lights just under the tinted windows, and a light-up sign on the front of the bus can display the bride's first name or a message such as, "Melinda and the girls are here!" All make for fantastic photos and increase the fun factor exponentially by virtue of being a celebrity-style effect for the bride.

Booking It

Follow the exact same method as described in booking limousines, with all essential questions asked and requests put in writing on the contract. Read the fine print, know the overtime and tipping rules, and provide an itinerary for the company's driver either now or closer to the party's date when you have more specifics arranged.

A deposit will be due upon booking, and since this is a large order you may be asked to pay one-third a month before the party and one-third on the night of the party. The company does need to protect its bottom line, guarding against last-minute party cancellations. A limo is easy to reassign with just a few days' notice if a group cancels; a party bus is not as easy to rebook in so little time. So be prepared for slightly different rules.

No More Drama

"My groom was *so* much happier about us having a stripper pole in the party bus, since he knew that some of my friends get wild when they drink, and he didn't want any trouble at a club or bar if they were to get on stage and attract guys to our group. We promised that we'd only have fun on the pole inside the bus, with no guys joining our party, and I avoided a huge drama with him." – Teresa, bride

Fun Extras

The bus may have a refrigerator as part of its wet bar option, so stock that fridge with your liquor and mixer supply, along with a buffet of treats and snacks to please your crowd. Since you do have a refrigerator here, consider surprising the bride with a cake, stashing a small, circular chocolate mousse cake or other flavor of cake in the fridge. As the evening progresses, you pull the cake out and present it to her with your group's chosen sing-along song, a champagne toast, and generous slices cut with a plastic cake cutting knife and served on the plates you've brought along. I say plastic because the rental agency has rules about no weapons on board, so that big, sharp knife could be taken from you before the ride begins.

Some party buses, again, have stripper poles in place, so everyone can take their turn and spin on the pole with far more bravery than they would at a club that has a pole onstage. Your braver and wilder party guests might be happy to pole dance before strangers, but in the privacy of your party bus, your milder friends may take a daring spin as well.

Exotic Car

Let's start with the big stretch vehicles, the all-eyes-on-us Lincoln Navigator Stretch, Cadillac Escalade Stretch, Ford Excursion Stretch, Hummer H2 Stretch—the cars that many people think are just for the guys to use for the bachelor party. These big, bold cars are now a hot choice for the bachelorette party! If you have more than fifteen people on the party guest list, these may be your best and smartest options.

Pricing will be higher than that of a standard stretch limousine, and these vehicles come with some of the perks found in party buses: satellite TV and radio, sound systems, lighting, a bar on the side. If your bride loves statement cars, this is the choice for her.

Another statement vehicle is a trolley. Reserved just for your group, a trolley allows you to celebrate in the open air as you cruise down the strip or down a bar-lined street.

And if your group will be a small circle of four or five best friends, you might follow the trend of renting a Bentley or Rolls-Royce—with driver—or a hot-pink convertible. Check with limo companies to see what's in their exotic fleet, and you may be surprised to find the bride's dream ride—the one she couldn't get for her wedding.

For any car you rent, again ask all of the questions listed in the limousine section, and work with the rental agent to secure a solid contract with deposit and payment rules spelled out, details in print, and refund/cancellation rules understood.

Your Car

Your own car can be a free, fun solution if your party is liquor-free or if you'll be the designated driver. Even brides are enjoying the freedom and savings of using a privately owned vehicle for their wedding transportation, decorating it with fun soap pen designs and messages on the windows. You and your team can decorate the car with lots of fun magnetic signs, such as Bride on Board. Got Groom? and Bachelorettes on the Loose, and

Money Mastery

Be wary of individual car owners who rent out their "baby" to make side income. Their prices may be attractive for that exotic car they show at car club events, but you don't want to risk any dilemmas stemming from a lack of insurance, licensing, and association rules that actual vehicle rental agencies must abide by.

write messages on the windows in your swirly handwriting that makes the car a work of art—and a must for taking lots of photos.

Any type of car will do, but the minivan wins the vote for shuttling six to seven partygoers with ease and comfort. Collect a few volunteers and their minivans, and you have your own decorated fleet of vehicles. With washed cars and polished wheels, even an older car transforms into a festive ride for the big party.

Parking Required

With your own cars transporting you, parking is going to be an issue. The restaurant, club, or casino you go to may have its own parking lot or garage for free parking, or you might be required to find a for-pay parking garage. So bring plenty of quarters no matter what. The restaurant's lot may be full, and circling the block would make you miss your reservation. Yes, you can pay with a credit card in a public parking facility, but many people hesitate for fear of their credit card's security. So stock up on cash for the lot, or quarters for meter parking for you and the other drivers. A great host is always prepared.

No Transportation Needed

And of course, your party's plan may require no transportation at all. If the celebration takes place at your home, guests are invited to drive themselves to you, then spend the night if they'll be drinking. A party that's set in a hotel suite also means no limousines are required to transport your group from place to place, and a getaway bachelorette party at a resort could have everything you need within walking distance on the resort's grounds.

A bed-and-breakfast booked by your group eliminates the need for limousines if your relaxed weekend keeps you on the well-gardened grounds, terraces, and by the sitting room fireplace. A ski resort could have you hopping on its shuttle bus for rides to the lifts, shopping, and restaurants. And a quaint wine country destination could have all of you biking from vineyard to vineyard, with your only for-pay ride being a lift in a hot air balloon to survey the lush, lovely ground below you.

No transportation needed adds up to no transportation budget needed, and your party funds can be shifted to more enticing and enjoyable sectors of the planning, such as a case of the finest champagne to wish the bride well.

CHAPTER 6

Invitations

In This Chapter

- ➤ Traditional print vs. electronic invitations
- ➤ Invitation do's and don'ts
- ➤ Design your invitation
- ➤ Giving directions
- ➤ Crafting your own invitations

Designing invitations for the party is one of the first exciting tasks in your preparations. You get complete artistic freedom to choose the style and colors as the perfect complement to the party's theme. In this chapter, you'll decide if you wish to send out traditional printed invitations through the mail, or if you prefer to send e-invitations such as through Evite. com's quick and easy service that also organizes guest responses. There are perks to both choices, and here is where you'll set your method first, then proceed into design and sending, making sure you adhere to all-important invitation etiquette rules.

Print or E-Mail Invitations

Simply put, one method costs money and the other most often does not. Granted, the financial investment in printed invitations isn't enormous, but there are some budget land mines to watch out for. Some professional invitation companies will charge upward of $3 per invitation for brand-name, custom-designed and printed cards, and then additional postage adds up to perhaps another $15 or so, depending on the size of your guest list.

Put It in Print

Many planners say they enjoy making print invitations that will arrive in guests' mailboxes, thrilling them with the tangible style elements of fabric, texture, shine, and custom graphics. The envelope alone conveys a sense of excitement, and some planners feel that print invitations make them look better, impressing guests with the effort taken to acquire and send them.

So, print invitations arrive in the mail as a bright spot among bills and catalogs, and they give guests something to admire in the bride's honor. Party guests say they've posted the invitations on their refrigerator as a daily reminder that they have an exciting event to look forward to. A printout of an e-invitation just doesn't have that same kind of official feel to it.

Printed invitations may be made on recycled cards or on textured papers, allowing your artistic side to shine, and some co-planners like to make the invitations as their share of the party preparations. It's their creative contribution to the celebration. An e-card doesn't allow them the option of a work-in-trade share of the plans.

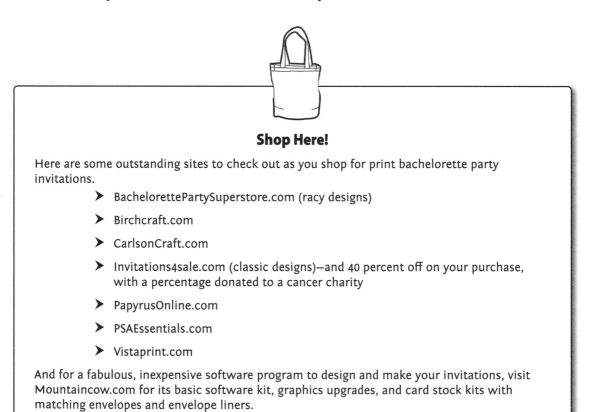

Shop Here!

Here are some outstanding sites to check out as you shop for print bachelorette party invitations.

> ➤ BachelorettePartySuperstore.com (racy designs)

> ➤ Birchcraft.com

> ➤ CarlsonCraft.com

> ➤ Invitations4sale.com (classic designs)—and 40 percent off on your purchase, with a percentage donated to a cancer charity

> ➤ PapyrusOnline.com

> ➤ PSAEssentials.com

> ➤ Vistaprint.com

And for a fabulous, inexpensive software program to design and make your invitations, visit Mountaincow.com for its basic software kit, graphics upgrades, and card stock kits with matching envelopes and envelope liners.

If you choose to make print invitations—as you'll explore later in this chapter—your expenses may include invitation design software (not a budget-wrecker at under $30, but still an entry in your expenses column), papers, envelopes, and the ink it takes to print them out, plus postage. The payoff of print invitations is that you get more creative control than you would choosing from a set number of e-invite templates on your chosen site.

E-Invitations

On the opposite side of the coin is the e-invitation, which arrives as an e-mail inviting guests to click their way onto a private invitation posting, filling their screen with a stylish invitation announcing the party details. They can often see the names of other guests invited, click on their response, and add a fun personal note that everyone can see. In this age of Internet-everything, this method is extremely popular. It does, after all, keep your guest list updated and totaled automatically, and it gives you the easy option of resending the invitation to late responders. Print invitations don't offer that service, and you'd have to call or e-mail people who haven't RSVP'd.

Another perk of e-invitations is that they're interactive, often featuring music, animation, and special effects. Keep in mind, though, that not all of these are free. At Hallmark.com, for instance, a selection of e-cards costs 99¢ apiece to send. It does have free styles that you can select, but some of its upgraded sound and animation cards do carry this additional expense.

If you've used, or received, Evite.com invitations in the past for your own parties, you're quite familiar with how it works. But keep an open mind to other sources and sites that your group may favor for their design styles and other perks. Here are just a few:

➤ BlueMountain.com: The collection includes pretty pastels of lavender, pink, and purple at the time of this writing. You can choose musical or singing invitations and even add a photo of your choosing

➤ Vistaprint.com: This popular site now has free e-invitations in a range of image categories and is a favorite of party planners hosting culinary-themed parties due to its wide range of foodie graphics. Other designs include tropical drinks with tropical flowers, florals, 1950s martini glasses with retro lettering and swirls à la *Mad Men*, and your chosen design printed on matching envelopes and return labels. Freebie notecards printed in your choice of design can be given to the bride

➤ Punchbowl.com offers a range of fashionable e-invitations and allows you to keep track of RSVPs, as well as see who has viewed their invitations but hasn't yet responded. It also has additional party-planning tools, just like Evite.com offers

➤ PurpleTrail.com has a range of modern graphics in its e-invitation collection and is among the sites that give you the option of designing your invitations online and e-mailing them or ordering them in print form to mail out

➤ PrintFree.com allows you to choose from a selection of bachelorette-themed invitations, fill out and print out single-panel or multifold designs

➤ Pingg.com is one of those on-the-rise invitation sites offering multiple levels of service from e-invites to design-and-order and even design-and-print methods. This site is a fast-growing favorite among bachelorette party planning groups for its modern, stylish collection of themes and images, including animal prints, shirtless men, and martinis, as well as invitations for tamer-themed parties such as restaurant nights, travel for a destination party, florals for an afternoon tea, and shoes for a fashion show party. For just a small amount more in budget, you can arrange a personal event web page for guests to log onto, with easy Facebook and Twitter update tools. This site is on the pricier side, but it does give you a large number of options.

Not to leave out Evite.com, take a look at that classic site's ever-growing collection of invitation styles. Its team has paid special attention to bachelorette parties lately, offering designs on the racier side: black lace, pink-and-black animal print, girls' night out cosmopolitans in neon colors, and more.

Some sites like Hallmark and Pingg allow you to design your invitations, and send them your mailing list, and then they mail out your invitations for an extra charge. While this might seem like a great time-saver, many guests don't like it when their contact information is shared with any third party. So think about the aftermath, which may include angry guests who are now on multiple mailing lists and receiving a flood of junk mail, and an angry bride who can't believe you would submit her friends' information to a website.

Getting Contact Information

The bride is going to be your number one resource when it comes to collecting the current contact information for her bachelorette party guests. You tell her the method by which you'll send out invitations—

Style Savvy

Those packs of invitations that you find in the card store and party supply store, with Date:_____, Time:_____ and other fill-in lines may be inexpensive for a pack of twenty-four invites, but some hosts feel that they're too labor-intensive, requiring them to write out the same information lines over and over again. Some also feel that fill-in-the-blanks invitations look like a cost-cutting measure, and make them look like they didn't care to put much effort into arranging the invitations.

e-mail or mailed print ones—and she provides you with either the e-mail or street addresses of each person on her guest list. It couldn't be simpler.

Just one warning: not everyone checks their e-mail every day, and some may have multiple e-mail accounts. And of course, e-mails sometimes wind up in the spam folder or don't get delivered at all. So when you do e-mail invitations, send them with a receipt request for when guests view their invitations so that you have some proof that they received them. If you haven't seen a receipt notification for any of the guests, send once more, then ask the bride to call her friend(s) for their current contact information.

This is why many party hosts like Evite.com and other invitation sites that show the list of who is invited to the party. If a particular guest hasn't

No More Drama

Taking steps to ensure that guests have received their e-invitation prevents the drama that grows when a friend of the bride hears about the party, thinks she hasn't been invited, and causes a gossip mess. It sounds petty, but it can really upset the bride. So think of these receipt notifications as insurance against unnecessary turmoil.

received an e-mailed invitation, another guest she talks to about it can assure her she's listed with the other party guests. She then logs in and, relieved to make the party list, can RSVP.

Invitation Etiquette

You're not bound to the same strict invitation etiquette that the bride faces, with long lists of rules on the proper way to work an invitation, but you do need to remember a few basic party invitation etiquette rules:

➤ Send an invitation to each individual woman in a group that lives together, not one e-mail to the three friends who share one apartment

➤ There's no need for titles on the invitation, such as Ms. or Mrs. Susan Jones. Address the invitation by the name the invitee goes by, whether it's Susan Jones, Susie Jones, or Sue Jones

➤ Double-check to make sure you've spelled everyone's name correctly. Guests get very offended when invitations show up with a misspelled or completely wrong name. Take your time!

➤ Hand-written envelopes are best. It's still considered tacky to print out address labels and stick them onto invitations, even if these are informal invitations

➤ Send the invitation six to eight weeks prior to a local party, or twelve weeks prior to a destination party, to give guests the chance to make their travel arrangements and perhaps put in for a day off of work

➤ Let guests know in the invitation what will be required of them, such as a split of the limousine cost, and provide the amount they will need to pay before the party date. Guests do assess if a party will be too expensive before they RSVP

➤ Let guests know what the plan is for the party, sharing location names and websites

➤ Let guests know the dress code, such as by saying, "Put on your little black dress, because we're taking Penny out to (upscale restaurant)!"

➤ Set an early RSVP date, giving yourself at least two weeks to know the final head count and make any plans for catering or favor shopping

➤ Ask guests to RSVP via e-mail or through Evite.com's RSVP tool. There's no need to order or make response cards and ask guests to mail them back to you

Invitation Style

Now it's time to design your invitation. You're first big decision is whether you will focus on graphics to match the theme of the party or simply use color and font styles. There's a big difference, as each conveys a different feel in its composition. Think about an invitation to a spa party. The invitation could feature a graphic of a woman in a spa robe, sipping champagne. Or it could be a pure white invitation with sage-green lettering and an italic font, with just a simple bamboo graphic in the bottom corner. Both are attractive designs, yet each depends on a different element to convey a feeling of what the party will be like.

In this section, you'll explore some style inspirations for different party themes, with color, graphics, and font in mind.

Color Palette and Card Style

Together with your co-planners, you'll decide on a color scheme for the party, and that color will be integrated into the invitation design. You don't have to use the colors the bride has chosen for her wedding scheme, since you don't have to coordinate this party to that event. You have complete freedom to choose a color scheme that works for the party's style.

The most popular choices for traditional bachelorette parties are bright colors. Fire engine reds. Hot pinks. Bright purple. Take the color you've chosen for the party décor, and bring several shades of it into your invitation design. So that could be a range of pinks, from light pink as accent shades to a medium pink for your background to a neon pink for the lettering. And consider black to be your base color that works in any color mix design. You can design that trio of pinks in the invitation motif and have black as the standout lettering. Other hot color combinations for invitations include orange and yellow, orange and red, aqua and purple, and the popular black/white/red mix.

When you're considering invitation style, keep in mind that single-panel cards—as opposed to greeting card fold-out styles—will cost less to order or make, since they require half the card stock. They're also easy to design and print four to a page if you're DIY-ing. Dual- or tri-fold invitations are stylish options if you're willing to spend a bit more on your invitations or if you need more space than the four-inch width of a single-panel card to convey all of the details of your party, including hosts' names and RSVP information. A party with multiple phases—such as dinner, a show, an after-party, or bar hopping—may require a standard card style to share details without a single-panel card looking crammed with small print. A smart solution: provide your event's personal page URL on a single-panel invitation, so that guests can easily click there, bookmark it, and always have easy access to driving directions and other party data.

Style Savvy

Look online for The Pantone Color Report to see its seasonal lists of the hottest colors for weddings. It posts swatches of the hottest hues coming right off the fashion runways and into the wedding world, as a leading trendsetter for weddings, bachelorette parties, and bridal showers. If you're baffled about which color combinations are hot right now, your answer is at Pantone.com.

Later in this book, you'll find chapters on different themes of bachelorette parties, and each provides ideas and inspiration on creative graphics to use on your invitations. Here are some universal concepts on matching your party's theme and the bride's personality in the design of your cards, whether they're printed or e-cards:

Spa Party

This invitation lets guests know that they're invited to an indulgent pampering party, so use spa-white cards printed with a font in soft pastel colors. Brightly colored print doesn't convey the soothing, calming effect of a spa day, so look at actual items you'll provide at the spa party for inspiration on your colors. For instance, that spa-white robe is the main inspiration for a pristine, white invitation. The soft greens of bamboo, or the tans and browns of Zen garden sand, are the two most popular color schemes to use for the font.

Choose a swirly handwriting font in a creative form of italics to convey an upscale feel to the invitation, and borrow the design style of actual spas' websites to see the use of marble

Steal My Party Idea

"We looked at the website for the spa where our party would take place, and we wrote down all the colors that stood out for us. We came up with the bamboo green and white, and also the golden color of champagne, so that's the main color we went with for the invitation. And we used the *same* colors on the personal event website we set up. It was great to have them match!" —Delilah, bridesmaid

Money Mastery

Don't bother buying scented items to include in your spa invitations, since some people have sensitivities to perfumed products. It's not worth spending the extra money to enclose packets of scent strips or thin envelopes of scented bath salts.

tile effects as their background, which can become the background inspiration for your invitations.

Another color and design inspiration to use is the mani/pedi. Your invitation may feature a fun illustration of a woman's hand with nails painted in a soft pink French manicure. You can then use that same shade of pink to create a border for the invitation, and a slightly deeper but still soft pink in your font.

One universal rule about spa party invitations is don't use too many colors. Stick with a light, neutral background and use only two shades of color, tops, in its design.

A fun trend for bachelorette party spa invitations is enclosing a printout of aromatherapy "cures," such as lavender to ease anxiety, or tangerine to boost your energy level. If someone has a laminator in their home office, use it to give these cards a simple, free upgrade in style, a real keepsake for your guests. Check out the aromatherapy lists at AuraCacia.com to list five or six scents per card made with matching or coordinating colors.

Fashion Show

Fashion show parties call for fashion-inspired invitations. While you will find a list of theme-specific invitation graphic ideas in the chapter on Fashion Parties, start off here thinking about the colors you'll use for this invitation. I love to look at fashion magazines such as *InStyle*, *Vogue*, and other fashion sources to get the current hot colors, textures, and combinations most easily. For instance, at the time of this writing, purple is the in color of the season, and I could look at *InStyle* (as well as fashion catalogs!) to benefit from seasoned fashion professionals' genius combinations of fabrics, colors, accents, and textures. So I could then design a shiny card stock invitation in a rich purple shade, and DIY glue-on little purple Swarovski crystals interspersed with the hot style of silver studs that I was seeing paired with those purple fashions, often on hot purple boots.

The fashion editors did all of the styling for me. I just took those trends and built my invitations from them.

If the bride isn't high fashion and doesn't follow runway reports or wouldn't be caught in purple studded boots no matter what the celebrity trends are, ask her who her favorite dream designers are. When you get her list of top designers, you can then use their brand logos in the design of the invitation, or use a single brand logo on a shopping bag that you've created or ordered from a custom bag-printing operation, and include the invitation, itinerary, and other goodies in each small bag that you deliver or mail to party guests.

If the bride is a ravenous fan of best-dressed lists and fashion police scores of celebrity fashions, you can use a photo of the bride dressed up—such as from a prior wedding or when she was a bridesmaid—and use

Steal My Party Idea

"When I was watching one of those *Real Housewives* shows with the bride, she swooned over one of the reality stars' elite black credit card, one that only the ultra-wealthy are given and spend six figures on in a single shopping trip. I had my invitation idea right there! I made the invitations look like one of those elite black credit cards, and that was perfect for wording the invite to say, 'Come shop with us at Nancy's private fashion show and boutique shopping evening. Friendship has no *limits!*'" —Bianca, bridesmaid

PhotoShop or another self-publishing program to create a faux magazine page with her as the star in the fashion spotlight. You can make up glowing reviews of her style, attributed to fashion icons like Tim Gunn and Stacy London, and also print "I'd love to dress (bride!)" from celebrity stylist Rachel Zoe. This fun full-page spread will thrill the bride and the guests, and then you can share the party details by taking lots of pictures of the bride during the event and sending her another fashion review spread after the party. What will the fashion icons have to say about that hot dress she tried on at the boutique?

Nightclubbing

Use the logos from the nightclubs you're going to, all surrounding an image of a limousine, a bottle of champagne, or an image of the bride drinking champagne in a limo from a prior event! You can invite guests to "Hit the town and show everyone how it's done, at Lisa's barhopping bachelorette party!" If your group is older than the twenty-two-year-old

No More Drama

Let me help you avoid a potential conflict. When it comes to a bride's partying style, don't poke fun at her conservative ways without first checking with her. I've seen party planning groups print invitations saying, "Darla's going out past 11 pm!" which may amuse some friends but can be taken as a criticism of how Darla hasn't been going out for late-night jaunts with the girls but has been staying at home with her man. This joke would be great if it fits Darla's sense of humor, but keep in mind that Darla probably has a lot of wedding-planning stress making her a little bit more sensitive. So check this with the bride first, and don't risk unintended drama and hurt feelings.

post-college clubbing scene-stealers, and if the bride approves, you might even make light of the bride's age and partying personality with a fun announcement that "The cougars are on the prowl! Join us as we revisit our old stomping grounds for drinks at the top five hottest clubs in town!"

Destination Party

In the chapter on getaway parties, you'll see ideas on using the colors of the island, that pink sand beach of Bermuda, the brights of tropical flowers, the shimmering orange and gold of the ocean at sunset. Use the location for your invitation style, going to the website for the resort you're booked at, and emulating the design its own experts have chosen to convey the feeling of the resort.

If the resort's big attraction is its clear blue ocean with spectacular snorkeling, your destination invitation can borrow the same aqua color palette from the website. Showing a private beach with an arch of untouched blue water tells your guests to be ready for a relaxing weekend by the water. If your destination is the party-central city of New Orleans, use the bright colors of beads, or the hue of a hurricane drink, lots of golds and purples and greens. Borrow your colors from the environment and the experience you plan at the location.

You can also choose the colors the bride has selected for her destination celebration color scheme. While it's not a must to match colors to the wedding tones, this style choice simply honors the bride's chosen palette, which she may have chosen from the location's feel as well.

At-Home Racy Party

Here is where *your* choices of party décor colors and patterns come into play. As you'll see in the racy party section of this book, an essential step is matching your décor and accent plans to what the bride considers and likes as racy. She may not like the all-penis décor items that are so prevalent on bachelorette party websites. That's an essential piece of information to have from the start of your plans and to honor throughout the décor plans, then continue to honor in the invitation motif you choose.

Guests look at an invitation to find out the theme, style, and tone of a wedding, and they do the same for a bachelorette party. So if your racy party's invitation shows X-rated graphics, you're conveying an X-rated party that guests will assume is going to be one of those raunchy drinkfests with a male stripper. If the party will be racy without being raunchy, your invitation needs to convey this by showing your theme in racy colors and patterns, such as hot-pink and black-tiger stripe borders on a hot-pink card with a bold, decorative black font. This style of invitation conveys that the raciness is in the colors and patterns of the party.

A racy, bold, stylish color scheme on an invitation comes off as infinitely more sophisticated than stereotypical X-rated racy parties and may be more pleasing to the bride's mixed crowd that may contain the groom's female relatives, her own mother, and little sister.

As you'll see in the racy parties chapter, sexiness can be subtle, such as using a pearl necklace as a barely-there sexual innuendo, and it can also bring in what the bride considers sexy. So your invitation would honor her vision and comfort level if you feature a sexy corset or sexy sky-high heels.

Maps

Guests have to be able to find the party location, whether it's a restaurant or your house, so be sure to include a smart method of sharing a map. It may be as simple as sending party guests the URL to the restaurant's website where it has driving directions perfectly listed coming from every direction, providing your street address with your zip code so that guests can GPS to your locations, or you might use the same smart website, WeddingMapper.com, the bride and groom are using on their personal wedding website.

WeddingMapper.com lets you create a free map of all of the locations your party involves. You can enter the names of each bar you'll be stopping at along the way, and the map posts a cute icon with the location's address and directions, with your personal note about each location targeted on your map. You can also target your house as the starting and ending point of the party.

A very wise move in creating this map is including the parking facilities near your place or near the restaurant where everyone will meet up. Guests say they love it when party hosts think of their every need, and when the party's in a city or town they're not familiar with, knowing exactly where parking is makes them feel so much more comfortable.

With WeddingMapper.com, your guests get detailed directions and can print them out or access them on their phones for an easier on-time arrival without having to call you for directions.

If you prefer, you can use this site or your favorite mapping site like MapQuest.com, Google Maps or RandMcNally.com and print out maps on colored paper, folding them and tucking them into your mailed invitations.

Making Invitations

Craft-savvy party planners love to embrace the entirety of the invitation creation task. Designing and making the invitations may be their gift to the bride, or their share of the planning in a team's decision to have each co-planner take on and fund an element of the day. Three co-planners may take on the décor, two planners may stock the bar, and one planner may request crafting the invitations.

The first step in invitation creation is making sure you have the right tools. Every computer has basic graphic design-type tools, such as access to clip art, the insertion of your own images, a range of graphic styles and a rainbow of colors to use on fonts. It is possible to design an attractive invitation using just these free tools.

It gives you an advantage when you use invitation-making software that makes layout easy, such as giving you a template for a greeting card-style invitation. You fill out the wording on each of the four pages, and it assembles them in the proper configuration for a quick printout. Invitation software will also help you size and space your fonts, showing you the outer borders of your invitation page sizes, helping you design a layout that allows your content to fit stylishly on the page.

Invitation software has pretty graphics, such as line drawings of dresses, cakes, champagne bottles, and other iconic images, and the benefit in these collections is that they are not immediately recognizable by guests as the free clip art that's found on every computer. A fresh collection of images in a software package, as well as in that package's additional clip art kits that you can buy for under $20, allows your invitation to stand out, and look professionally made. I use Mountaincow.com's inexpensive invitation-making software because it creates classic, timeless designs, and its card stock and envelope collections come in the current season's hot colors. You can create and save several different versions of your party invitation, and then use the

No More Drama

Before you commit your design to paper, be sure to send your design file to your co-planners, sharing your first draft with them and inviting their input with regard to the image, font, and colors you've used. Even though you're the invitation designer, they're still equal co-planners and as such should be allowed to chime in on the look and feel of the invitation that will bear their names.

software to design additional print items like the itinerary, direction cards, place cards, and other items.

What you'll most likely find is that a simpler invitation style is best, with your wording printed clearly in a legible font. This is the number one mistake in DIY invitations. The creator finds and falls in love with a swirly artistic font, and in that ornate style the numbers and letters may be hard to read. A zero can look like a six, which would be a disaster if an address was read incorrectly by half the guests. So test your wording in several different styles of fonts and see if the detail is lost when bolded before choosing the style that's easiest to read.

The next important issue is card stock. Go to the craft store or the office supply store to pick up packages of single-panel or dual-fold invitation card stock. Single-panel cards may also be called menu cards. You'll find a vast array of colors in card stock collections, and even pre-patterned ready-to-print cards, such as those with two-inch zebra-striped borders.

The world of invitation cards has expanded so much in the past three years that you'll be surprised to discover so many different patterns, and even cards with pearlized borders just like the bride has seen on pricy designer wedding invitations. Why is there such a huge market of card stock? The explosion in DIY invitation plans for budget-crunched party planners is the main reason, with DIY entertaining blogs showing fabulous homemade designs.

Another factor is the hugely popular scrapbooking audience. Scrapbook enthusiasts love these cards—marketed as invitation cards and menu cards—as pretty, inexpensive frames for details they wish to share about birthday parties and anniversary celebrations. They may use them to print out the party's menu, for example. If you look at the massive aisles of scrapbooking supplies in craft stores, it's easy to see the hobby's popularity. That's to your advantage as a bachelorette party-planner, since you can use standard invitation panels and cards, and dress them up using the self-stick accents from the scrapbooking world.

Once you design your invitation layout on your card template and are happy with it, it's time to print. Start with one test sheet, to see if the four single-panel cards per sheet fit the page as

Style Savvy

Don't use large graphics that require lots of ink in the printout because some printer inks apply in thick layers, creating a saturated, wavy effect. That's not professional looking. So keep graphics smaller to avoid this unwanted effect. Remember, ink is pricy!

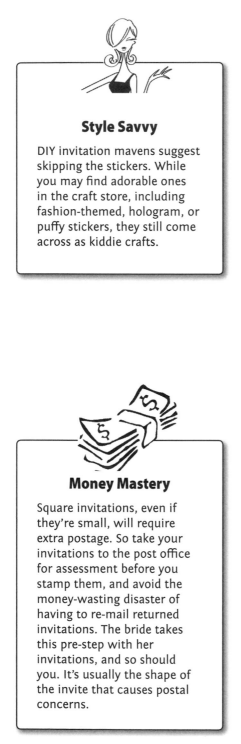

Style Savvy

DIY invitation mavens suggest skipping the stickers. While you may find adorable ones in the craft store, including fashion-themed, hologram, or puffy stickers, they still come across as kiddie crafts.

Money Mastery

Square invitations, even if they're small, will require extra postage. So take your invitations to the post office for assessment before you stamp them, and avoid the money-wasting disaster of having to re-mail returned invitations. The bride takes this pre-step with her invitations, and so should you. It's usually the shape of the invite that causes postal concerns.

promised by the program. DIYers say that sometimes the bottom invitation can extend too far into the bottom of the page or even be cut off. You may need to use just the top two cards in your final design. Always, always use a long-handled paper cutter to create straight-line cuts in your invitation creation, since they have ruler markings on top and can guide you into creating perfectly shaped and perfectly sized invitations. Cards cut with scissors will always turn out wavy and homemade looking.

Print out 15 percent more cards than you'll need to provide for extra keepsakes as well as replacement cards should your next DIY steps create a flaw. By next DIY steps, I'm referring to any hand-created accents you'll add. These include:

➤ Shaped hole punches: At the craft store, you'll see a wide range of hole-punch tools that allow you to pop out stars, circles, shoes, or other theme designs. You can punch out these shaped holes in one corner for a subtle effect, or make a punched-out border along the top or bottom edge of the invitation. (For a more stylish look, choose either top or bottom, not both.) A trend in hole-punch design is to get three different sizes of, say, star-shaped hole punches to create a varied starburst effect in a corner of the card

➤ Stamp art: Using a colorful or metallic ink pad, create a simple added accent with a rubber stamp. Again, the craft store has hundreds of these to choose from, or you can visit a crafter friend who owns a collection of them that you can borrow

➤ Rub-on designs: You'll find everything, including theme shapes such as shoes, tiaras, handbags, stars, champagne bottles, and accent swirls for the top or corners of the invitation. Take each sheet of rub-on décor in solid or metallic styles, lay your chosen accent on top of the invitation, then rub it with a special rubbing tool onto the page. Lift off the sheet, and voilà!

➤ Glue-on crystals: Tiny clear or colored crystals can add a bit of sparkle to the invitation. Follow graphic designers' lead and affix a tiny crystal to the swirl of a font such as on the first initial of the bride's name to give her a sparkling presence on the card. A single or trio of crystals at the top of the invitation adds a pretty pop as well

➤ Cut borders: Special craft scissors can be used to freehand a scalloped border at the top or bottom of the invitation. Again, it's a more stylish effect when you add this touch to just one edge of the invitation rather than all four

Your next concern is the envelopes. Purchase envelopes that match your invitations from the same line of invitation cards. By *match*, I mean you can choose the exact same shade or add visual interest by inserting your invitations into envelopes that match the color of your accent or font instead of the shade of the invitation card.

Style Savvy

You can affix regular postage stamps, or have customized stamps made. At Mountaincow. com, you can order official postage stamps designed to match the invitations you created using their software. At PersonalStamps.com, you can order customized stamps using your chosen theme-matching graphic, or even a photo of the bride herself. Yes, these will cost extra, but guests are impressed with these fun, customized details on the invitation package.

Keep in mind that dark shades of envelopes, such as black—on which you plan to write with silver pen—can pose a processing problem at the post office, so try to stick with lighter-colored envelopes that make it through postal processing with a minimum of challenge.

Always affix a return address sticker to these invitations to assure their return if you've sent to a guest's prior address. While you can order themed return address labels—an especially easy and inexpensive step if you've ordered your invitations through Vistaprint.com, a great source for low-cost labels—you can also use your own existing simple return address labels. It's perfectly okay to use what you have, provided your existing labels don't have distracting graphics on them or illustrations of your family, a photo of your dog, or any other decorated styles.

PART TWO

Wild Bachelorette Parties

Barhopping

When the ladies hit the town, *look out!* You'll be instantly recognizable as a bachelorette party group by your bride's tiara and veil, a T-shirt proclaiming her as the bride, and any number of theme props you're bringing along for the ride. When a group of bachelorette partiers walk into a bar or club, all eyes are on them—which creates VIP treatment for the bride and sometimes free drinks for the ladies as well.

In this chapter, you'll plan your bar or club crawl as you take the party from one hot nightspot to the next, drinking, flirting, dancing, and celebrating at each one. The scene can get wild, and your co-partiers can get wilder—if you plan the party well. You don't want to be one of those bachelorette parties that winds up at a too-quiet club that's playing bad music and serving watered-down drinks, with a bunch of smarmy old guys at the bar trying to send you drinks.

So use the advice and warnings in this chapter to pick the perfect nightspots with the perfect scenes for your wild barhopping party, and also arrange for unforgettable VIP status for the bride at each stop along the way.

Style Savvy

Starting the party too early means the clubs won't be in full, wild action. Starting too late means the clubs will be overly packed and the bouncer might not be able to let you in due to fire codes. Ask your club-going friends, if you're not a frequent partier yourself, to help pinpoint a good starting time for the clubs on your itinerary. Most often, these in-the-know ladies will suggest the smartest start time, reportedly 10 pm in most places. In big cities, that's a really early start time. So mine your partying friends' wisdom to start the party off smartly.

Choosing Your Location

In order to go barhopping, you need other bars to hop to. It's a big mistake to plan to go to just one club and stay there all night, because you never know what the scene will be like at that place on that night. The deejay could be weak. The crowd can be subdued or made up of bachelorette parties that are way more raucous than yours. The party guests might not be used to the sweaty crowd you're used to and could be pretty miserable. And the drinks might be way more expensive than you thought. Any number of factors can render a particular nightspot a snooze or a shock, so it's best to have multiple hot spots on your itinerary.

Even if you have to drive further away than your favorite local bar, find a nearby city that has a strip of nightclubs and bars. In many centers of many towns, especially in towns accessible to college crowds, you'll find an array of different nightclubs from dance-centric clubs to cool, chic nightclubs, country western bars, and clubs that have theme nights. The crowds at each will be different, the energy different, and the music different—and that variety makes for better odds of finding multiple fun hot spots on a given weekend night.

Ask your partier friends and co-planners to recommend the nightspots where they've enjoyed great music and dancing, or where they attended bachelorette party pub crawls. These experienced party girls will know the personalities of the club, and perhaps even the bouncers who can get you past the velvet ropes. Picking the right club for your group's personality is best done when you have firsthand information on which sites suit your party style.

What the Bar Does for Brides

When a club requires reservations—as some of the higher-end clubs do—it's smart to let them know you're booking for a bachelorette party. The staff then makes a little note or adds a special icon to your name to indicate preferential treatment for your group, a free bottle of wine for the table, or a drink for the bride. Some clubs will even usher you into their VIP section or waive your cover charges.

For walk-in clubs, two things can happen: either the bartenders will see the bride's bachelorette party shirt and veil and give her free drinks, or you'll request some perks and special attention for your bride.

Bars and nightclubs have a roster of perks for brides that include free drinks, VIP seating, and a lot of attention.

Free Drinks

The bartender might bring over that special shot just for the bride, or your entire group might get a tray of test tube shots delivered to your table. Some bars love to make a show of not just your group, but what they're doing for your group. So the bartenders might put on a big performance of spinning bottles, lining up flaming shots, making their signature neon-colored drinks for your group, and even letting the bride take hers as a body shot off the bartender who's known to be the one to treat bachelorette parties to that particular perk.

Steal My Party Idea

"I checked the websites and Facebook pages for several local bars to find out what their theme nights and specials were for the party weekend, and I was able to find both clubs to include in our barhop—a hip-hop night, an 80s-themed night—and which clubs to avoid—a karaoke night and a beer pong tournament night. Frat boys are awful with bachelorette parties in the room!" —Melinda, bridesmaid

At one bar in New Jersey, the bride is invited up to the bar, where a shot is placed on the bar top. The bartender hops up on the bar and—fully clothed—spreads his legs in front of the shot. The bride then bends down to grab that shot with her mouth, flips it back into her mouth, and her friends take pictures from the right angle to make this shot look extra racy. The sirens go off in the bar, the lights flash, making the bride the center of attention.

The bride, at another bar, might be presented with a huge drink. At many bars, the potent group drink of choice is a bright-colored mega-cocktail served in a fishbowl. The bride and her friends grab a straw and "do the fishbowl" as a group, with friends taking pictures.

Steal My Party Idea

"We told the bartender that our friend was the bride, and we asked if he'd put a Reserved sign on the first table that cleared. He not only did that, he sent over a few hot bartenders to give our group some shots. They know how to treat their bachelorette parties!" —Amy, maid of honor

Depending on the bar's policy, the bride might drink for free. That club wants to keep your group there, rather than hopping to the hot bar down the street, so they'll keep the bride in free martinis, shots, and other drinks while your group pays for yours. They make money from your tab, and it still turns out to be a great deal for your group.

VIP Seating

Your group may be led to the VIP area, which in some clubs is just a platform seating area with the telltale velvet rope making it a permission-only exclusive area. Other partiers in the crowded bar can only look on as your group enjoys lots of elbow room, a big table, and a server bringing drinks to you.

Attention

If the bar has a spotlight dancing space, such as an elevated platform, the staff might invite the bride to hop up there and dance while your group takes pictures of her big moment.

No More Drama

Bachelorette party codes of silence include bar top dancing, not just male strippers. Even though you know her dance was pure fun and that she wasn't taking off her clothes or eliciting money from men, her groom might not appreciate knowing that his sweet bride was one of *those* types of girls. He may not envision her dancing to a Duran Duran song at the 80s club, so this is one of those party details that's best left to your code of quiet, unless he's the type to be amused—not threatened—by the bride's *Coyote Ugly* moment.

Some of these platforms are lighted, some are four feet off the ground, and some involve a cage or a pole.

The deejay might announce that all eyes should go to the bride on the platform, and he may play a song you've requested for her spotlight dance. If she has a few drinks in her, she can get wild and play out a club dancer fantasy while you and the other guests surround her so that nightclub predators don't move in.

The bride might be invited to dance on the bar or on a table just like you've read celebrity party girls are wont to do, and this too gives her those priceless "wild girl" photos your group can take of her. With a hand from the bartender, she then steps down from the bar and rejoins your group.

The deejay might bring the bride up to the booth to help him spin some songs, and she'll have a spotlight moment her clubbing friends will love as they snap tons of photos of her with the character running the music. Celebrities often jump up to guest-deejay at nightclubs, so this is a dream opportunity for many club goers and can be especially fun if the bride isn't a practiced club goer and can't name any professional deejays. She's not going to be asked up if she's sloppy-drunk, so lead her toward the deejay booth earlier in the night to dance in front of him and participate in his leading of the crowd with "*Yeah!*" and other lyrics that everyone sings. She'll be noticed, and she may be plucked from the crowd for her celeb moment.

Owning the Scene

If the bar doesn't have any rituals or perks for brides, then you can create your own excitement by dancing as a group, cheering for the bride as she takes a drink, and standing out as the hottest group in the club.

Wearables

Some bachelorette party groups choose to wear matching hot-pink T-shirts announcing themselves as part of the bride's entourage, and they will tailor their tees for extra hotness. This means cutting off the bottom of the shirt to show off a belly ring or tying it at their waist or writing on the shirt with a fabric pen. They may also wear glow-in-the-dark necklaces, and they too can wear candy necklaces just like—or instead of —the bride.

Owning the Dance Floor

If there's a dance floor, your group needs to get on it and show your best moves. When a dance floor is slow to fill, the deejay feels the pressure of not pleasing his crowd, so when you take to the floor and show your love for the music, you'll jump-start the party atmosphere, enticing other bar-goers to join you as well. You make the party.

Befriending Fellow Club Goers

You don't want hangers-on who order drinks on your tab, but if there's a fun group at the club who gravitates to you, welcome them to

Style Savvy

The candy necklace has long been a prop given to the bride, meant to entice men in the club to bite candy from the bride's neck after buying her a drink. Wilder brides still go for variations of this tradition, but a growing number of brides say they'd rather have their single friends get all of the attention from the men in the club. So they request that their party guests get the candy necklaces and the nibbles from the guys, all in good fun. Some brides turn the candy necklace into a candy bracelet, so that drink-buying men can take a bite from candy located at the more innocent forearm instead of at her neck or on her chest. Always stick close to the bride, or party guests, who have on candy necklaces, to be sure they're not inviting trouble from too-aggressive men at the bar. If things are getting too wild, the necklaces come off.

No More Drama

Don't expect to corral the party guests' attention by forbidding them to talk to men, dance with men, or get phone numbers. It's a big mistake when party hosts get mad at guests' flirty agendas, thinking everyone should pay attention to the bride at every moment. Even she would be unhappy with that. So if a guest seems to be chatting up a guy over in the corner, just give her the space to connect. You could be a story at their wedding someday. But do make it a rule that no one is to leave the premises with a guy to go back to his place. Especially when there's a lot of alcohol flowing, good judgment can go out the window, so step in and keep your fellow partiers from a dangerous error.

your circle. Your group of ten could turn into a wild, dancing, drinking group of twenty, having more fun together than you would have in your own crowd. Perhaps your original group consisted of a few freer spirits who want to dance all night, and more conservatives who tend to sit at the table and observe the crowd. They're having fun, but it's not a wild style of fun. So those women at the next table who are dancing make a great addition to your group, and together you own the place.

The same goes for a circle of hot guys who are eyeing the single women in your group. If you welcome them to dance with you all, not just with the bride, your circle owns the place. Plus, the single women might get some phone numbers and future dates. Granted, men are not ideally welcome to spend the entire evening with your group, or, again, hop onto your bar tab, nor should they be used to pay for your drinks. But it can make for a fun portion of the evening at one club if you have a brief mixed crowd for hotter dancing and sexy shots served up. When that brief time is over, or if the men start acting inappropriately, your party moves to the next location.

Behind the Scenes

When your group is at a bar or club, you'll be asked for your credit card to run a tab. That has financial disaster written all over it, especially if you don't have a lot of room left on your card for a pricy expense to be covered. You don't want that embarrassing moment of being informed that your card has been declined, and you don't want to wreck your credit by going over the limit.

A smart solution is prepurchasing a Visa debit card with your co-planners in wise pay-ahead strategy that you can load with a generous amount and use for the night's tabs. Your credit stays healthy, your cards stay in your wallet, and your team knows that it's partying on a set budget.

The next behind-the-scenes issue is tipping. While I'll always suggest that you tip servers generously, I must warn you that many establishments automatically include a gratuity of

18 percent or more for large groups to protect their servers from getting stiffed. Before the big night, check with each stop on your journey via its website to see what its tipping policy is. You'll then know which club is automatically taking out a tip, and you'll avoid the pricy mistake of double tipping.

Who else gets a tip? Coat-check gets $1 per person, valet workers get several dollars apiece, and in some upscale clubs a restroom attendant is there to hand you a warm towel. She should be tipped as well. So even if you're not going to a strip club, have plenty of singles on hand for the entirety of the night.

CHAPTER 8

Celeb-Style Wild Parties

In This Chapter

> Where to go for party packages
> Getting the celebrity treatment
> Taking the party to strip clubs

Us Weekly, OK!, and other celebrity gossip magazines feature photos and stories from stars' big birthday celebrations and appearances at Vegas hot spots like Pure and TAO. The news of what goes on in VIP rooms—with partying stars dancing on tables and downing magnums of champagne with their entourages—fills those nightly gossip shows like *Access Hollywood*. For the bride who wants to party like a rock star, or a Kardashian, a wild celebrity-style bachelorette party is in order.

This chapter will inspire you not just to find the hottest nightclub, but also to get the bride VIP access and celebrity treatment once she walks past the velvet ropes. The bachelorette party inside then turns into the same kind of wild night out that celebs indulge in, which makes the bride a superstar when the club treats her and her group the same way they do celebrities and their partying groups.

Finding the Perfect Hot Spot

When you think VIP nightclub, you think Vegas. So let's use Vegas as our example of how to find the hottest club that suits the bride's partying style. In Sin City, you have almost too many nightclubs to choose from—LAX at Luxor, TAO at the Venetian, Risqué Club at Paris, Pure at Caesar's Palace, Tryst, Blush, Surrender, and XS at Wynn. That's not even half of them. How do you choose the best location for the bride's party?

You can't just show up at Pure and expect to get in with your group, and you *really* can't expect to tip the doorman and be shown to a private booth in the VIP room. You have to make reservations first. Way in advance.

In Vegas, and in many big partying cities, you'll discover various bachelorette party planning companies online that promise VIP packages of several hundred dollars each. And with a package, the company becomes your concierge and books you VIP access to your choice of hot clubs. Sounds perfect, right? Well, if only that were so. While there are established events groups out there, specializing in bachelorette parties, there are also scam companies that will happily process your credit card through their site and send you a packet of what turns out to be fraudulent VIP passes.

A smarter move is to contact the nightclub directly to arrange for specialty access and VIP perks through its own bachelorette party planning teams. Most of the top nightclubs have events professionals on staff, and the resorts certainly do. So as lead planner of your team, go right to the source and make arrangements with the establishments themselves to plan a celebrity-style night out for the bride.

No More Drama

Assure the other co-planners that you're going to plan this party through the actual club or hotel or through an events planner so that you don't get flooded with nightmare stories of bachelorette party groups left out on the street in a long line, never gaining access to a club. Ask your co-planners to suggest any coordinators they know, or friends who've booked through sites or coordinators to add that extra layer of safety to your plans.

Another smart move is to locate a professional events coordinator, accredited by the Association of Bridal Consultants (BridalAssn.com) or the International Special Events Society (Ises.com). Log onto those sites to locate a coordinator in your party area, in Vegas, or in any other city, and you'll find a list of accredited professionals who have studied and passed exams and have years of experience in good standing with their association. These pros have expanded their party-planning repertoire to include bachelorette parties, and some even specialize in this type of party. They know all the hot spots, they have connections with the sites, and they can connect you with valid VIP passes and other perks as part of their package. Book with a professional vendor, not a novice, and your investment in their fee will provide the access you desire.

And of course, ask your own friends where they attended similar bachelorette or destination wedding parties, thirtieth birthday parties, and other celebrations at resorts, hot nightclubs, and other dream locales. Firsthand experience is always a smart part of your site research.

As mentioned earlier, the site has to match the bride's tastes. And she may have a dream location in mind, having dreamed of partying at Ghostbar or at the VooDoo Lounge in Vegas, or at celebrity favorite haunts in New York City, at casino resort nightclubs, or wherever her favorite celebrity deejay is performing. She may cut your search short by pointing right to the club where she'd like to celebrate.

Arranging the VIP Experience

No matter who's helping you plan the bachelorette's bash, you'll find certain celebrity-style elements to be alluring, a must for giving the bride that VIP experience. The resort or coordinator can help you arrange that for her.

An Arrival Surprise

If your celebration has you checking into the resort for the night, you can arrange for the bride's suite to have flowers, a bottle of champagne, and a free pass to the resort's spa. If the bride has been involved in planning her party, providing an indulgent surprise keeps the mystery in her party.

Another arrival surprise is having some of the bride's long-distance friends whom she didn't expect to attend her party awaiting her arrival, either at the lounge or in her suite. Seeing her closest friends there to share in her celebration will thrill her, and they get to join her VIP entourage.

Steal My Party Idea

"We were able to get a fabulous deal on an upgraded suite for the bride using my boyfriend's club card at the resort. For the price of a regular room, we got her a penthouse with a private terrace pool, a full bar, and an amazing view of the Strip." — Linda, bridesmaid

A Limousine

One of the most popular celebrity-style party elements is transportation in a hot car. It could be a stretch Escalade or a hot-pink limousine, a real all-eyes-on-us car that delivers you right to the nightclub's door. You step out of the car and bypass that long line behind the velvet rope to get right into the club.

VIP Passes

VIP entry to a club is the golden ticket. The bride will certainly feel like an A-lister when she and her group get to walk right into that exclusive, celebrity-filled club without waiting

Money Mastery

Expert help and connections in getting VIP passes may also free you from having to pay hefty cover charges at the club. One great source for free entry is the local tourism department, found through TOWD.com. It gives out freebie passes, especially to bachelorette party and wedding groups, on a regular basis.

in any line or being judged by a clipboard-holding bouncer who—let's face facts—may have been instructed to let in only the youngest, blondest, plastic surgery-enhanced model types to create a hot crowd inside the nightspot. With your passes in hand, the doors open, and you're not subjected to any scrutiny.

Entry to the VIP Room or Balcony

While other partiers stand shoulder to shoulder in the general party space, sweaty and finding it hard to get a drink, the bride and her group are led to the leather banquettes and private booths in the VIP room, where countless celebrities may be partying as well. You get breathing room and the rarified atmosphere that Oscar-winners and socialites enjoy as they sip their champagne and enjoy the complimentary caviar.

In some clubs, the VIP area is a balcony overlooking the action below, allowing your group to see and be seen—the envy of all below.

Bottle Service

If you're not familiar with the nightclub lifestyle, bottle service is the ability for your group to order entire bottles of wine, liquor, or champagne at your table, rather than having to order glass by glass. Bottle service is a special offer at most clubs, pricy to regular patrons but often provided to bachelorette groups.

An Assigned Server

While everyone else in the club has to fight to get to the front of the bar line, and then fight to get the bartender's attention, your group has a dedicated server assigned to your table, bringing you drinks and rounds all night long.

A Party Host

Some resorts or coordinators will send a party concierge out with your group. She'll be dressed in clubbing attire to blend in with your entourage, and she'll flash her credentials at various nightclubs to get your group in the door and into VIP rooms. She'll also handle the business end of your evening, taking care of the tab and tipping on your account, call the limo for you when you're ready to head to the next club, call over the bouncers if someone in your group is getting hit on too aggressively by a club patron, and otherwise act as the bride's personal assistant.

Meeting Celebrities

When you're in the VIP room, the next table over may be filled with today's hot celebrities. While it's never a good idea to scream and make a scene, it is okay to nod a quick hello, wave, and have a moment connecting with the star. Remember that he or she is on private time, socializing with friends, and perhaps even entertaining a producer or director while trying to land a role. If anyone from your group becomes a hyperfan barging in on their private time, your group may be asked to leave. It happens all the time. The star is an upper-level VIP, perhaps a regular. All he or she has to do is motion to the bouncer, and you're gone, with your drinks left behind.

No More Drama

Since this host will become one of your group, it's important to like her style and demeanor. So if she's not clicking with your crowd, or if she's not getting you into the places you'd like to go—as promised—you can thank her for her guidance and send her on her way. There's no law saying she has to stay with you all night, even if you booked her for five hours. It's worth it to be free of a disappointing or overbearing host who makes the bride uncomfortable.

Some celebrities are friendlier than others and will start a conversation when you offer a "regular person" greeting like, "We'll try to keep it down. It's Anne's bachelorette party, and we have champagne on the way." The celebrity may wish Anne a great party from where he sits, or he may be the type to send over a drink for the bride. What he's not going to do is offer to take photos with your group. That's a D-lister move. So how do you get a photo? Slyly, such as having a friend take a photo of your group at the table, with the star clearly visible just past you.

Should you send a drink over to a celebrity's table, to try to get him to come over and party with your group? You could, but that can be seen as bothering the famous patron. It's far better to motion to your shots when they arrive, and the star will either gesture that he'd like to join you for a toast or decline. Many celebrities love interacting with their fans, but you never know what frame of mind this celebrity is in. He might have had a bad day, so if he declines, your interaction with him is done for the night. Act like stars yourselves and just have a great time, knowing *you're* in the room.

Going to Male Revues or Strip Clubs

Especially in Vegas, but in any celebrity-style wild party, part of the evening's activities may include going to a male revue or to a strip club where muscled-up hunks pay special attention to the bride, dancing with her or for her as she tucks dollar bills into his costume. Your resort concierge can build a party itinerary for you that includes tickets to a male revue, or you may need to buy individual tickets for each of the bachelorette party guests. This wild portion of the night may or may not include drinks—some clubs are dry to keep patrons from getting too wild—so preplan with the group how the tab will be paid.

Bachelorette party groups are sworn to secrecy about the bride's dances with male strippers, and some groups even download an Oath of Silence off the Internet, having each guest sign it and hand it in. This is a reassuring step taken so that the bride can enjoy her evening without any gossip getting back to her fiancé.

Money Mastery

Will it be your job to hand over your credit card, leaving you cringing every time a party guest orders another drink, bottle, or round? That essential business can take the celebratory mood right out of you and crush your credit, so talk with your co-planners about how you'll handle the costs of this wild party event. Perhaps they can prepay $50 each to cover bar tabs, and you then have a cushion on your card.

What about photos? Remind the group that it's bad form to post photos from a bachelorette party on Facebook or other social media site, and those who are caught posting embarrassing photos of the bride or any of the guests will be banned from all future parties. You can't take people's cell phones away, and Kodak even makes a bachelorette party single use camera for snapping images of the fun. All you can do as a good host is let the group know that there's a privacy code regarding any racy photos. Pictures taken at the table and in the limo are fine, but please don't snap photos of the bride getting a lap dance.

What goes on at wild parties can get pretty wild, so that's why it's important to keep the guest list just to the bride's most trusted friends, the ones who would never find it funny to post incriminating photos of her on Facebook, embarrassing her and potentially upsetting the groom.

If you see party guests snapping photos of the bride and posting them online, be a great host and step in, demanding that they take down that photo and delete it from their phone or camera right away.

What if the bride, like some celebrities, loses control, parties too hard, and is now getting too close to a male dancer? Be a good friend and guide her away from him, giving him a tip and a request to step away. It's your goal as a party host to show her a wild time, but there's a line that you're not going to let her cross. If only some celebrities had such protective friends around them!

No More Drama

Kodak is really onto something with the single use cameras it's designed for bachelorette parties. Photos are taken during the celebration, and the cameras are then collected by the host. She gets the film developed and acts as the gatekeeper for which safe images she'll post on a photo share website. Anything damaging doesn't get posted or included in a photo book. Check out the single use cameras at Kodak.com, stock up for the party, and give them to guests with instructions that these are the only cameras allowed for the night.

CHAPTER 9

Male Dancers

It's astounding how much wrong—*dangerously* wrong—information is out there on the Internet when it comes to finding and hiring male dancers for a bachelorette party. For example, I discovered one source who suggested calling a male *escort* service to see if any of their "workers" also strip at parties. That is *definitely* a don't for your party, but that's the kind of advice that's out there. This chapter will guide you through the process of finding and hiring male dancers for the bride's bash, in the safest and smartest ways. You don't want to give your credit card information to a scammer or invite a potential criminal into your home. Shop wisely for this particular part of your plans, since it's up to you to protect your identity, money, and guests.

First Things First

Before you do anything regarding this form of entertainment, you first need to find out whether or not the bride even wants a male dancer at her party. It used to be a surprise planned for a bride by the party hosts, but in this age of sensitivity and with many brides being older and past their wild partying days, or simply not the type to want a male dancer at her party, this portion of the plans becomes the bride's domain. She makes the decision if she wants a dancer or not.

No More Drama

Your responsibility above all others as a party host is to make the bride happy. When you ask her if she'd like a male dancer booked for her party, don't attempt to subtly (or not-so-subtly) sway her decision by telling her how much all the other girls are looking forward to having a stripper at the party. This may guilt her into saying yes. You've then created big problems for her, especially if the groom is against the idea of his bride having a male dancer at the party.

Also, take into consideration who the bride would like at her bachelorette party. Does she have the groom's sisters on the guest list? His mother? His grandmother? She may not want R-rated entertainment taking place in front of them, since it would be wrong for her to accept a lap dance from another man in front of her future in-laws.

If the bride is on the fence, propose to her that she has the option of a two-part bachelorette party, as was mentioned in an earlier chapter. The moms and grandmoms can join the group for a ladies'-night dinner at a fine restaurant, and then the bride's friends continue on to a private, racier party or to a strip club for male dancer night. That way, the bride can have her cake and eat it, too (so to speak), celebrating with her more conservative guests, then letting loose with her friends later in the night. Be sure she's aware you can arrange any plan that works for her.

An important consideration before the bride chimes in: Does the location allow for male dancers? If the bride has requested a fabulous dinner out in a restaurant's VIP room, you likely can't book a gyrating male dancer to show up to perform his act. The restaurant manager will throw you all out! It may seem like a simple concept, but you'd be surprised at the party planning groups that find themselves in hot water when a hot guy starts stripping in a restaurant, having arrived dressed like a waiter.

No More Drama

It may seem funny to a co-planner who never considers consequences and thinks this scenario would get millions of hits on YouTube, but it's one of those danger spots you need to keep in mind—and mention to your co-planners before they book any entertainers without first checking with you. Be sure the group accepts that you are in charge of this category, and no strippers will be booked by them. They can and should share their contacts with you, but you're the one who keeps every piece of this plan on the safe and secure side.

Out On the Town or Ordering In?

If the bride does want a stripper at her party, the next decision is do you go to a club for an all-male revue or a ladies' night featuring wandering male dancers in skimpy costumes dancing for groups? Or do you have a male dancer come to your home or hotel suite to perform privately?

There are pros and cons for each plan:

A Public Club

For this party style, your group goes to a club that features either male dancers performing music/dance numbers on stage—where you can run up and tuck dollar bills into their costumes—or male dancers who come to your table to give your group up-close and personal dances. The bride is pointed out to the dancers, and she gets tons of attention from an array of beefy hunks in skimpy outfits. You have a VIP table up front to be close to the action so the bride and her guests get a full night of access to dozens of hot guys.

The pros:

> ➤ Clubs feature a group of male dancers in varying sizes and looks, a candy store of hot guys to ogle

> ➤ Clubs feature excitement-building music courtesy of a deejay, plus dance numbers by groups of male performers or solos by their specialty acts (like the stripping fireman)

> ➤ Clubs may have special effects such as lasers, strobes, and fog machines to enhance the atmosphere

> ➤ Clubs can accommodate any size party, from four women to more than 50

> ➤ Male dancers perform for hours, not just for the one hour you paid for a dancer who comes to your private location

> ➤ Celebrating at the club means you don't have to clean, decorate, prepare, or protect your own home

> ➤ If the club serves alcohol (some clubs don't!), your crowd likely has access to a greater variety of drinks

> ➤ Tickets per person may be quite affordable, especially when you factor in group discounts that clubs offer to bachelorette party groups

> ➤ Some clubs throw in freebies for brides-to-be, such as boas and tiaras and free drinks

> ➤ If you have fun groups of women around you, they can elevate the party atmosphere when their lively guests interact with yours

The cons:

> ➤ With many other groups of women in the room, including other bachelorette parties, the male dancers' attentions will be divided

> ➤ Again, the club may not serve drinks during the show, in an effort to prevent patrons from getting too drunk and aggressive with their dancers

> ➤ If they do serve drinks, the cost per drink may be very high

> ➤ You'll need to hire a limousine or party bus to provide a safe ride home from the club

> ➤ If groups of partiers seated near you are wild, loud and unruly, your group may get annoyed

> ➤ If you don't book tables at the front of the room or a table large enough for your group, you may be divided or far from the action

Private Home or Hotel Suite

Planning your party at home gives you control over the environment, the music, the décor, and the space where the male dancer will perform for your group. You may decide you like the privacy afforded by your home or hotel suite, and the greater amount of attention paid to be the bride by the dancer you hire. As the only party in the place, you get the entertainer's undivided attention.

The pros:

> ➤ Again, the entertainer pays more attention to the bride

> ➤ You're not subject to too much chaos around you, such as other groups of partiers, a fog machine, and blinking lights that can make guests dizzy

> ➤ You control the bar and the cost of drinks

> ➤ You don't have to hire a limousine or party bus, and drinking guests can get a safe ride home or spend the night at your place

> ➤ If you wish for male dancing to be a brief portion of the party, this option allows for just an hour of attention to the bride, or even for a quick dance and a swift departure

The cons:

> ➤ You only get the dancer or dancer you specifically hire, not the range of men you'd find at a club

➤ The dancer may not arrive at your location on time, causing a delay in your party's timeline

➤ You have to deal with the noise factor. If you live in an apartment or condo, will the neighbors call the police over all the screaming coming from your place?

➤ You may have to book by the hour at pricy rates, so the dancing may not last as long as you'd like

➤ You have to arrange for a space in your home where the dancer can perform for your group, which may mean clearing out the living room

➤ Some hosts feel awkward about a strange man gaining access to their home, and asking for private time to get ready in a bedroom

Dancers for Hire

Now that you have the bride's permission to book dancers and you know where the party will take place, it's time to begin your search for a reputable entertainment company or quality club that has male dancers. Key word: *reputable*. Other key words: *entertainment company*.

You never want to hire a freelance male dancer from Craigslist or some other social media site because you won't get the type of screening, insurance, and other protections offered by an official entertainment group. We live in a dangerous world, and you don't want to be the tragic story on the morning news when the person you invite into your home turns out to be not a dancer but a danger. Criminals lurk everywhere, so stick with a reputable, licensed entertainment company as your source for locating and booking your male dancer or any other type of entertainers for your party.

Word-of-mouth is always going to be your best resource for locating a good club or entertainment company, so ask the wedding coordinator and local friends who have held or attended other bachelorette parties.

And, of course, if you're going to a club, once you have a collection of club names, ask the

Steal My Party Idea

"The Internet was filled with all kinds of ads for clubs with male revues, and we had no idea which ones were good, which were seedy, which were rip-offs... so we had the bride ask her wedding coordinator to suggest a few quality clubs. Wedding coordinators plan bachelorette parties, so we knew she'd have a list of the best clubs in town."
—Angie, bridesmaid

No More Drama

It is best to ask the party guests—not friends of the bride who aren't invited—and contacts who don't know the bride and, therefore, won't be offended by not being invited to the party. Be sure to start asking for club or entertainment company references only after the bride has finalized her guest list.

Shop Here!

If a company is reputable, it will be a member of a professional organization like the International Special Event Society (ISES.com). Entertainment agencies that are members of this organization must follow strict business practice rules and codes of ethics, and have insurance. Check out its website, and you'll likely discover a company that can fulfill your party wishes.

manager if you can stop in just to see the show in action. At the prospect of booking your group, you'll likely be granted cover-free entry to survey the scene, judge the performances, take a walk through the club, and decide if this is the perfect place for the party.

If you're going the private route, once you have the names of some entertainment companies, ask the bride if she wants to participate in choosing the look of the dancer. Will he look like the groom, or fulfill a fantasy by looking like her favorite celebrity or athlete? Some brides look at the entertainment company's website to pick out the dancer she'd like for her party; others leave it up to the party planners.

That's Entertainment

If you don't hear about a reputable entertainment agency from a trusted source, look in the Yellow Pages or online under "Entertainment: Adult" to collect the names and locations of agencies in the area. Then investigate each one, looking for essential signs of their legitimacy. They need to not only have a website, but a street address must be listed as well.

Don't be fooled by an attractive site filled with photos of hot male dancers. A talented website creator can steal images from other companies' sites to make it look like the agency is loaded with the hottest guys in the state. Never book a company based solely on its website design.

Look for an agency that will allow you to come to their building, look through their portfolios, view videos of their talent's performances, and review their price packages. Event entertainment is big business, with the most reputable agencies offering not just male dancers, but other forms of entertainment as well, from musicians to celebrity impersonators, comedians, and other acts.

The Third Degree

To be a good consumer and make a smart decision as to who to hire from where, you need to ask smart questions at each company or agency you investigate:

➤ Can I see photos of the male performers and pick out the one(s) I want to hire?

➤ Do you offer a guarantee that I will get the dancer I select, or do you offer three or four choices?

➤ If a dancer can't attend my party at the last minute, how will a replacement be arranged? Do I pick a No. 2 choice now?

➤ What are your rates? Is it flat-fee or per-hour?

➤ How long a performance time do I get for the flat-free rate? Does it go by time or by number of songs?

➤ Does the dancer include travel time in his fees?

➤ What are the themes I get to choose? (Fireman, policeman, other personas)

➤ How revealing is his act? Does he strip down to briefs, or does he strip down to nothing? Can I request no nudity?

➤ Does the dancer use props, and can I approve of them before the party? (Your crowd may be game for the dancing, but not for X-rated props the dancer may include in his act.)

➤ Does the dancer bring his own sound system, or will we need to provide one?

➤ What else will we have to provide for the dancer's act?

➤ How do you handle billing? Do I pay a deposit now? A percent at the start of the night? The final amount after he performs?

➤ Which forms of payment do you accept? Do you accept payment through PayPal? (Beware a company that only accepts cash, as you'll have no official, protected record of your payment and a disreputable company can claim you never paid them. Pass by any cash-only operations.)

➤ Do you offer a contract? A contract is an essential document protecting your plans and investment. A reputable company offers a detailed contract, and a reputable agency owner will let you write in specific details of your order, such as what time the dancer will arrive and how long he'll perform. Take the time to read this contract, and if it's a detailed one, take it home for a legal-minded friend to review. Never give in to pressure from an agency owner to "just sign our standard form," and walk away from an owner who writes out an agreement and calls it a contract. This is a business deal. And in this era, you need to protect yourself by reviewing the contract and acquiring signatures before handing over any payments

Party Planning Fail-Safes

➤ Book at least a month in advance to hire the dancer you've chosen

➤ Call the entertainment company two weeks prior to your party to be sure your chosen dancer is still available

➤ Have the entertainment company's phone number with you at the party so you can call them directly if your dancer doesn't arrive on time

➤ Provide your party's full location, including zip code so the entertainer can locate you via GPS

➤ Prepare for the dancer's "no photos" rule. Since many male strippers work day jobs or are in relationships, they don't want photos and video of their act to appear online, embarrassing them and their families. Many male dancers say they're happy to pose for photos after their act, once they're fully dressed again

➤ Speak to the dancer like the professional he is. Just because he's showing up to strip for the bride doesn't mean he should be spoken to with any disdain, or encouraged to "get a real job." Male dancers hear all kinds of things and raunchy comments are part of the act, but he doesn't need anyone's advice about the path he's on

➤ Tell guests to bring plenty of singles so they can participate in the dancer's act. It's also a good idea for you to go to the bank ahead of time and get $100 worth of singles for guests to trade their $20s for

Shop Here!

For logo T-shirts in an array of colors and styles, check out the high-quality shirts at CafePress.com, and visit the sites mentioned in the Resources section of the book for all additional bachelorette props you might want her to wear as the star of the party.

In the Spotlight

The dancer is going to focus on the bride in his act, using his persona, such as fireman, construction worker, or another fantasy role you choose for her. While she sits in a straight-backed chair, he'll dance around her, maybe on her, certainly in front of her, and she may even get up and dance with him. Make sure he knows her name so he's not calling her by the wrong name all night!

To make things even more fun, consider outfitting the bride in a special ensemble. You might have her wear a special logo T- shirt such as one that says, "*I'm the Bride*," a tiara and party veil, or a white or hot pink feather boa. You could do this if you go out to a club as well.

Some groups also outfit themselves with coordinated T-shirts declaring "*I'm a Bridesmaid*" or "*I'm With the Bride*," which also garners attention for the group, but gives the male dancer the clear message that his attentions to the ladies of the group are of course appreciated, but The Bride is the clearly-identified one on which he is to lavish most of his focus and routines.

CHAPTER 10

Menu for Sexy Parties

In This Chapter

➤ Fabulous menus

➤ Sassy ways to present food

➤ Foods that rev you up

➤ Sexy food names

➤ Recipes

The food at a bachelorette party is too often an afterthought by party hosts who get caught up with the entertainment and the drinks, and that's one of the biggest party-planning mistakes you can make. It's a sign of poor planning when the food is cliché or blasé or simply not there beyond some bowls filled with chips. This chapter will save your party-planning reputation by helping you create a fabulous menu that pleases your diverse crowd, offers unique choices, fits within your budget, and impresses guests with its perfect fit to the party's theme. Since this is the section on racy, sexy parties, you'll focus here on creating a sexy, racy, even aphrodisiac menu that the bride and her guests will never forget.

Menu-Planning Basics

Before you start selecting appetizers from a catering list or cookbook, you need to set some foundational rules that are essential to a successful party menu. There's a smart science to choosing menu items that work together and that meet the tastes of your guests, and of course you need to create a plan for acquiring enough food to last through your entire event. Now, you might be planning the snacks for a preparty at your place, just an hour before you all pile into the limo and head out on the town, or you might be arranging the menu for a five-hour party at your place. You'll find the formulas for buying enough of the right combinations here.

Serving a Variety

Smart menu creation happens when you combine different kinds of dishes, providing a variety of foods to please your varied guests. If you've ever been to a wedding cocktail party at which every platter that came around was filled with fried, greasy appetizers in phyllo puffs, you know that it's a party don't to offer only greasy, heavy foods, no matter how easy they are to pop into the oven tray after tray.

A great rule of thumb for appetizers is to provide one or two—tops—frozen appetizers in phyllo puff style, in addition to six to eight fresh, tasty, refreshing appetizers such as a crisp curl of shrimp or a tomato bruschetta on a toasted circle of Italian bread. So the ratio of greasy to fresh foods is 1 to 6. Your guests will thank you for not tempting them with too many fried appetizers.

No More Drama

We're avoiding the drama of nauseated guests. When alcohol is flowing and cocktails mixing, the addition of greasy, fried foods can result in guests feeling queasy and actually getting sick at the party.

Next, mix up proteins and produce. A square of lemon chicken, a curl of smoked salmon and then lush, veggie-filled salads, stuffed mushrooms, artichokes and dipping sauces, mango salsa and chips, veggie crudités with an amazing array of gourmet dips, and the crunch of seasonal watermelon with a feta cheese crumble gives your guests guilt-free menu choices that don't leave them feeling greasy and heavy.

Consider a bread buffet to be an essential addition to your cocktail party spread, since guests who snack on breadsticks, rolls, grissini, pita triangles, and other absorbing foods do their bodies a service when they're drinking at the same time. So load up on fresh breads at the bakery, grocery store, or eateries like Panera Bread, and serve your collection warm with softened butters and spreads, plus a dipping plate of olive oil with a dusting of black pepper.

Finally, a great host takes into account the menu restrictions of her guests. These days, a smart catering list includes multiple choices for vegetarian, vegan, gluten-free, dairy-free and other guests with specialty diets. While it can be a challenge and a stressor to try to please everyone, it's quite easy to arrange a menu featuring multiple vegetable-based options, more pasta than red meat, brown rice sushi with veggies inside, and offer a dairy-free dip in addition to traditional sour cream dips. Providing an array of vegetarian foods that nonvegetarians can enjoy, for instance, makes your party spread a success for all guests.

Next is the spicy factor. Part of a racy sexy-themed party is the theme of adding a little spice to your life, so it's a smart idea to add a few spicy-hot items, dips, or sauces to the menu. Just be sure to label these items so that guests don't get an unwelcome surprise when they take a bite.

Style Savvy

Talk with your co-planners to get their lists of dietary restrictions and use their firsthand expertise to compose a list of foods and brands that they love, such as a soy spread or gluten-free chips. Next, include on your invitations a mention that invites guests' input, such as, "Please let us know if you have any special food restrictions or allergies so that we can make you happy with the party menu!" They e-mail in with the important warning that anything seafood is going to send them to the hospital, so you know to label that salmon dip well and provide a hummus alternative for party guests.

Serving Enough

It's better to have more food than you need than not enough. Planners on a budget run the risk of party failure when their food selections are skimpy, so it's wiser to go a little bit overboard with the spread you create. Leftovers can always go home with guests, hosts, and the bride.

Here is the formula that many caterers use when they help clients order the correct amount of food for their party's style:

➤ At an all-appetizers cocktail party with no dinner served, plan for each guest to take between ten and fifteen appetizers

➤ Guests will eat 20 percent more when the food is arranged on a buffet table, as opposed to appetizers that are hand-passed by waiters or hosts

➤ When you're having an hour-long cocktail party before a sit-down dinner, plan for four to five appetizers per guest

➤ For a dinner party, plan one entrée plus three side helpings per guest, in addition to those four to five predinner appetizers

➤ For a luncheon, plan for three to five appetizers per guest, plus one entrée and two sides

If you're going to a discount warehouse store like Costco or Sam's Club—a popular choice for hosts on a budget—the catering staff will help you plan the types and sizes of appetizer and sandwich platters for your guest head count. A platter of twenty small sandwiches, for instance, will be calculated as being enough for ten guests.

Don't forget that making some of your own dishes to add to catered or store-bought choices helps you expand your menu. So ask each co-planner to bring along a dip or a veggie platter or a plate of cheese slices, since these are the big three party staples that cost more to buy premade in your grocery store than they do to make on your own. Often, the price can be a stunning 50 percent more for those plastic-wrapped trays, so encourage your co-planners to cube, slice, and blend a generous amount for the party.

Creating a Menu on a Budget

Catering can be expensive, even for a cocktail party with appetizers on the menu. A box of twenty-four pastry puff appetizers can cost $8 or more, and those two dozen bites will be gone in a flash. A good menu will add up to one of the larger percentages of your party budget, if not the largest, so promise yourself and the bride that you will not let money get the better of your party. You'll utilize smart menu planning according to many of the same wise rules the bride is using to cater her own wedding events. Here are some smart money choices:

➤ Smaller amounts of a variety of foods always make it look like you're offering a bigger, more exorbitant spread

➤ Come up with creative ideas for pastas, since pasta is one of the least expensive menu items. Serve mini ravioli filled with goat cheese and spinach or basil and mozzarella—unique tastes in toothpick-speared pastas

➤ Serve plenty of fresh veggie dishes, such as artichoke leaves with dipping sauce, jalapenos (deseeded and filled with garlic spread), mushroom bites, and veggie sushi, buying in-season veggies and making the most of these less expensive options

➤ Make hummus to triple the amount you'd get in packaged hummus. Find great recipes at FoodNetwork.com and AllRecipes.com

➤ Top inexpensive chicken bites, pastas, and other foods with creative sauces, such as a drizzle of Alfredo, a marsala sauce, a creamy seafood sauce, or a creamy spinach sauce to make low-budget bites seem like you spent more

Money Mastery

The greater the variety of dishes you offer, the less you'll have to buy of each one. At bachelorette parties, guests do eat heartily, so don't make the mistake of thinking that guests will be more interested in the drinks than the food. Buy enough for everyone to eat well at the start of the party, and then come back for seconds a few hours into the party.

➤ Rather than buy a three-foot sub to provide sandwiches for guests, buy three or four individual submarine sandwiches—such as turkey, roast beef, Italian, and veggie-filled—slice them in two-inch pieces, and then arrange them on three different platters to make your sandwich choices look like twice as much food. You'll save over 40 percent with this strategy

➤ Hand-pass expensive items like shrimp cocktail in just two or three walk-throughs of the room so that guests get a bite or two without going wild on a buffet-displayed bowl of shrimp

➤ If you set up several food stations around your party space, those smaller groupings will actually look like you have way more food

➤ Arrange appetizers spaced out on larger platters or oversized plates so that it looks like an upscale restaurant display and you spent more than you really did on the food

➤ Bulk bags of frozen waffle fries create a crowd-pleasing baked treat on a low budget, when you find those family-sized bags at warehouse stores like Costco or Sam's Club, and use coupons to get them. Then, dress up those fries with a dusting of flavored spices such as Old Bay or a small amount of cayenne pepper for that spicy kick

Sexy Food Presentation

On any bachelorette party website, you'll see the ubiquitous penis-shaped cake molds and penis-shaped platters for party food. You can certainly create your bachelorette party food presentation to include a number of phallic designs, giving your menu a racy edge, or you can go for a sensual rather than sexual theme with your food. And, of course, you can create a combination of the two approaches.

In this section, you'll plan how you'll present your party menu items in sexed-up, sensual, or

Money Mastery

Coupons will save you a fortune on party food items, so ask all of your co-planners to clip coupons for menu items and send them to you if you're the menu shopper, and load up on fabulous coupons—starting now—at Coupons.com. Plus, Target has a grocery section with immensely discounted frozen foods ($1.99 for a package of fries as opposed to a grocery store's $3.99 price), and coupons available on its website can take your grand total down by a sizeable amount. Don't be afraid to venture away from your usual supermarket to net great deals on party food, and research the dates of double- and triple-coupon days. Coupon timing is not just for moms and grandmoms; imagine getting your party menu for under $10. It could happen with your supply of coupons tripled.

sassy ways. The food itself might be made or molded into the shape of a penis, or you might garnish with phallic items. Of course, you might find that the penis is not your chosen motif. For the bride, *sexy* is lingerie, stilettos, a pearl necklace, feather boas, the dress-up interpretation of sensuality. And the third most popular design motif for sexy menu presentation is animal print, with plates, platters, napkins, and other essentials coordinated in leopard print or zebra stripe, including black and hot-pink zebra stripe. So if that's your party décor, bring those sexy stripes into your food presentation as well.

Style Savvy

Cookie cutters are available on the top bachelorette party websites listed in the back of this book, but keep in mind that size matters! The cookie cutter kit I found at Bachelorette.com provides three different sizes, but the largest one is about the size of a cookie sheet. Look at the measurements of each cutter in the kit you find online to be sure they'll be good for cutting smaller food items. And get several sizes of cutters. Having a range of sizes, rather than just one cutter, lets you create a more varied and impressive presentation of dishes.

Cutouts and Shapes

The craft store is not likely to stock phallic-shaped cookie cutters, so look online to discover a collection of penis-shaped cookie cutters in different sizes and designs, and use these not just to make cookies, but also to cut out shaped foods. For instance, you can use these cookie cutters to stamp out slices of watermelon, cantaloupe, honeydew, or pineapple. Smaller varieties of cookie cutters can be used to stamp out shaped sandwiches, pita bread sections, garlic toast made from slices of wheat, rye, or pumpernickel bread. The creativity possible with these shaped cookie cutters is unlimited, so think about tailoring your menu to include foods that can be cut into your racy-themed shapes.

You can, of course, create phallic-shaped foods without an official penis cookie cutter. Just use two small circular cutters—very available at craft stores—and use a knife to create the rest of the shape. It's time-consuming, but the results will be worth it.

If you'd rather go a bit more subtle with your food cutouts, use a cherry-shaped cookie cutter instead. You'll find a wide variety of sexy-styled cookie cutters, including bras, panties, high heels, and dress shapes that can be iced with passionate hot-pink frosting to look like a camisole, with white frosting used on the edges to look like lace. It's important to create the bride's style of sexy, never going too raunchy for a conservative bride.

And of course, the food itself may be phallic in shape. Again, bananas may be the most obvious choice, but anything with length such as breadsticks shaped before baking will provide that hint of manhood.

Sensual Sauces

As another more subtle option for sexy food presentation, without any phallic items on the menu, provide sensual sauces for foods. Some suggestions include a creamy Alfredo sauce for mini ravioli and other pastas, marsala sauce, vodka sauce, and other rich flavors that appetizers can be artfully drizzled with or served in. The indulgence of a sauce is what makes the simplest of pastas, meatballs, chicken fingers, and other hors d'oeuvres sexy and sensual.

Aphrodisiac Foods

A sexy party calls for sexy food, and what
could be sexier than aphrodisiacs on the menu?
With libido-launching foods at the party, your
guests will take their revved-up sex drives out
on the dance floor, up to the male revue stage,
and home with them at the end of the evening,
where their boyfriends, spouses, or partners
will enjoy the side effects of the menu you
planned. Here are the most popular foods that
studies say include aphrodisiac elements, either
relaxing inhibitions, stimulating blood flow to
all regions of the body, or creating feel-good
and arousal hormones:

Steal My Party Idea

"We decided to go with a
'penetration' theme for the food,
so we served coconut shrimp
inserted into a ring of pineapple,
full sour pickles inserted into
the top of a butterfly-shaped
sandwich, carrot sticks inserted
into shot glasses full of onion
dip, and other styles to show
our racier party theme, which
included a few 'get it in' games."
—Marcia, bridesmaid

Seafood

➤ Oysters: Oysters are one of the best-
known aphrodisiacs, and they're best
served raw with champagne for a real
dose of libido boosting. While raw
oysters are on the pricy side for a party,
you can make an oyster dip that delivers almost as much perk

➤ Salmon: Salmon, that staple of wedding and party menus, is high on the list of
aphrodisiacs, so add some smoked salmon to your hors d'oeuvres or buffet, as well
as mini salmon cakes, salmon-filled sushi, and salmon dips

Fruits and Vegetables

➤ Avocado: A creamy guacamole is a sensual food to eat, with its smooth texture
and a bit of spicy kick. For that reason alone, guacamole becomes a top party food
choice. Looking back in food history, avocado has a racy past. The Aztecs thought
that avocados looked like testicles, so they called the avocado *ahuacuatl*, which
translates to "testicle tree." And early Catholic priests in Spain were so offended by
the testicular resemblance that they banned the fruit entirely. A fruit banned for
looking like male parts? That has to be on your sexy food menu!

➤ Bananas: Just the shape of them make them a must for your party, and some
hosts even make a phallic centerpiece out of a big bunch of ripe bananas. Banana

chips and banana chunks in fruit salad bring a burst of vitamins, potassium, and magnesium that is said to enhance libido, especially in men. That's a smart little FYI to share with party guests

➤ Watermelon: It's true. The summertime snack is filled with libido-lifting hormones, which is why you might feel randier in the warmer months. Add slices of watermelon topped with Brie, gorgonzola, or garlic cheese spread on top, or make a watermelon salsa with mangos and shallots for a refreshing shooter that packs a punch

➤ Celery: Celery is currently being studied to see if it truly does arouse women with its hormone androsterone, which is a hormone produced in males. It's most often on the okay list for dieting party guests, so provide a pretty platter of celery with dip to give your healthy eaters a boost

➤ Figs: Figs carry a long history of being associated with the female sex organs, and food experts say that the sweet fruit was Cleopatra's favorite. Many cultures hold the fig as a symbol of love and fertility, so add a fig dip to your menu, or bake a Brie in brioche with a fig sauce inside

➤ Pomegranate: The sweet and tart juices of a pomegranate are a potent aphrodisiac, so blend up not just pomegranate martinis but add some pom seeds to your salads. Pomegranates also can be used to make a fabulous sauce for appetizers, with a particularly good pairing being goat cheese ravioli

➤ Asparagus: An ingredient in asparagus has long been believed to boost the production of histamines in the body, which leads to a stronger orgasm. In the nineteenth century, grooms were given several different preparations of asparagus to get them prepared for the wedding night. For your party, add asparagus tips to salads, or bundle mini asparagus tips in chive-tied bunches for a crunchy veggie side, or wrap large asparagus spears in prosciutto for a salty and crunchy snack. Dried asparagus chips don't pack the freshness power, but they still deliver potassium, thiamin, folic acid, vitamin B6 and more for a libido-raising crunch in the snack mix

Nuts

➤ Almonds: Legend has it that almonds arose passion in women and have long been a fertility symbol. Think about the traditional wedding favor of candied almonds—brides have been handing out "love aids" to their guests for years. Now, almonds and their libido-boosting magnesium and vitamin E can be a love aid for your guests in snack and drink form

➤ Walnuts: The belief that walnuts have aphrodisiac properties has been around for so long history says they've been used in ancient fertility rituals. The natural oils of these and other forms of nuts are said to give a glow when added to beauty products, and the antioxidants in nuts are said to stimulate blood flow, which is always good for the sex drive

Additional foods

➤ Chocolate: Chocolate contains a number of libidinous compounds, notably phenylethylamine, which is said to promote feelings of subtle well-being, plus hormones that release dopamine—the same chemical that is released during orgasm. The perks go on and on, with dark chocolate ranking number one in the good-for-you category. So fill your menu with chocolate options, from desserts to chocolate martinis, and consider chocolate as your guests' take-home favor as well

➤ Basil: It's the sweet smell of basil that's said to be the aphrodisiac here. So load up your pasta appetizers with plenty of fresh basil, serve ravioli filled with goat cheese and basil, and make my bruschetta recipe found later in this chapter for a big dose of blood-pumping basil

➤ Garlic: It doesn't impress with your breath, but garlic included in your dips, bruschetta, appetizers, and on good-for-you garlic bread gets your blood flowing with its ingredient allicin

➤ Additional aphrodisiacs: Honey, hot chili peppers, onions, peaches, peas, cherries, ginger, oranges, pears, vanilla, and truffles all add a little excitement to your step

Giving Food Sexy Names

Add an extra dash of sexiness to your party's menu by placing food ID cards in front of each platter. You'll come up with creative, sexy names for each dish—such as Slippery Shrimp, Orgasm Orange Chicken, or Stud Mushrooms. You can make the names of each dish personal to the bride and groom, such as Not on the First Date Nachos, or Fifth Date Fajitas. Brainstorm with your co-planners in a fun series of e-mails (which you can keep and give to the bride later as a fun look into your planning process—but let the co-planners know you plan to do so!), and pick the best sexy names of the bunch.

Use place card sheets from the office supply or party supply store to print out your tented food ID cards using ink that matches the party's color scheme and a cute font, and you have the kind of smart party detail that makes it look like a pro helped you plan.

Recipes

If you're going to make any food items for the party, you can bring out your personal favorite recipes to share with the crowd, or you can find plenty of fabulous recipes at the top sites like FoodNetwork.com, MixingBowl.com, AllRecipes.com, FoodandWine.com, and BHG.com. Party recipes are also plentiful at MarthaStewart.com, RachaelRayMag.com, PaulaDeenMagazine.com, and other celebrity chef sites.

Dips

Dips are perfect for cocktail parties, since you can inexpensively offer so many different flavors on a budget. The top dip styles to choose from are artichoke dip, bean dip, crab dip, guacamole, hummus, pâté, salsa, shrimp dip, spinach dip, artichoke and spinach dip, buffalo chicken dip, roasted red pepper dip, smoked salmon dip, and seven-layer Mexican dip. Provide an array of chips from black bean chips to whole grain and veggie chips, as well as different breads such as pita triangles and crunchy melba toast. Grissini and soft bread sticks, as well as fresh veggies, are perfect dippers as well.

Here are just a few recipes:

No More Drama

Ask your co-planners to tell you what they'd like to make for the party, which is a far smarter option than assigning dishes or categories. Everyone has her own signature dishes that she feels confident making and may already be the bride's favorite treats. When you give your co-planners the freedom to make what they wish, they're happier cooks and the results show in their dishes and presentations.

Artichoke and Spinach Dip

> 4 whole cloves garlic, unpeeled
> 1 10-ounce package frozen chopped spinach, thawed and drained
> 1 14-ounce can artichoke hearts, drained and chopped
> 1 10-ounce container Alfredo-style pasta sauce
> 1 cup shredded mozzarella cheese
> 1/3 cup grated Parmesan cheese
> 1/2 8-ounce package cream cheese, softened

Preheat oven to 350 degrees F (175 degrees C).

Place the garlic in a small baking dish and bake for 20 to 30 minutes until soft. Remove from the oven. When cool enough to touch, squeeze softened garlic from skins.

In an 8 x 8–inch baking dish, combine the roasted garlic, spinach, artichoke hearts,

Alfredo-style pasta sauce, mozzarella cheese, Parmesan cheese, and cream cheese.

Cover and bake the dip for 30 minutes or until cheeses are melted and bubbly. Serve warm.

Hot Crab Dip

    2 cups crabmeat

    1 cup sour cream

    1 8-ounce package cream cheese, softened

    1 cup buttermilk

    1 cup mayonnaise

    1 cup shredded Monterey Jack cheese

    1 cup white cheddar cheese

    1/2 cup capers, drained

    2 8-ounce cans artichoke hearts, drained and chopped

    2 tablespoons minced garlic

    1/2 teaspoon ground black pepper

    1/2 teaspoon dried dill

    1/4 cup grated Parmesan cheese

    1/2 teaspoon Old Bay Seasoning

    1 round loaf sourdough bread

Preheat oven to 400 degrees F (200 degrees C)

Lightly grease or nonstick-spray an 8 x 8–inch square baking pan.

In a large bowl, combine crabmeat, sour cream, cream cheese, buttermilk, mayonnaise, Monterey Jack cheese, cheddar cheese, capers, artichoke hearts, garlic, black pepper, and dill. Stir until well mixed, then spoon dip into prepared baking pan.

Sprinkle with Parmesan cheese and Old Bay Seasoning.

Bake in preheated oven until top is slightly crusty, about 15 to 20 minutes.

Cut the top off the loaf of bread. Hollow out the loaf. Cube the removed pieces so that they may be used for dipping. Spoon the hot dip into the hollow bread loaf. Serve immediately with bread pieces for dipping.

Hummus

    1 15-ounce can garbanzo beans, drained, liquid reserved

    2 ounces fresh jalapeno pepper, sliced

    1/2 teaspoon ground cumin

    2 tablespoons lemon juice

    3 cloves garlic, minced

In a blender or food processor, combine garbanzo beans, jalapeno, cumin, lemon juice, garlic, and 1 tablespoon of the reserved bean liquid. Blend just until smooth. Makes 2 cups of dip.

Hors D'Oeuvres

Stuffed Mushrooms

24 mushrooms
1 container Alouette spread in garlic flavor or spinach and artichoke flavor
1/2 cup Italian-flavored bread crumbs

Preheat oven to 350 degrees F (175 degrees C).

Carefully remove stems from each mushroom, leaving a hollowed cap.

Wash mushrooms well, removing any dirt or debris, and gently pat mushrooms dry with a paper towel.

Using a teaspoon, fill each mushroom cap just to the top level with Alouette spread.

Sprinkle bread crumbs over the tops of the filled mushrooms.

Bake for 10 to 15 minutes and serve immediately.

Makes 24 stuffed mushrooms.

Coconut Shrimp

2 quarts vegetable oil for frying
10 ounces orange marmalade
3 tablespoons prepared horseradish
3 tablespoons prepared mustard
3/4 cup all-purpose flour
1/4 teaspoon baking powder
1/4 teaspoon paprika
1/4 teaspoon curry powder
1/8 teaspoon salt
1/8 teaspoon cayenne pepper
1/3 cup beer
1 pound large shrimp, peeled and deveined with tails attached
1/4 cup all-purpose flour
8 ounces unsweetened flaked coconut
Duck sauce (optional)

Heat oil in a deep fryer at 375 degrees F (190 degrees C).

In a small bowl, stir together marmalade, horseradish, and mustard, and set this dipping sauce aside.

In a medium bowl, combine 3/4 cup flour, baking powder, paprika, curry powder, salt, and cayenne.

Stir in beer to create your batter.

Dredge shrimp in 1/4 cup flour, dip each piece in beer batter, and then roll each piece in coconut.

Fry the shrimp in hot oil until golden on both sides; break one open to check for doneness.

Drain and serve with dipping sauce or duck sauce alternative.

CHAPTER 11

Drinks

In This Chapter

➤ Smart bar setup

➤ Mixing and pouring cocktails

➤ A menu of alcohol-free libations

Bachelorette parties are known for being wild, drink-filled fun fests, and that means you need to offer an impressive bar. At traditional bachelorette bashes, the hosts choose potent cocktails and racy-named shooters, neon-colored jello shots, salt-rimmed margaritas, bottles of tequila, and the Margaritaville machine gets pulled down from the cabinet. When you're at a bar or club, you don't have to think about ingredients and recipes; everyone just orders what they want, and the martini glasses and test tubes just keep coming to the table. But when you plan an at-home party of any style and raciness level, you do need to put careful thought and preparation into your bar list.

In this chapter, you'll plan a crowd-pleasing bar menu featuring everything from martinis to margaritas, sangria to shots, and you'll also take the smart steps to create a bar menu that includes nonalcoholic drinks for those who wish to pace themselves or who don't drink alcohol. A great party host provides perfectly for every guest's preferences.

Planning Your Bar

Here, you'll create a winning plan to offer a wide variety of drinks, and you'll also find out how to easily calculate the amount of alcohol and mixers you'll need to buy to keep your guests happy throughout the entire length of the party. You don't want the bride, or the guests, disappointed when the bar goes dry an hour into the celebration because you underestimated their drinking power or cheaped out at the liquor store. This chapter will guide you to two of the top drink calculators that will do the math for you.

You'll also create a smart bar setup, with guests easily able to prepare their own drinks because you've given them plenty of room to do so. It's a big party flub when your bar is a counter crowded with bottles of alcohol and barely enough room for drink glasses. Guests don't want to stand in line at a bar, so they definitely don't want to wait in line at your house party. A smart bar setup lets everyone access their drink choices quickly and comfortably.

And you'll even make your drinks pretty. All in this section.

Variety of Drinks

You may have your own favorite drinks that you always enjoy at parties, and you may know what your friends' usual drinks are, but you're hosting a party that may include the groom's sisters and friends of the bride whom you've never met before. That means setting up a diverse bar list with at least eight different kinds of drinks available to the guests. The usual formula is four different cocktails, two different kinds of wine (red and white), and three different kinds of soft drinks. That's the basic bar plan. You might choose to add a variety of flavored shots such as Lemon Drops, Mind Erasers, and, of course, the vividly colored Jell-O shots your crowd has indulged in during your barhopping days—no matter how long ago that was. Brides in their thirties say they love to throw back throwback drinks from their party days, although perhaps not as many.

Look at the recipes section in this chapter for a starter list of drink inspirations, and make it a rule that you'll provide drinks in varying levels of potency, or drinks that guests can mix themselves in their chosen levels of potency.

Many hosts decide to display a bar card featuring the five different cocktails on the drink menu for the evening. If you'd rather give guests their choices, you can provide a variety of hard liquors alongside standard mixers so that guests can mix their own concoctions. To do this successfully, it's smart to provide, along with all of those bottles, a printed recipe sheet sharing basic drink combinations for guests to try. An example of this is a bar card sharing the half-and-half blend of a rum punch made from orange and pineapple juice, with a flavored rum bar at hand. Cruzan rums come in a variety of flavors such as vanilla, mango, and guava—to name a few. Many tropical resorts serve this brand of rum. So your tropical mixed drinks will taste like the ones you'd be served on an island.

Hard liquors to stock on your bar include:

➤ Rum

➤ Vodka

➤ Gin

➤ Tequila

➤ Whiskey

➤ Southern Comfort

➤ Amaretto

➤ Chambord

➤ Kahlua

➤ Bailey's Irish Cream

Mixers to offer on your bar include:

➤ Colas, regular and diet

➤ Lemon-lime soda

➤ Tonic water

➤ Club soda

➤ Seltzer

➤ Orange juice

➤ Pineapple juice

➤ Cranberry juice

➤ Grapefruit Juice

➤ Lemon juice

➤ Lime juice

➤ Collins mix

➤ Sour mix

➤ Triple sec

➤ Margarita mixes, flavored

Style Savvy

Think also about the colors of the drinks. You may wish to offer drinks in the color scheme of the party, such as pinks, reds, or blues. Or you may love the look of a dazzling festive, neon collection of bright blue martinis, sunshine yellow shots, and emerald green Jell-O shots rather than a monochromatic collection of drinks.

Style Savvy

Create a stylish mixers bar by pouring juices into half carafes—found at the dollar store or inexpensively at Pier 1 or Crate & Barrel—and labeling each carafe with a computer-designed and printed label. The effect is more upscale bar than "I pulled things off of my refrigerator shelf."

Style Savvy

An important supply to estimate as well is ice. For a larger guest list and for drinks served on the rocks, plus frozen blended drinks, you'll go through a lot of ice. Ask your co-hosts to each bring several bags of premade ice to the party and store them in dedicated large coolers that you keep outside on your patio. Your freezer's ice maker is just not going to be able to keep up, and no host wants to keep filling ice trays all night. For the style element of this essential supply, get or borrow a fabulous ice bucket with a lid, plus easy-to-use ice tongs. To refill the ice bucket from the coolers, use a metal ice scoop, never your hands.

Getting Enough

It can be difficult to estimate how much liquor and how many bottles of mixers to buy for your at-home party. You may have guests invited who you know to down a drink every five minutes, and guests who you know to nurse their cocktails for an hour. And you likely have guests invited whom you've never met. That's why party hosts are wild about drink calculators found at Evite.com and at ThatsTheSpirit.com. You enter the number of guests, broken down by heavier and lighter drinkers, and the length of your party—and ThatsTheSpirit.com even asks you to enter the cost of each bottle of liquor—and the sites automatically tally a shopping list for you. To be on the safe side, add 15 percent more to each total. It's better to have a liquor and mixer supply that is too large than too small, so that a guest won't have to run out to the liquor store during the party.

Serving Style

As mentioned, guests want to access your bar easily and quickly, so here is where you design your bar's serving style. While some party hosts hire bartenders to work the party—for expert drink creation and perhaps even to have hot men serving the room—many find it more budget friendly to arrange a self-service bar.

Assess your party space for the location of your bar. Your dining room table will likely be taken up by the food and by plates and serving items. So that's often out of play. Your kitchen counter may offer a good amount of counter space, but can guests move into and out of the kitchen easily enough?

Many guests solve the bar problem by having a friend bring in a dedicated table to set up in the living room, where the bar will be displayed. Set it first with an attractive tablecloth to give the tabletop a uniform and clean look, since that extra table may have scratches, paint, or other mars on it. Then set liquor bottles on one side, mixers on the other side, ice in the middle and glasses set in front with garnishes also handy.

A big trend, and a smart strategy, is to set up several bars around the party space, just as you have seen at wedding receptions. One corner may feature a wine bar. Another corner may feature the cocktail bar. Another table on a side wall may feature trays of Jell-O shots. And yet another table may offer soft drinks and punch. Guests then go to their chosen station, without long lines and long waits anywhere.

If you'll have guest tables for eating, you can set pitchers of sangria or iced tea right on the tabletops for easy access.

Presenting Pretty Drinks

No matter what's on your drinks menu, take care to create a pretty presentation for each. Margaritas can be served not just in salt-rimmed glasses, but in red salt-rimmed glasses to convey that hot and sexy theme of your party. Tropical drinks can get a little drink umbrella (which you'll find in the party supply store for under $3 per pack of fifty or so). Olives can be prespeared on bachelorette party-themed neon-colored toothpicks, also from the party supply store.

Each and every style of drink you serve— including soft drinks—can be garnished in any of the following ways:

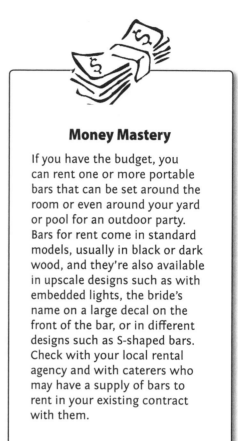

Money Mastery

If you have the budget, you can rent one or more portable bars that can be set around the room or even around your yard or pool for an outdoor party. Bars for rent come in standard models, usually in black or dark wood, and they're also available in upscale designs such as with embedded lights, the bride's name on a large decal on the front of the bar, or in different designs such as S-shaped bars. Check with your local rental agency and with caterers who may have a supply of bars to rent in your existing contract with them.

> ➤ Salt-rimmed glasses

> ➤ Sugar-rimmed glasses (such as the sugar-dipped shot glass used for a Lemon Drop shot)

> ➤ A half circle of fruit wedged onto the rim of the glass

> ➤ Tiny fruits such as raspberries, blackberries, and pomegranate seeds dropped into glasses to sit at the bottom of champagnes, martinis, other cocktails, and soft drinks

> ➤ A stick candy such as a candy cane placed in each glass

> ➤ Jelly beans or hard candies dropped into each glass

Here is your essential shopping list for a well-stocked bar's edible garnish supplies:

> ➤ Lemon slices/wedges

> ➤ Lime slices/wedges

Style Savvy

Allow each drink to share a message. Use your computer and printer to print out on adhesive address labels your choice of words or messages in a pretty style and color of font. Then attach two labels to the top of a toothpick (like a flag), use a creative hole punch to pop out a heart, star or other tiny accent at the end of the message flag, and have these stylish, inexpensive accents ready to pop into each of your drinks.

➤ Orange slices/wedges

➤ Pineapple slices/wedges

➤ Strawberry slices

➤ Raspberries

➤ Olives

➤ Maraschino cherries

➤ Red hot candies and other candies such as jelly beans, Gummi bears, hard candies in fruit flavors or butterscotch, and more

➤ Margarita glass rimmer kit with regular, colored or flavored salt (the circular salt container allows you to easily dip a moist-rimmed glass into the salt for an even, attractive garnish.)

Another way to dress up your drinks is to add store-bought or DIY charms to each glass's stem. You'll find pricier wine charm collections in gift shops—often $20 for six or so charms—and those elegant styles may be perfect for your party theme. You might not find that expensive at all. You'll also find inexpensive plastic glass charms at the party supply or craft store, in such theme shapes as stilettos, handbags, flamingoes, bright butterflies, dice for a Vegas-themed party, and a vast range of other designs. And, of course, a big trend in party supplies is the DIY wine charms kits at craft stores that allow you to make twenty or more custom glass charms for your party.

The styles of glasses go a long way to making your bar stand out. You could simply buy packs of colorful plastic drink glasses at the party supply store; some shades would work perfectly with your theme. Plastic party collections include cups sized for cocktails, soft drinks, shots, even champagne toasts. A coordinated supply adds a pop of color to your bar setup, and some party hosts like the ease of cleanup after the party.

For a higher price, you can rent collections of modern, sleek, chic, real drink glasses, from highballs to shot glasses to wineglasses, martini glasses, and more. Why rent? So that all of the glasses match, coordinating perfectly, giving your party a more refined feel right down to the details. That's way better than bringing out lots of mismatched wineglasses and shot glasses of different shapes and heights, each stamped with a liquor brand in different colors. That's the style of a college party, and this occasion calls for a step up in effort.

So go to a reputable rental agency and assess the different styles of red and white wineglasses—and if you'll be serving sangria as well as wine, tell the rental assistant to multiply the number of wineglasses you'll need. The rental assistant will help you calculate how many glasses you'll need in each style as well as help you find the perfect new designs in martini, margarita, shot, and other specialty glasses. The rental shop might have those amazing modern stemless wineglasses you've seen in the Crate & Barrel catalog and have always admired—and party hosts say they love that style for wine service, since drunk guests tend to plunk down their wineglasses a little too hard, snapping the stems and costing them lots of replacement money. Using stemless glasses lessens the breakage factor.

Money Mastery

Of course, for rented glasses you do need to configure the replacement costs due to breakage. Even at tame parties where alcohol doesn't flow wildly, glasses sometimes get dropped or cracked. So get the replacement cost for damaged glasses in writing. It's important information to have when renting.

Most rental agencies don't require you to wash and dry their glasses before their return. On that day-after-the-party recovery day, your easy task is just rounding up glasses, dumping unfinished drinks, and placing each glass into the compartmented cases they came in. You'll arrange for their return via drop-off or pickup with careful attention to the time they're due to be returned. Don't be one of those hosts who gets stuck paying double because an afternoon drop-off counts as a second day's rental.

Drink Recipes

You'll find an impressive array of drink recipes online at FoodNetwork.com, Cocktail.com, CocktailTimes.com, and AllRecipes.com. Don't forget that the websites for individual brand-name liquors feature extensive collections of drink recipes to be made with their products in their various flavors, so those sites are priceless resources for your well-stocked bar as well.

We've started you off with a few recipes in the top drink categories here:

Champagne Cocktails

Cosmopolitan Champagne Cocktail
    10 ounces Grand Marnier

10 ounces cranberry juice
32 ounces chilled champagne
5 ounces fresh lime juice
3 tablespoons superfine granulated sugar
ginger sugar (optional)

Combine sugar and lime juice until sugar dissolves. Add cranberry juice and Grand Marnier. Then chill, covered, for an hour. Just before serving, divide mixture among ten champagne flutes, approximately 2-1/2 ounces per glass. Top off each with champagne. For an added flavor effect, first rim glasses with ginger sugar. Makes 10 servings.

French Flirt

8 ounces Alizé Gold Passion liqueur
2 ounces Chambord
1 ounce ginger liqueur
1 750-ml bottle chilled brut champagne
raspberries

In a large pitcher combine first three ingredients. Stir well. Chill for at least an hour. Just before serving, carefully add champagne. To reduce loss of effervescence, tilt pitcher and pour along sides. Stir gently to combine. Serve in champagne flutes with berries dropped into each flute. Makes 10 servings.

Arctic Kiss

2 parts vodka
3 parts champagne

This recipe creates one drink, so use the 2 to 3 formula to make your desired amount of champagne cocktail. Pour chilled vodka into champagne flutes and fill each with champagne.

Bellini

1 ounce peach schnapps
6 ounces champagne

This recipe is designed to make one drink. Pour peach schnapps into champagne flute, and fill flute with champagne. No need to mix; the bubbly will take care of that. Makes 1 serving.

Mimosa

> 1/2 ounce orange juice
> ice
> 4-1/2 ounces champagne
> orange slice (optional)

This recipe makes one drink. Pour orange juice over ice in chilled champagne glass and fill with champagne. Garnish with an orange slice on the rim of the glass. Makes 1 serving.

Caribbean Champagne

> 1/2 teaspoon light rum
> 1/2 teaspoon banana liqueur
> 1 dash orange bitters
> 4 ounces champagne
> 1 slice of banana

Pour rum, liqueur, and bitters into a champagne glass, fill with champagne, and garnish with banana slice. Makes 1 serving.

Fruity Margaritas

Mango Margarita

> 1/4 lime
> 1/2 cup peeled sliced mango
> 1/2 ounce Cointreau
> 1-1/4 ounces tequila
> ice
> splash Chambord
> lime wedge

In a blender squeeze juice of lime, then add the mango and blend. Add the Cointreau and tequila and blend. Combine with ice, then serve topped with a splash of Chambord and garnished with a lime wedge. Makes 1 serving.

Pear Margarita

> 1 whole fresh Bartlett pear, peeled and sliced
> 1 ounce tequila
> 1/2 ounce triple sec
> 1/2 ounce lime juice
> 1-1/2 ounces sweet and sour mix
> ice
> lime wedge

In a blender, combine all ingredients with ice and garnish with a lime wedge. Makes 1 serving.

Pineapple Margarita

1/2 cup fresh pineapple
1-1/4 ounces tequila
1/2 ounce triple sec
1/2 ounce orange juice
ice
lime wedge

In a blender, combine all ingredients with ice and garnish with a lime wedge. Makes 1 serving.

Hawaiian Margarita

1 whole pear, peeled and sliced
1-1/4 ounces tequila
1/2 ounce amaretto
1/2 ounce blue curacao
3-4 slices cored pineapple
2 ounces sweet and sour mix
ice
lime wedge

In a blender, combine all ingredients with ice and garnish with a lime wedge. Makes 1 serving.

Cranberry Margarita

1-1/4 ounces tequila
1/2 ounce Cointreau
2 ounces cranberry syrup
splash orange juice
ice
lime wedge

In a blender, combine all ingredients with ice and garnish with a lime wedge. Makes 1 serving.

Raspberry Margarita

1/2 cup fresh raspberries
1-1/4 ounces tequila
1/2 ounce Cointreau
1/2 ounce orange juice

1-1/2 ounces sweet and sour mix
ice
lime wedge

In a blender, combine all ingredients with ice and garnish with a lime wedge.

Shots

Literally hundreds of shots recipes exist, many with X-rated names that may suit the racy style of your party. Check BacheloretteParties.com and Cocktail.com to locate potent shots for your wild bash.

Lemon Drop

1-1/2 ounces vodka
lemon wedge
sugar

Pour vodka into a shot glass. Coat a lemon wedge with sugar. Drink the shot of vodka, then follow up immediately with a bite into the sugary lemon.

You can also coat the inside of a shot glass with lemon juice and pour sugar on top of the liquid. Shake out any loose sugar and juice. You then get a sour sugar-coated shot glass to pour your shot into and drink.

Orange Drop

1 shot Stoli orange vodka
ice
Pixie Stix
1 orange slice

Chill vodka over ice. Pour in a shot glass. Pour contents of Pixie Stix on orange slice for a bite after you drink the shot.

Alabama Slammer Shot

1 ounce amaretto
1 ounce Southern Comfort
1/2 ounce sloe gin
dash of lemon juice

Pour the amaretto, Southern Comfort, and sloe gin in a chilled highball glass with ice. Add the dash of lemon juice and stir well. Strain into a shot glass.

Blow Job

1/4 ounce Baileys Irish Cream liqueur

1/2 ounce amaretto almond liqueur
whipped cream

Pour the liqueurs into a shot glass and top with whipped cream.

Jolly Rancher Jell-O Shot

1 package green apple Jell-O
1 cup boiling water
1 cup DeKuyper Sour Apple Pucker schnapps, chilled

Mix the boiling water with a package of green apple Jell-O and let dissolve for one minute. Add chilled DeKuyper Sour Apple Pucker schnapps, and stir until well combined. Pour into 1-ounce disposable shot glasses and refrigerate for several hours until Jell-O sets fully. Makes 20 servings.

Tootsie Roll Jell-O Shot

1 (4 ounce) box orange Jell-O
1 cup boiling water
1 cup Créme de Cacao

Dissolve Jell-O in boiling water. Add Créme De Cacao and stir. Pour into 1-ounce shot cups and chill for approximately four hours till it's set. Makes 20 shots.

Mojito Jell-O Shots

6 sprigs fresh mint
3 ounces light rum
4 teaspoons sugar
6 tablespoons fresh lemon juice or fresh lime juice
1 cup boiling water
2 packages lime Jell-O

In a cocktail shaker, crush the mint to release the oil. Add the rum, sugar, and lemon or lime juice, and shake thoroughly. Mix with the water, strain, and mix in Jell-O until well dissolved, then pour in 2-ounce shot glasses three-quarters full and refrigerate till set. Makes 20 servings.

Sangrias

Standard Sangria

1 bottle red wine
2 ounces lime juice
4 ounces rum
Slices of fruit

Mix together the wine, lime juice, and rum in a pitcher and add the fruit slices. Serve in wineglasses. Makes 4 servings.

Spanish Sangria

> 1 sliced orange
> 1/2 sliced lemon
> 1 sliced lime
> 1-1/2 ounces brandy
> 2 tablespoons sugar
> 1 bottle of chilled red wine
> 12 ounces chilled club soda
> ice cubes

In a large pitcher, combine the fruit slices, then add the brandy and sugar, and stir until sugar is dissolved. Pour in the wine and stir, then refrigerate for at least two hours. When ready to serve, add the club soda and stir gently. Fill wineglasses with ice and pour sangria over the ice to fill each glass. Makes one pitcher.

Hot and Spicy Sangria

> 1 sliced Granny Smith apple
> 1 sliced peach
> 1 sliced plum
> 1 sliced apricot
> 3 thin slices of seeded jalapeno
> 2 ounces tequila
> 2 tablespoons sugar
> 1 bottle dry white wine
> 12 ounces club soda
> ice cubes

In a large pitcher, combine the fruit slices, jalapeno slices, tequila, and sugar. Stir until sugar is dissolved. Pour in the wine, gently stirring, and refrigerate for at least two hours. Before serving, pour in the club soda, stir, and pour into ice-filled wineglasses. (Keep the jalapeno slices out of drink glasses, though!)

Cosmopolitans

Classic Cosmopolitan Number 1

> 1 ounce citrus flavored vodka
> 1/2 ounce Cointreau
> 1/2 ounce cranberry juice

1/4 ounce lime juice
ice

Combine all ingredients in a shaker, shake well, and strain into a cocktail glass to make one drink.

Classic Cosmopolitan Number 2

1-1/2 ounces vodka
1/2 ounce Cointreau
1 teaspoon fresh lime juice
1-1/2 ounces cranberry juice
ice
1 lime twist

Pour first four ingredients into a shaker with lots of ice. Shake vigorously for several seconds and strain into a cocktail glass. Garnish with a lime twist.

South Beach Cosmo

3 ounces Absolut Citron or some other vodka
1 ounce Cranberry Juice Cocktail
1 ounce Chambord raspberry liqueur
ice
lime slice

Pour everything over ice. Shake or stir until chilled. Strain into a chilled martini cocktail glass. Garnish with a lime slice, if desired.

White Cosmopolitan

1-1/2 ounces vodka
1 ounce white cranberry juice
1/4 ounce Cointreau
splash of fresh lime juice
ice
lime wedge

Mix all ingredients in a cocktail shaker with ice. Strain into a chilled martini glass. Garnish with a lime.

Style Savvy

CocktailTimes.com's recent survey reveals the breakdown of cosmopolitan drinkers' favorite flavors:

➤ Mango: 25%

➤ Citrus: 21%

➤ Berry: 21%

➤ Apple: 18%

➤ Orange: 15%

Martinis

Standard Martini

> 2 ounces gin
> 1/4 ounce dry vermouth

> Add ingredients to a cocktail shaker, shake, and pour into a glass for one serving.

Gibson

> A standard martini served with a cocktail onion

Sweet Martini

> A standard martini served with an orange peel

Zen Ginger Martini

> 2 ounces vodka
> 2 ounces Zentini Syrup, recipe follows
> small sprig fresh mint
> 1/2 lime, juiced

> In a martini shaker, add the vodka, Zentini Syrup, mint, and lime juice. Shake and serve in a chilled martini glass for one serving.

Zentini Syrup

> 4 cups water
> small piece fresh ginger, sliced into coins
> 2 cups sugar

> In a small saucepan combine the water, ginger, and sugar, stir and bring to a boil. Continue to heat on a simmer, stirring occasionally to make a simple syrup, about 20 minutes. When ready, strain and transfer to a glass container and allow to cool to room temperature.

Key Lime Martini

> 2 shots vanilla vodka
> 1/2 shot key lime juice
> 2 tablespoons cream of coconut
> 1 shot pineapple juice
> ice

> Add all ingredients to a martini shaker filled with ice. Shake well and strain into a martini glass. Makes 1 serving.

Apple Martini

> 1 part vodka
> 1 part sour apple schnapps
> 1 part apple juice
> ice
> sour apple hard candy
> apple peel curl

Pour vodka, schnapps, and apple juice into a cocktail shaker with ice. Shake well and strain into a pitcher or a chilled martini glass. Drop a sour apple candy in a glass and garnish with a curl of apple peel. Makes 1 serving.

Pomegranate Martini

> 6 ounces chilled gin
> 1 lemon, juiced
> 1 orange, juiced
> 1/4 cup pomegranate syrup
> pomegranate seeds

In a medium pitcher stir the gin, fruit juices, and syrup together. Divide among four martini glasses. Garnish with pomegranate seeds.

Organic Martini

> 6 ounces organic cucumber vodka
> ice
> 2 sliced strawberries
> 4 slices of cucumber
> lime slice

Pour vodka over ice and blend in strawberries and cucumber. Top with lime slice.

Nonalcoholic Drinks

A great host always makes sure she has plenty of nonalcoholic drink options available to her guests. Some might enjoy one or two cocktails during the party, and then for presence of mind or dietary reasons switch to soft drinks. Some may power drink for a few hours and then need to switch to alcohol-free libations. And some may not drink alcohol at all, by choice or by age. In this section, you'll continue your bar list with a variety of nonalcoholic beverages.

Colas

Guests may use them as mixers, but they may also drink them straight. So to make your cola choices stand out, add some unique colas to the standard diet and regular colas, colorful choices such as orange soda, black cherry-flavored cola, root beer, and the fun and fruity organic sodas such as pomegranate Fizzy Lizzy (FizzyLizzy.com).

Iced Teas

A big, gleaming pitcher of iced tea is a welcome sight for a partygoer who wishes to skip alcohol and carbonation. So offer regular sweetened iced tea along with unsweetened iced tea, plus flavored iced teas such as peach, apricot, green tea, and white tea. And if you're serving sangria as part of your liquor list, dress up one pitcher of iced tea with the same colorful fruit slices that you used in the sangria.

Style Savvy

Treat colas like any stylish cocktail, garnishing them with slices of fruit, lime or lemon twists, fun drink stirrers, and offer color-coordinated cocktail napkins to accompany each ice-cold drink.

As a style note, it's always more impressive to offer iced teas in glass pitchers—have co-hosts bring theirs for the party—rather than offer a plastic ice-filled cooler containing those little glass bottles or cans of iced tea like you'd see at a picnic or tailgate party.

Juices

While juices are most often used as mixers at bachelorette bashes, a guest or two may prefer to drink undiluted, nonalcoholic juice in her martini glass. So for these 100 percent juice lovers, add extra bottles of the juices seen on the mixers list— orange, cranberry, and pineapple, plus a collection of Pom juice drinks.

Punches

Punches are back in style as a choice party drink that's unique, festive, and easy on the budget. Check FoodNetwork.com for a variety of punch recipes, and check out these nonalcoholic punch recipes for a fun alternative to a boozy bar list.

Style Savvy

Add a touch of color to champagne with just a splash of cranberry, peach, raspberry, or pomegranate juice added to each champagne flute before you pour in the bubbly. Drop in a small slice of fruit, and your champagne cocktails will impress.

Classic Punch

>1 can frozen lemon juice concentrate
>12- to 15-ounce can crushed pineapple
>1 package frozen strawberries
>84 ounces ginger ale

In a blender, process lemon concentrate and fruit until well mixed. Pour into a punch bowl. Slowly add ginger ale and stir gently. Makes approximately 30 servings.

"Sangria" Punch

>4 ounces lemon juice
>4 ounces orange juice
>32 ounces grape juice
>32 ounces club soda
>lemon slices
>orange slices

Use a blender to mix all the fruit juices and pour into a punch bowl. Add club soda, then garnish with fruit slices. Makes 18 servings per bowl.

Caribbean Punch

>equal parts orange juice and pineapple juice
>orange slices
>pineapple slices
>ice ring
>scoops of orange sherbet to float on top

(If you'd like to offer an alcoholic Caribbean Rum Punch, add your chosen amount of Cruzan rum)

Combine fruit juices in a punch bowl; add fruit slices and ice ring, then scoop sherbet on top for a frothy surface. Adjust your recipe to suit your guest list, offering one nonalcoholic Caribbean punch and one well-labeled alcoholic version so that guests can enjoy the same taste in garnished punch glasses or wineglasses.

CHAPTER 12

Racy Desserts

In This Chapter

➤ Size and shape of your cake

➤ Options for getting a penis-shaped cake

➤ Sexing up the cake

➤ Small and sexy desserts

No racy bachelorette party ends without something sinful and sweet, and that most often means a cake designed in the shape of a penis or other sexy design. In this chapter, you'll design your dessert style, size, and taste, putting the perfect finishing touch on the party. Guests say that when a dessert is fabulous, the entire party seems more fabulous; and when a dessert is disappointing, the entire party loses its luster. So pay special attention to the desserts you serve, and, again, tailor the racy factor to the bride's personality. She may not be the type to appreciate a penis-shaped cake, but she'd love a cake topped with a sexy stiletto made from rich Belgian chocolate and designed with that signature red sole of a Louboutin. To her, *that's* sexy.

Planning the Size and Shape of the Cake

Before we get into individual dessert styles and flavors, let's focus on the most important factors: the size and shape of the cake you order or make.

Size Matters

You want a cake that's big enough to impress with its design and big enough to feed your guests, but you don't want to overdo it with an enormous sheet cake that costs a fortune and dries out in your refrigerator in a few days. Here is a smart guide to assessing cake sizes:

Size	Number of Servings
Round pan:	
6″	8
8″	15
10″	30
12″	40
Square pan:	
6″	12
8″	24
10″	32
12″	40
Heart-Shaped pan:	
6″	8
9″	18
12″	30
Petal-Shaped pan:	
6″	9
9″	18
12″	30

If you're going to order a professionally made cake, and this is your first time doing so for a large group, choose your flavors and fillings from the bakery's list of standard cake and filling flavors such as lemon cake with buttercream icing or red velvet cake with cream cheese icing. When you look across the menu at the more gourmet flavors such as rum cake or cappuccino-flavored filling and frosting, the price goes way up.

You don't have to attend a tasting like the bride often chooses to do for her wedding cake, but it's a smart idea to order this cake from a bakery you frequent, not one you found online and have never sampled before. A great cake is moist and tasty, in addition to being decorated in great detail, so think about taste before design when you order. Since it's the bride you aim to please, let her choose her cake flavors, but it's a smart idea to keep the cake design a surprise for unveiling at the party.

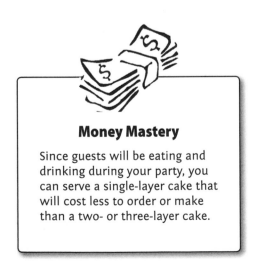

Money Mastery

Since guests will be eating and drinking during your party, you can serve a single-layer cake that will cost less to order or make than a two- or three-layer cake.

Penis-Shaped Cakes

The ultimate in racy cakes is one that is shaped and iced to look like a penis, and you'll find plenty of designs at specialty cake bakers who make cakes for bachelorette parties. They make them tall, wide, arched, even dressed up like cowboys and firemen in ultra-creative presentations. When you're shopping for the designer of a professionally made penis-shaped cake, it's often best to go right to a specialist, since your regular hometown baker might not make this particular design.

To spare themselves any discomfort in going to a baker, many bachelorette party planning groups opt to make their own penis-shaped cake, using a cake mold and kit they find online at a bachelorette party planning site or through Amazon.com. You'll find these kits in a range of materials from anodized aluminum to nonstick to silicone, and the packages share special baking instructions such as adjusted cake baking timing. You then frost the cake and add your choice of accents to it to perfect your own personal creation.

Style Savvy

Overwhelmingly, the most popular cake flavor for racy bachelorette parties is red velvet, with its sexy red color and moist, sweet taste, filled and topped with a vanilla buttercream or cream cheese frosting. Second choice is a plain vanilla cake with cherry or raspberry fruit filling and sweet buttercream frosting—classic and simple. The third choice is a boozy cake filled with rum, topped with vanilla vodka buttercream or iced with mango rum buttercream frosting, or you can choose among other flavors.

Sexy Cakes

Again, the penis-shaped cake might not be your choice of racy cake design, so consider the new class of bachelorette party racy cakes that convey a sexy style without crossing the line. These designs include corsets, bras, animal-print camisoles, panties, and sky-high stilettos.

Specialty cake bakers will show you a portfolio of sexy cake shapes and colors to coordinate with your party décor and colors, and your own hometown bakery may be able to help you out with this level of sexiness for your cake. Lingerie, fashion, and shoe designs may be within their repertoire, and you get to co-create with them in your choice of frosting artistry and additional accents.

Don't forget that the entire cake doesn't have to be made in the shape of a bra, corset, or shoe. That's quite time-consuming for a pro or for a DIY cake baker, so start with a round or sheet cake and place a chocolate-molded bra, shoe, or other item on top of it. You can

Steal My Party Idea

"I used a large heart-shaped cake pan as the base for my corset cake, and I also baked two smaller cakes in sphere cake pans to make the 'breasts' that I shaped a bit more and placed on the top arches of the heart. It made the perfect corset look, and I then iced it in hot-pink frosting and piped on a black zebra-print design using a bit of lighter pink frosting to make the 'skin' part on top, plus tiny stars of deeper hot-pink frosting to make a lace effect along the top edge of the corset. It was incredibly easy and fun, the bride loved it, and now everyone wants me to make that cake for their own parties!" —Elizabeth, maid of honor.

also use shoe, bra, lips, or other cookie cutter shape to stamp out a thinly baked cake layer (from a 6″ x 9″ pan that you've filled only halfway and baked, ice the shaped pieces, and place them on top of your frosted main cake. The collection of sexy shoes, or ruby-red lips gives your cake a sexy style that's one of a kind.

Another popular way to sex up a standard cake is to insert several sexy-shaped lollipops into the top like a bouquet, only it's X- or R-rated. Check out BachelorettePartySuperstore.com to browse the shapes and colors of racy lollipops, choosing from those penis-shaped pops, stiletto-shaped, bra-shaped, and other candy styles.

Cupcakes, Cookies, Chocolates, and Other Desserts

In this section, you'll look beyond the cake, or perhaps in addition to it, at other types of desserts that you can order or make in sexy styles. Since guests tend to eat more than just one of these smaller treats, as opposed to the one slice of cake that most guests will take, it's smart to make enough for each of your guests to enjoy two to four of each type of these desserts. When the liquor is flowing, inhibitions go out the window, and guests don't worry about looking overly indulgent by grabbing two cupcakes or four cookies. They taste sweet perfection, and they're going to indulge.

Cupcakes

What surprises many bachelorette party planners is the incredible variety of X-rated cupcake molds that are out on the market right now. Sexy-shaped baking supplies are big business, and you'll find cupcake tins in the shapes of penises and breasts at bachelorette party websites like BachelorettePartySuperstore.com and at specialty cake baking websites. These inexpensive aluminum or silicone molds are often bought by party groups, then shared with other party-planning friends. So ask friends you know who have hosted racy bachelorette parties if they have a supply of cupcake molds that they can lend you.

Cupcakes are a hot dessert trend right now, and so are cupcake toppers. Those well-stocked bachelorette party sites and specialty bakers often sell racy and subtly sexy items that you can top standard iced cupcakes with. You'll find little sugar paste or plastic penises, stilettos, bras, lips, cherries, and other stick-in décor pieces that add a theme touch to your cupcakes.

Since sexy has so many interpretations, don't forget that you can order from a baker cupcakes that are iced in tiger stripe, leopard print, or zebra stripe patterns and flattened on top for a stylized look. This style choice brings in a sexy fashion angle to your dessert collection and may be ideal for the bride who dislikes the trend of penis-centric bachelorette party accoutrements.

A trend with cupcakes is to fill them with a piping of buttercream so that guests get a creamy center when they bite in, and another option is to fill the centers of cupcakes with a rich chocolate mousse for an indulgent, sexy dessert.

Cookies

Cookies stamped into racy- or sexy-themed shapes are also winning ideas when they're iced to fit the party's theme. One new style is to ice dress-shaped cookies in coordinating colors with some negligees being solid-colored, such as hot pink, and others iced in a hot-pink and red design. You'll display these cookies on a platter—perhaps mixed in with shapes such as shoes, dresses, and handbags—for party guests to select on their own.

Style Savvy

These smaller sweet treats also make great party favors, since edibles are the number one favor style. So triple your baking, set out two-thirds of your cookies, cupcakes, or chocolates for the party's dessert collection, and bag or box the remaining treats as take-home favors.

Style Savvy

One trend in sexy cupcake design—as well as cake design—is having your baker pipe on little icing pearl necklaces on your desserts. Your baker can make them pure white or a bit iridescent to resemble real pearls, and your subtly sexy design idea will get past conservative moms and grandmoms who may be in attendance, thinking you've just added a classy, elegant touch to desserts.

Chocolates

Chocolate shops are fabulous sources of molded bras, panties, shoes, and other sexy shapes in a variety of dark, milk, and white chocolates. You'll also find larger molded chocolate pieces such as a high-heeled shoe. Party hosts like to get one big chocolate stiletto to set in the center of the dessert display platter, and then surround that with smaller, bite-sized chocolate stilettos.

The chocolate shop may also sell molded truffles in sexy shapes or in traditional rounds or hearts filled with decadent chocolate fillings or cherry cordials.

If you'll be DIYing your own chocolates, you'll find a variety of X-rated chocolate molds at bachelorette party websites that you can use to make small- to medium-sized chocolates or even chocolate lollipops in a variety of sexy shapes. If you'll bypass the sexy shapes, your local craft store has plenty of standard chocolate molds and different colors of chocolate chips to melt down for your own chocolate creations. The art of chocolate molding allows you to paint details onto these molds, such as white chocolate zebra stripes painted onto the insides of each mold, then dark chocolate piped into each mold. The next batch would have you painting each mold's zebra stripes with dark chocolate and then pouring in white chocolate to fill each mold for a coordinated variety.

Additional Desserts

In addition to cakes, cupcakes, and chocolates, you also have a variety of additional desserts to consider. Here are the most popular dessert choices for bachelorette party menus:

➤ Fresh, whole strawberries and whipped cream

➤ Chocolate-covered strawberries in chocolate swirl designs and dipped in mini chocolate chips

➤ Ambrosia and whipped cream

➤ Meringues with raspberry dipping sauce

➤ White chocolate mousse with raspberry sauce

➤ Dark chocolate mousse with raspberry sauce

➤ Chocolate fondue with fruit and pound cake dippers

➤ A candy bar with lots of different types of candies from jelly beans to red hots in a variety of bowls arranged as a candy buffet

Find fabulous dessert recipes at FoodNetwork.com, AllRecipes.com, MixingBowl.com, MarthaStewart.com, and other favorite food sources, and bring your own special dessert recipes into the mix. The bride will love it that those racy-shaped cutout brownies are your signature recipe, made just for her party.

CHAPTER 13

Preventing Trouble

In This Chapter

➤ Consider the groom

➤ Avoid male dancer mayhem

➤ Handling party crashers

➤ How to handle a drunk bride

Many grooms get very tense when they find out their brides have a bachelorette party planned for them. No man wants a greased-up male stripper gyrating in his woman's face, and if he's heard about the raunchy parties the bride's friends planned for other members of their circle, the bride might have a very anxious and angry fiancé on her hands. While the couple's trust issues are between them, you do have a responsibility as a bachelorette party co-planner to minimize the potential for conflict in their relationship. It's a simple matter of respect: if the bride says no strippers because she has promised her groom so, you must honor her rules. Don't give in to your co-planners' pressure to hire a male dancer anyway, with their reasoning that the groom will never know. You don't want to be party to deception in the couple's partnership.

In this chapter, you'll find out how to plan the party while keeping the groom in mind, and you'll also pre-empt other potential trouble. The male dancer may get a little carried away with his act, or not show up at all. Uninvited guests or strangers may crash your party. The bride may accept a few too many free drinks from strangers and become a complete mess.

While it's true that you can't control everything that could happen during the party, especially when alcohol is involved and guests are getting wild, there are some essential steps to take and plans to consider so that you can lessen the odds of party pitfalls and disasters. You don't want this party to turn into a nightmare, and you don't want to spend the entire night on edge, so use this chapter to help you and your like-minded co-planners devise ready-to-go strategies during the celebration.

Groom Drama

The groom's feelings about male dancers, or just his fiancée's partying in bars that are packed with men, have everything to do with his maturity level and his trust in his bride. Some grooms, though, have been burned before by their prior girlfriends who attended bachelorette parties and acted badly. So that wound can reopen now. Again, these are his issues, but you can help the bride assure him that all will be well.

No More Drama

If the bride says she's handled the problem by promising to call in to her groom several times during the night, you might see that as an awfully pathetic plan, a sign of his control over her. But it's not your place to say so or take her cell phone away from her. Bachelorette groups in the past have done just this, claiming to be looking out for the bride, objecting to her checking in, and that created a monumental fight between the bride and the groom who didn't get the calls he was promised. Leave the bride to her own plan for relationship peace. This may not be a sign that she's in an abusive relationship. She may be doing this in an equal trade that makes her feel better: he will call her several times during his own bachelor party night or weekend.

Explain the Party

The first step is to let him know about the nature of the party. If it's a traditional barhopping night, he knows what to envision. If it's a hotel suite party with that male dancer booked for only an hour, it's best to give him full disclosure. It might seem logical to subscribe to the "what he doesn't know won't hurt him" philosophy, but that plan can lead the in-the-dark groom to imagine a far worse scene than you've planned. Never keep the party a mystery from him. He doesn't have to know every detail, or get a photo of the male dancer you booked, but it's best to give him a vision of the type of party it will be. If you're planning a fine dinner out, or any other tame party, his fears plummet, and he can ease up on his worries.

The bride will be your best guide on this. She knows him best. She knows what scares him, and she can advise you on how they run their relationship. Maybe he'd be totally fine with the male dancer. It may be you assuming he wouldn't be. Talk with the bride to discuss how you can put the groom at ease about the party plans. She'll be touched and impressed that you're looking out for her relationship.

Give Him the Guest List

Another thing that can eliminate conflict with the

groom is telling him who will be attending the party. Grooms may have strong feelings about the wild antics of some of the bride's friends, but he may also know that her best friends are G-rated women, conservative, nonpartiers, never the types to act like tramps. In his mind, if Jen's going to be there, it can't possibly be a wild party, and that gives him some comfort.

Grooms say they don't want to be embarrassed in front of their sisters, sisters-in-law, and female friends (even their moms!). Again, a groom may have total trust and admiration for the bride, but it's her raunchy friends he doesn't like, the ones who flirt dangerously with strange men and drink too much, who often cause trouble during girls' night out. He doesn't want that element's influence turning this party into a humiliating event, especially if the bride is likely to dance on tables with them, do shots, and show her wilder side. The groom knows this is just a small part of her, but his family would certainly raise an eyebrow over this behavior. Sorry, groom, you can't control everything, either. But as the party host, if you do see the bride starting to go too wild and the groom's sisters and mother getting mortified, it's smart to step in and remind the bride that her future in-laws are taking mental notes. The line to use: "You don't want them to think badly of you long after this night is done, so climb down off the bar."

Style Savvy

If a bride feels that it would be far better to avoid the entire issue of what's happening at each party—hers and the groom's bachelor party—she may request a combined bachelor/bachelorette bash—a party at which all the men and women celebrate together in almost any style included in this book. The traditional bar crawl is often the most popular choice, with dinner and a show party being choice number two, and tickets to a special event such as a concert or even a sporting event being the third most popular coed party plan. On a bigger budget, everyone goes to Vegas or to the beach together. No secrets, no drama, thinks the bride who knows she would worry about what's going on at the guys' bash—knowing what her groom's friends are like.

Male Dancer Drama

The various dramas that could be associated with hiring a male dancer are covered in Chapter 9, so go to that section if you're concerned about the business transaction. Here, you'll think about how to handle what must be done—if anything—if the dancer gets a little too racy during his show, or if select guests get too racy with the dancer.

Reputable dancers from reputable agencies have a long list of rules within their contract. Most importantly, they don't engage in any sexual activity with the guests. None. They're not male escorts, so if the dancer who shows up at your party offers anything more than dancing, you are urged to demand that he leave immediately. Step forward without touching him—this is important, because some disreputable dancers have shown a red grip mark on their arms as signs of assault—and tell him that his time is done. Pay him the contracted amount, and show him the door. Do not turn off his music, because that is his property. And if guests get angry at you, liquored-up as they may be, they're just going to have to drink their sorrows away.

You promised a certain level of entertainment—namely dancing and a dancer paying special attention to the bride and the guests—and as the host of the party, you keep disasters from happening. If a male dancer strays from his contractual obligations, he's finished for the night. If he protests, sensing a generous crowd he can profit from and egging them on to jeer you, simply threaten to call hotel security or the police. Reputable and disreputable male dancers want no trouble, so they will take their money and go.

If the male dancer is performing according to plan and contract, but it's the guests who are acting inappropriately, pawing at him, tugging at his costume, being too aggressive with the dollar tucking, it's his job to remove their hands expertly and move away from the too-drunk woman who's overdoing it. Male dancers get that all the time, and they've perfected the art of dodging a grope and moving on to the next guest.

It must be said that your judgment and expectations of how people behave with a male dancer in the room could be the dilemma. The ladies are going to get wild, scream, shake money at the dancer, dance with him, touch his abs when invited, and get lap dances. If you're the ultraconservative type who would never behave in this way, you may just need to accept the nature of a wilder bachelorette party entertainment scene.

But do keep in mind that if you put your discomfort on display, such as stepping back into the corner or wrinkling your eyebrows, the male dancer will target you as someone to approach and win over by gyrating

Steal My Party Idea

"We knew that our friend Stacy can go over-the-top when she's drinking, and we've seen her practically maul the male dancers at other bachelorette parties we've been at. So when the male dancer arrived, we stepped out into the hallway where he was preparing for his entrance and told him to keep his distance from the girl in the white top since she's out of control this evening. He thanked us for the warning, and we were amazed at how perfectly he was able to do his act without her gaining too-close access to him."
—Emma, bridesmaid

too close to you as the rest of the guests cheer for him and urge you to loosen up. It happens at many a party. So stay within the group, have some singles in hand for the dancer, and play along for the bride's happiness. She'll notice if you're scowling the whole time.

Party Crashers

There are two kinds of party crashers: people the bride knows who weren't on the guest list but showed up anyway, and strangers who join your group and tag along from bar to bar with their drinks going on your tab.

Uninvited Friends

The first category of crashers likely read about the party plans on Facebook or Twitter. When your guests post that they can't wait to start Megan's party at the Blue Bar on Friday night at 10 pm, nervy friends invite themselves and show up with a faux innocent "what are you doing here?" agenda that gets them added to the party. It happens too often, so do tell guests to keep the party plans hush-hush. Specifically tell them not to post on Facebook and Twitter for this very reason, so that they don't get stuck splitting bills for too many people. That usually keeps the party plans quiet, even if you don't intend to let guests pay for their drinks.

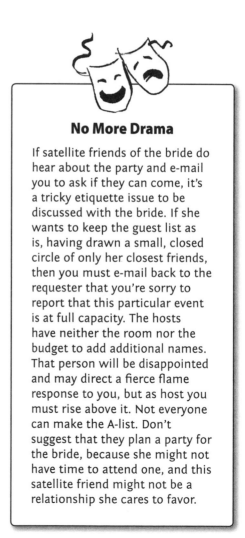

No More Drama

If satellite friends of the bride do hear about the party and e-mail you to ask if they can come, it's a tricky etiquette issue to be discussed with the bride. If she wants to keep the guest list as is, having drawn a small, closed circle of only her closest friends, then you must e-mail back to the requester that you're sorry to report that this particular event is at full capacity. The hosts have neither the room nor the budget to add additional names. That person will be disappointed and may direct a fierce flame response to you, but as host you must rise above it. Not everyone can make the A-list. Don't suggest that they plan a party for the bride, because she might not have time to attend one, and this satellite friend might not be a relationship she cares to favor.

The Party Clingers

The party clingers who join your group at a bar, sit with you, drink with you, and tail you from location to location are a new breed of con artist. Believe it or not, groups make it a practice each weekend to latch onto bachelorette party groups and other tipsy crowds and—ordering drinks among your orders—drink for free.

If you notice this cluster of hangers-on joining your party, it's best not to confront them to pay for their round of drinks, since con artists are well practiced in starting arguments and fights to distract from their thieving ways. You don't want one of these troublemakers to incite your group into violence that can end in ejection from the bar or even arrest. So if you sense that you've attracted more than just a friendly trio of bar patrons who happen to be with your group for a round, it's time to take the party to another section of the club or to another club altogether.

Pay your tab first, then say your good-byes to the crashers by shaking their hands and telling them you're taking your private party onward. If they ask if they can join you, it's okay to say that your group is just friends of the bride, but you hope they have a really great night. Good-bye. Then gather your people and leave. This is why it's important to close your tab first. If you say good-bye to the crashers then have to wait for your bill to close, they'll stick around and latch onto other guests in your group. It's a devious trick. They compliment the other guests, and say they wish they could stick with your group. The tipsy guest in your circle invites them to join you, "the more the merrier," and the crashers have won.

If you're having trouble shaking con artists or sleazy guys who have targeted your group for their woman-stalking ways, have one person in your group go to the bouncer and explain what's going on. The bouncers—protecting the establishment from potential lawsuits—will step in and ask those sleazy guys to leave your group alone. If you have a limousine taking you from stop to stop, call your driver and ask that he be waiting for you at the curb. Explain that you're making an escape from a group of men, and the driver will stand outside the car to escort you safely to your ride.

If you'll be walking to the next bar, make it tough for that group of sleazy guys to follow you by having a friend tell the bouncers your group needs some time to get away. Bouncers are great at slowing down a group's exit, which allows your group to make a safe exit.

The Drunk Bride

The bride who can't handle her liquor makes for a quick end to the celebration. If she's stumbling or sick, the party cannot go on.

It may be a long road from sober bride to stumbling bride, with a lot of wild behavior in between. So if your bride has had a few too many too quickly, with well-wishers giving her free shots and an array of drinks, and she's getting embarrassingly loud, slurring her words, knocking things over, bumping into other bar patrons, picking fights, or otherwise acting not her usual self, you and the other hosts need to reel her in. Because this will not end well.

Your trouble-avoiding strategy is first to slow down the stream of drinks heading the bride's way. Tell the others in the group that she's on a no-shots policy for right now, because she's not used to this speed of drinking. Order some breadsticks—not cheese steaks or greasy foods—for the bride and your group to snack on. Move away from the bar, where it's been too easy for everyone to order up round after round. Waiting for a server to approach or having a co-host go to the bar (taking her time) to get the next round slows down the speed at which drinks are getting to her.

No More Drama

By the time you notice the bride's inebriation, it may be too late. The alcohol is in her system and is still affecting her. What often happens is that the bride doesn't feel as drunk as she's about to be, so if you're taking drinks out of her hand or telling her to switch to water, she may get angry. You're daring to ruin her good time, and she feels judged. She may demand another drink, and other party guests who are equally tipsy may be happy to get her the drinks she demands. How do you stop them from bringing over cocktails? Remind them that the groom will be very angry at all of you if the bride winds up in the hospital getting her stomach pumped, and he may uninvite the group to the wedding. Remind them that they will be the ones who the bride gets sick on in the limo. Remind them that the bride has a busy schedule tomorrow, and she won't want to be hung over to the point of immobility. Drunk guests may not care as much as you want them to, and the idea of a sick bride might actually make them laugh. Be the one who's looking out for her, take her away from the party even if it's for a good long walk out in the fresh air, slow down her pace, and even if she protests, you're being a good friend.

And, of course, remember to have small trash bags in the limo or in your car for the bride's—or any overly drunk person's—use if she should need it.

If you need to take the bride home early, get your tab closed at the bar first. The rest of the guests can continue on with their Friday night if they wish, but their tab isn't going to show up on your credit card. If your limo is their ride, they do need to come home with you, even if they don't wish to because the limo is not going to go back for them. Simply put, the party's over.

PART THREE

Tame Bachelorette Parties

CHAPTER 14

The Spa Party

In This Chapter

➤ Choosing where to have your spa party

➤ Choosing the right spa treatments for your party

➤ Details for a successful spa party

The bride and her guests change into comfy, luxurious spa robes and spa slippers, and they mingle by the pool with champagne glasses in hand as uniformed servers present them with canapés and shrimp cocktail on silver platters, and professional manicurists, pedicurists, and massage therapists welcome each guest to their stations for indulgent pampering. That's how celebrities plan their spa parties, and it's quickly becoming *the* party style of choice for the tame bachelorette party.

If the bride is past her partying days and doesn't wish to pile into a limo to go to hot and sweaty dance clubs, this calming and decompressing party may be just the celebration style for her. What could be better than being served by smiling waiters and primped by friendly beauty experts in a gorgeous outdoor setting? All that's missing is the paparazzi.

In this chapter, you'll plan the spa party of the bride's dreams, one the guests will call a highlight of their year as well. It's not the most inexpensive party, but for a select group of friends and family, a group of ten to fifteen, the cost does average to the same as a country club brunch for thirty or more.

Choosing a Location

The location you choose for the spa party will determine the celebrity style of the celebration and will affect the types of treatments you can offer to guests. For instance, if everyone goes to a spa, you all have access to that spa's steam room and other on-site treatments. At your home, you can invite spa experts to treat your guests to pedicures, manicures, and massages—but the seaweed wrap could be too messy for your home. The options are varied.

Outdoors By the Pool

If you have a fabulous yard with an in-ground pool and lovely landscaping—or if a co-planner or one of the moms has this stunning scene set for your use, the search is over. Since many homeowners consider their backyards and pool areas to be an extension of their living room and a primary entertaining area, they invest a sizeable chunk of money in the best stonework, plantings, and spa-worthy lounge chairs—even poolside speakers with surround sound. They might have an outdoor wet bar as well, which would be amazing for your party's style. If the pool has an attached hot tub section, that yard becomes the equivalent of an A-lister's outdoor party palace.

Outdoors Without a Pool

The good news is that a pool is not necessary. You can manicure your backyard terrace and gardens—some hosts hire landscapers to come in and weed, level stone walkways, and otherwise primp their yards for the party—and clean and polish your deck furniture for an attractive outdoor spa party. There's something very indulgent about getting a massage outdoors—which is why so many top-name resorts offer outdoor spa treatments. So don't fear that your outdoor spa party dream is dead if no one has a $50,000 pool and entertaining area in their backyard.

Shop Here!

Save time and search for a fabulous spa at SpaFinder.com. Here you can click on spas near you and see their lists of treatments as well as special bachelorette party packages that provide a price break for wedding groups.

At a Spa

You might choose an upscale day spa with a wide range of treatment options from those seaweed wraps to paraffin treatments, hot stone massages, sauna and steam room, even chocolate body scrubs and white chocolate foot soaks.

Day spas might be stand-alone establishments, or they could be located at a golf resort or an upscale hotel. Most of these affiliated spas do welcome nonguests, so don't count them out of your research fearing that you must have a room key to get in the door.

Party groups who have been to a nearby spa center say that they felt transported, as if they had escaped their world to a getaway weekend, but no travel was needed. From the minute they walked in the door, were greeted by model-gorgeous staff members, and welcomed with Bellinis, mimosas, and champagne, then given Egyptian cotton robes to change into and led into a Zen garden to begin their decompression before treatments begin, they felt like socialites, royalty, celebrities.

It may be this getaway element that will elevate your party to spectacular heights. Think about how escapist your backyard would be. Would the bride feel transported? Would it seem as special and indulgent?

Reservations and treatment bookings need to be arranged far in advance, since quality spas are often booked solid. It would cost a fortune to book the entire spa for the day—especially on a convenient weekend—so your group's three or four hours of spa time need to be carefully arranged with the establishment's event manager who will effortlessly schedule each guest's treatments for a smooth flow.

At Home, Indoors

No yard, no pool, no problem. You can transform your or a co-planner's home into a personal spa with expert treatments offered in different bedrooms, the den, or on a balcony if you live in an apartment building or condo.

It will take some work to give your space a spa makeover, and that begins with stripping away many of the framed photos and busy knickknacks from around each room. Minimalist décor creates the most soothing environment, and clean counters newly set with a single floating lotus flower and flickering pillar or votive candles welcome the spa state of mind. Furniture may need to be cleared away into a no-access storage room so that the massage therapist can set up her heated massage table.

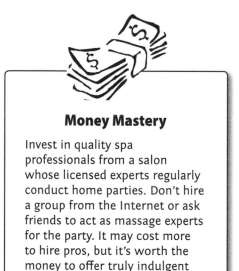

Money Mastery

Invest in quality spa professionals from a salon whose licensed experts regularly conduct home parties. Don't hire a group from the Internet or ask friends to act as massage experts for the party. It may cost more to hire pros, but it's worth the money to offer truly indulgent and enjoyable pampering treatments to party guests and the bride.

As mentioned earlier, the at-home spa party may not allow you to offer as many spa treatments as you can access at a spa site, but that might be fine with you. All your bride and guests need are half-hour massages, foot massages, stress-busting jaw massages, lavender foot soaks and pedicures, and nail makeovers such as a more modern French manicure on newly squared nails. Beauty experts can certainly do those at a non-spa location.

No More Drama

Be sure to let the bed-and-breakfast proprietor know that you plan to bring in spa and massage experts to conduct your morning spa party on the premises. Some B and B owners have partnerships with local spa experts to offer their guests privately booked pampering treatments, and they might insist you use their professionals. Rather than risk any conflict or ruined reservations, clear your plans with the location's authorities first.

Your home setting needs to have a dedicated area for drinks and menu items that is comfortably and attractively arranged. You might not have the need, or the room, for strolling waiters, so setting up an attractive buffet gives all of your guests the freedom to graze on healthy and delicious organic hors d'oeuvres. Most at-home party hosts say that a table out in the living room is best for the food display, and a table in the dining room is best for a bar featuring wine and drinks in pitchers. When you separate the two, you eliminate party-wrecking traffic jams in the kitchen, for instance.

At a Bed-and-Breakfast

This location borrows from the getaway celebration style and blends in the at-home feel. Check BNBFinder.com to locate a wonderful bed and breakfast that's not too far away—under an hour's drive is best—and guests can stay overnight in the rooms as you make a weekend of this combined spa getaway party.

You've taken over the bed-and-breakfast establishment, your spa party takes place after the included breakfast, then everyone changes to enjoy afternoon tea, goes out to dinner, then spends the evening on the porch, sipping champagne and enjoying together time. It's the best of two worlds when you choose the B and B location.

Choosing Spa Treatments

How many spa treatments does each guest need to make this party a truly indulgent one? It's usually not enough just to have a manicurist arrive with a collection of twelve polish colors, while a long line of guests await their turn for the one treatment. Ideally, you'll offer four or five different types of treatments with variations on massages.

For instance, a team of massage therapists can arrive at your party in uniform—often black pants with a stylish black T-shirt sporting the logo of their salon in a bright color—and set up their stations to offer several different kinds of massages, which might include:

➤ Full body shiatsu, soft or medium pressure

➤ Hot stone massage

➤ Foot massage and reflexology

➤ Craniosacral (head, neck, and jaw—a new hot trend in de-stressing massages)

➤ Hand massage

➤ Prenatal massage for your pregnant guests

Manicurists can offer a range of different manicures, which most often begin with a pampering hand massage and the guest's choice of a nail shape makeover and flawless French manicure—which is a real treat for money-crunched bridesmaids who haven't had the budget for $30 manicures.

Foot treatments can include standard pedicures, aromatherapy foot soaks, and the new class of chocolate foot soaks and other organic foot baths that spa centers offer. By virtue of being something that guests have never done before, it makes your party an instant best-ever hit.

A new trend offers eyebrow shaping done by a professional. The simple shaping of your eyebrows—the correction of your arch, tweezing too-full brows, threading—can make your face look fresher, your eyes look bigger and brighter, and your entire face look younger, so this spa treatment is a popular choice for its ease of on-site availability. All a brow-shaping artist needs is a room with great light, and he or she can transform everyone's brows and give out brow pencils in the correct shade for each person's coloring. Find a brow shaper at a professional salon, not at a mall kiosk, to be sure the expert is licensed and insured.

Bear in mind that arranging pedicures, massages, and brow-shaping for fifteen guests can cost hundreds of dollars. So this is not a fitting bachelorette party plan if you're on a light budget.

Steal My Party Idea

"I'm a graphic designer, so I offered our local spa my services in designing an improved look for its website. The owner knew that such service can cost over $1,000 when you hire a professional web designer, so I worked out a trade that our spa party would be completely covered by my time and efforts to give their site a fresh, new look and improved applications. It took me only a few hours and was *so* worth it to be able to give my sister an amazing spa bachelorette party without anyone having to pay a lot of money." —Veronica, maid of honor

Keep in mind that bartering arrangements may have to be reported to the IRS, so get a detailed contract with the value of your services spelled out, and share that document with your accountant at tax time.

Party Details

With your location and spa services picked out, and perhaps plans for transforming your home's décor or yard landscaping underway as you create your party's perfect setting, it's time to focus on the many additional elements of your spa party. Remember to keep your color palette soft and neutral with light greens, corals, sand colors, and lots of white. Softer colors say "relaxation" far better than hotter bright colors, and studies have even shown that rooms decorated in soft neutrals soothe mind and body, whereas bright colors raise blood pressure. So follow this rule when you design everything from your invitations to your décor, even your favors.

Invitations

The invitations you send out immediately convey the sense of relaxation that a spa party brings, and guests will be thrilled that they have a pampering event to look forward to. So stick with that soft color palette of sage green, light blue, and sandy beiges, the colors of sea glass to help you envision the shades.

Images to include on your single-panel invitation or Evite can range from an illustration of a woman in a spa robe getting her nails done to a fun illustration of a nail polish bottle in a sky blue shade.

The papers you use for your invitation can be softly textured to give that soft, earthy feel, so look at the different grades of recycled papers—and remember that not all recycled papers have that textured feel, so always go to the craft store to touch and feel different types of invitation paper stock. If you order online, you may not experience the true texture, or color, of the papers you'll use to make your invitations.

There's no need to be clever with your invitation wording. A simple "Jamie's Bachelorette Party is a Spa Day! Join us at Maria's house for poolside pampering and champagne!" shares all the necessary definition of the party's style. And an e-mailed invite can share a link to the spa's website so that guests can see the spa, look over the treatment list, and dream of that glorious, relaxing spa party with friends.

Menu Items

Don't assume that spa fare is a couple of sprigs of watercress on a plate with a slice of melon. No, healthy spa-lite foods are far more gourmet than that, and they serve as the guide to the dishes you can serve at your spa party.

Keep your appetizer choices light and fresh, organic if you can, since no one wants to eat greasy fried foods when they're in a well-being state of mind. Here are some menu inspirations for you:

- Hummus blends of garlic and artichoke with pita triangles
- Veggie quesadillas
- Mango salsa and chips
- Smoked salmon
- Shrimp cocktail
- Salads with mesclun greens, goat cheese, walnuts, shredded squash and carrots, and pumpkin seeds
- Veggie sushi such as a cucumber avocado roll, pumpkin roll, and sweet potato roll
- Veggie spring rolls with wasabi soy sauce
- Garlic cheese spread with an array of flat breads, grissini, and whole wheat crackers
- Fresh fruit platter with fruit slices cut into shapes (use cookie cutters to make heart shapes, star shapes, and circles)
- Bowls of single fresh fruits, such as pineapple, cantaloupe, mandarin oranges, and other toothpick bites

Money Mastery

Set up multiple buffet stations to give your party's spread a more upscale look and to make it look like you have a lot more food than if everything was crammed onto one long table!

Cake and Dessert

You *can* serve dessert. A life well lived includes some indulgences in moderation, so plan for a pretty themed cake in spa-white frosting, with white frosting roses. Cake bakers say they love the creativity that comes out with spa party cakes; they've designed sugar paste bamboo shoots to stand out of the top of the cake, and iced intricate leaves on the sides of cakes. They've also created organic cakes as well as cakes filled with sweet fruity fillings and served with fruit sauces and Chantilly creams.

A popular spa-white dessert is white chocolate mousse served in martini glasses and topped with strawberry or raspberry sauce. Petit fours—tiny squares of two-layer cakes—are also spa-worthy indulgences, as are Godiva truffles in such flavors as key lime and champagne. White chocolate-dipped berries can surround your cake or top your cupcakes, or you can skip the white motif and lead your guests into a dessert room that features an all-chocolate buffet of desserts from rich dark chocolate mousse cups to espresso-chocolate trifles, to dark chocolate-dipped strawberries and hazelnut Piroulines.

Drinks

The top three drinks for a spa party are, of course, champagne, mimosas, and Bellinis, but you can get more creative and stretch your budget with a fabulous champagne punch. Guests go wild for champagne punches, since it's not something they get every day. So check FoodNetwork.com, AllRecipes.com, and Cocktail.com to get the perfect measurements for a champagne peach punch with sorbet, a champagne pear punch, and the amazing tropical blend of orange and pineapple juices with a champagne kick.

For mixed drinks, borrow from tropical island resorts' bar menus, with a rum punch (orange and pineapple juices with rum) or a banana colada as a twist to the piña colada.

Spa party hosts love to serve green tea wine spritzers alongside alcohol-free green tea pitchers, unsweetened iced teas, and pomegranate cranberry juice.

Décor

A spa party at a spa makes use of the establishment's existing décor—both in common areas and in treatment rooms. Interior designers work their magic in these environments to create a calming, soothing feel to each area so you don't need to give extra décor a thought.

For a spa party that takes place outdoors in your yard, perhaps by a pool, your décor opportunities include placing potted plants around the pool—with inexpensive grasses like Bermuda grass leading the popularity list.

Create a luxurious scene outdoors by hanging curtains of soft, billowy fabrics to dance in the breeze as celebrity event planners have done for their high-profile clientele. The texture and movement of the fabric create an upscale feel, and planners say they arrange this by running a strong wire line between trees, then draping a length of fabric evenly over the wire that is double the height from the ground to the wire. They then staple the ends of the fabric together on the ends of each length to keep the length secured on the wire, and voila! The effect can be created for less than $15 per curtain.

Another inexpensive outdoor spa party décor option that packs an impressive visual effect for a low price is hanging crystals from a tree. Shop for medium to large multifaceted glass crystals in a craft store, choosing

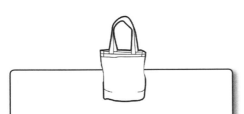

Shop Here!

Home improvement stores offer a great range of potted plants in scene-setting heights and movement, and they often offer a 100 percent guarantee on any plants you buy. Your investment in plants for the party, then, becomes an investment in your home when you later plant these grasses or palms in your own landscaping.

five or six per crystal string. You can choose from clear crystals or select an array of pastel-colored crystals to give your décor effect extra contrast in a colorful garden area. You'll then string these hole-cut crystals onto clear fishing line and hang each from an impressive tree or trees in the party area. When the light hits the crystals, starbursts and sparkles appear all around. This effect can be achieved for less than $30 for a dozen crystal strings. Just a few larger crystal strings make a great impression—you don't need to overdo it.

Ask if a co-planner has a portable waterfall feature that she can bring to your party's location. This inexpensive décor item—often found for under $40 at stores like Bed Bath & Beyond and Target— sets a relaxing atmosphere and is one of the most

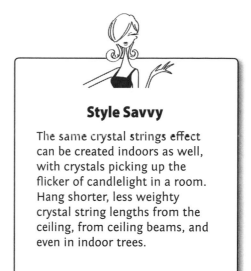

Style Savvy

The same crystal strings effect can be created indoors as well, with crystals picking up the flicker of candlelight in a room. Hang shorter, less weighty crystal string lengths from the ceiling, from ceiling beams, and even in indoor trees.

in-demand décor items for spa parties. Brides have even offered use of their own décor fountains, which were received as a bridal shower gift off of their registry.

Candles set a relaxing scene as well, but keep safety in mind as well as scene setting. Since guests will be walking around in spa robes, and curtains may be dancing in breezes both outdoors and indoors by an open window, be sure that all candles are safely ensconced in hurricane lamps and tall glass containers. Unenclosed candles risk too much, especially when you consider that guests will be reaching across a buffet table to fill a plate, or reaching across the bar to get an olive for a martini. One too-close robe sleeve and you have a grave danger. So do choose pretty pillar and votive candles for this party's style, but place each in a safe vessel.

Finally, stones are a popular décor item at spa parties. Smooth river stones in grays and blues are often used. You can easily and inexpensively find bags of these décor stones in craft stores for pouring into the bottoms of those glass containers that hold your pillar candles. A single $5 bag of river stones in 1-inch to 2-inch widths can decorate a half dozen glass containers. Since rocks are so popular, many hosts are filling 3-inch to 4-inch glass containers to the top with river stones for a minimalist look, or adding a dash of soft floral texture by tucking several tiny white flowers into the top of the stone-filled vase.

Finally, floral arrangements add freshness and scent to your spa party décor. So design one large cluster of dramatic white flowers such as lilies, roses, callas, or hydrangeas as a focal point at the party's entrance or on the dining table, and accent that piece with four-inch glass bowls containing a matching type and color of flower such as a single lily or gardenia floating on water. Simplicity is best for a spa party; overkill with floral or any other kind of décor creates visual "noise" and works against your goal of presenting a simple, soothing style.

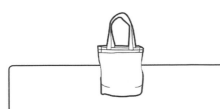

Shop Here!

You can find bags of smooth river stones in small, medium, and large widths at your local pet store chain, such as PetSmart or Petco, for attractive prices and in a nice range of colors.

No More Drama

No, giving a gift to the bride doesn't turn this into a bridal shower, and you don't have to ask all of the guests to pitch in for the group gift. If you decide to arrange a gift just from the bridesmaids or just from the bride's sisters or sorority sisters, you'll arrange the group-buy privately and give the bride her gift before the party, not during it. It's a big mistake to make other guests feel left out and shamed for not bringing a gift, so make this a private moment between your gifting group and the bride.

Theme Gifts for the Bride

If you'll be giving the bride a group gift—which is not essential but has become a fun surprise for brides who are increasingly involved in their bachelorette party plans—consider the following generous gifts:

➤ A gift card to the spa, good for any indulgent treatment(s)

➤ A luxury spa robe in the best and softest fabric possible with matching slippers

➤ A basket of massage oils, bubble baths, and lotions in her favorite brand's collection

➤ A spa item from her registry, such as a towel warmer for her master bathroom

➤ A gift card to her favorite natural-living store, such as Whole Foods Market or active lifestyle catalog, such as Gaiam

Favors

Party guests enjoy the pampering treatments at a spa party, but it's still nice to send them home with a little something. Think about the following popular spa party favors:

➤ Pedicure flip flops in candy colors without the floral decorations at the toe

➤ Lip balm trios

➤ Travel-sized lotions

➤ Envirosax tote bags in neutral colors with nature motifs (Envirosax.com)

➤ Truffles with three to a baggie

➤ Small bags of bath petals—dissolvable petals made of soap

➤ Bottles of lavender linen spray to make bedding and spa robes smell fresh and soothing

Entertainment

Soft music sets the relaxing tone for your spa party, so stick with the light sounds that spas pipe through their centers: instrumentals such as Asian wind flutes, piano, and a leading favorite among spa party planners is the Native American-inspired music by R. Carlos Nakai.

If your plan is for treatments during the first hour of the party—which is a great way to keep costs down, limiting your experts' per-hour charges—and a cocktail party afterward, switch from the new age music to your favorite iPod playlist for the second half of your party.

And take plenty of photos of the girls sitting by the poolside in their spa robes, toasting the bride with bright mimosas and champagne. These shots become framed favorites.

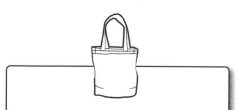

Shop Here!

Bath & Body Works is a top resource for tiny spa-themed treats. It offers lotions and spritzers and lip balms aplenty, in a range of fresh scents including award-winning fragrances. Shop online or go to a store in a mall to pick through its discount displays of lip balms, nail polishes, and pedicure toe pads with foot creams.

CHAPTER 15

Fashion Show Parties

In This Chapter

➤ Finding the right location
➤ Finding the perfect time
➤ Planning the details

The fashionista bride and her stylish friends get a private fashion show, complete with models on the runway and a postshow champagne reception at this style of bachelorette party. And it's far easier to arrange than you might expect. In this chapter, you'll take the steps to arrange for a VIP fashion event as the bride's last hurrah and perhaps her first time in the front row at a private runway event suitable for fashion week and *Project Runway*. Brides everywhere have seen *The Rachel Zoe Project* and have envied Rachel's fashion vision and access to the new collections, and this party lets your bride be the Rachel of the evening, the toast of the fashionable elite guests at the party.

Finding the Boutique

These days, small and chic boutiques compete with the big boys in fashion by offering these private VIP fashion show events to party and corporate groups. They shut down their store, hang a Private Party sign on the door, and walk their own models down the runway wearing their latest collections, accessories, and top-name designer shoes. The party guests sit in VIP chairs lining the runway, and like top fashion editors they leaf through descriptions of each fashion piece in the show to learn more about the details and decide if they want to buy it for their own collections. That's right, party guests can buy the fashions that have been modeled for them at a steep discount offered by the boutique for this special party.

It's the experience of the private runway show and shopping hours, aided by a team of personal stylists who mingle with your crowd, that turns this party style into an unforgettable celebration, something groups of friends have likely never imagined they'd be able to attend. And steep discounts mean party guests can shop to their heart's content.

All it takes to begin your plans for this party is finding a fashion boutique that's willing to host this kind of event for you. Some regularly hold private fashion show parties, and they have pages on their websites devoted to special event details and reservations. How do you find these? The bride's wedding experts can lead you right to them. Remember, everyone in the wedding industry knows everyone else. If they've been in the industry for years, they know the good and the bad in all of the surrounding professional categories, and the associations to which they belong promote these unique celebrations for the bridal market in their newsletters and at their conventions and networking events. Wedding coordinators, then, may have attended a regional meeting of their professional association, and a private fashion show was a highlight of that evening. So tap into the network the bride has—as well as the network of wedding experts your co-planners have—to locate a boutique that's known for its private fashion parties.

Steal My Party Idea

"I have friends who work in the fashion industry, and when I asked them to locate a great boutique for this type of party, they quickly came up with a dozen suggestions in our area! No one ever knew that those chic stores would close down for private parties. And they said to check with fashion institutes, which are also great resources for finding these shows, since they often send over their students to work these events, giving them field experience in an intern assignment at the boutiques." —Lila, bridesmaid

Don't get discouraged if you can't find a boutique that has an established fashion show social program. Many party planning groups have walked into their favorite fashion stores—including accessory stores—and asked if they could book the store's first such event! In a competitive market, store owners are always looking for an advantage over their competitors—as well as a newsworthy event they can promote in a press release to the local media—and your request may just get the store's owner inspired to plan a private fashion show for your group. Keep in mind, though, that untried boutiques may not be allowed to serve alcohol at their events, since each township has strict rules about the serving of liquor and sometimes even food on their grounds. So be prepared for township red tape when you're the first to suggest a private party at a store that hasn't hosted one before.

The criteria for the perfect fashion party site include:

➤ Enough room for a runway and seating

➤ A staging area for the caterer to work in

➤ A counter area or tables that can work as a bar

➤ Restrooms suitable for a party—not all stores have modernized restrooms, so take a look before you book

➤ Parking

➤ An attractive location, preferably on a strip of stores, on a main street, and not tucked away in a sketchy part of town

What's the Store's Signature Style?

Every fashion boutique has its own personality and its own target audience. A store may buy fashions and accessories for a twenty-one-year-old crowd's going-out outfits, or it may stock up on corporate classy pants and sweater sets. One may be an evening wear mecca, while another may be a heaven of designer accessories.

The accessories store is the newest hit in fashion parties, since earrings, bracelets and necklaces, scarves and handbags may be more in the affordable price range of partygoers. Few bridesmaids could afford to drop $200 on a jacket at a corporate-type boutique, but $20 for a trio of dangle earrings is doable. So party hosts are approaching accessory shops for the runway shows, and shop owners are enjoying the novelty of playing announcer and having their staff members thrill at the chance to be models for the event.

Talk with the bride and her co-planners about selecting the right style of store for the party, thinking also about what the party guests would prefer. Accessories are universally appealing for diverse groups, which is why accessory stores are enjoying a surge of party bookings. And those more stylized fashion shops with evening wear and accessories may be ideal for groups shopping on the higher end. Tailor your location to your crowd so that everyone enjoys the show and the shopping.

Now what about lingerie stores? Those too become ideal for the bachelorette party that moves closer to the racy line. Models can walk the runway in sexy lingerie ensembles worthy of the Victoria's Secret fashion show, with sheer modesty robes dropped down to the small of the back to cover their bottoms while wearing a G-string. Your friends may be fine with exposure, but you

Money Mastery

The shop doesn't necessarily need to hire professional models who can command hundreds of dollars an hour. Many shops invite their staff members to model the clothing and accessories, enticing them with a commission on the evening's sales. Staffers say they love working these events, since it's great fun and it allows them to make some extra spending money—sometimes a lot of extra spending money. And there's also the opportunity to have your co-planners act as the models for the runway show, if the shop owner approves of your freebie plan. Hey, sales for the store equal profits for her!

may have more conservative ladies on the guest list. So the sheer cover-up is always a great idea at a lingerie fashion show. Again, contact or visit the boutique's owner to arrange for a private fashion show and shopping event, and you may just inspire her to promote this very same party plan to the media, including regional bridal magazines and websites.

Rental Shopping List

You have to make the location work, to quote *Project Runway*'s Tim Gunn.

The vast majority of boutique-set fashion show parties will require the rental of chairs at the very least. If they say they have chairs, be sure to look at them to be sure they're a matching set of attractive chairs, not a collection of mismatched folding chairs with dents and paint splatters on them.

It's not essential to rent a raised runway platform, since even the top fashion designers have been known to simply have their models walk on floor level down an aisle created from the lineup of chairs. You can follow their lead and rent a top-quality aisle runner from a rental agency or floral designer, choosing any color of aisle runner from white to bright to pastel, even fashionable black and white with graphic swirls on the edges.

Additional items that may be on your rental list, and thus on your budget:

> ➤ A portable bar
>
> ➤ Glassware—enough for five glasses per person
>
> ➤ Appetizer plates—enough for three plates per person
>
> ➤ Dessert plates if you will serve cake— enough for 1-1/2 plates per person
>
> ➤ Utensils
>
> ➤ A portable bar
>
> ➤ Additional seating, such as couches, a big-ticket rental item for upscale fashion parties

No More Drama

Your home may not be the ideal site for this party. Yes, a number of boutiques will bring a collection of outfits and accessories to your home for a fashion soiree at your place. But be aware that the transport of their collection limits the amount of fashion finds that your party guests will have to choose from, and, perhaps more importantly, this plan can raise eyebrows and etiquette issues since it's now become one of those home sales parties that some women find tacky and unpleasant. So, for the sake of variety and an unpressured atmosphere that's more party than purchase-pushing, the boutique may be a more preferable location.

Party Timing

The boutique will need to close for your private party, so talk with the store owner to arrange for the perfect timing. Boutique owners say they usually host private parties starting at 7 pm, to allow their staff members time to go home and change or eat dinner after the store's closing time of 5 pm They also time their parties for this social hour because they know that the street outside their store will be filled with evening shoppers and people on their way to local restaurants. A big sign reading Private Party on their door and a greeter stationed at the door with a clipboard announces to the world that a VIP event is taking place right here, right now. It's good publicity for them, and it's also far more convenient for many of your guests to arrive at an after-dinner/after-work hour.

The second most popular time to begin is 2 pm on a Sunday afternoon when the store is closed on Sundays. The staff doesn't need to wake up early to prepare the site, and the afternoon time frame again captures weekend foot traffic attention in front of the store.

Money Mastery

Since this party calls in events professionals such as rental agencies, caterers, and bartenders, your weeknight party means lower costs from each of them. Caterers especially charge less per person for a cocktail party held on a weeknight than on a weekend, since a Wednesday night isn't their peak catering time. So they can charge 15 to 25 percent less, which is great news for your party budget. If the bride's closest friends can make it to a Monday, Tuesday, or Wednesday night fashion party, you'll save a bundle for a classy party that would cost much more if held during the weekend.

If the boutique is right down the street from a lovely restaurant, within walking distance to a shop-filled main street, your fashion show party might be the perfect phase two after a brunch or luncheon. After the meal, everyone proceeds to the boutique for the start of the runway show.

Party Details

Design your fashion show bachelorette party with the following stylish tips on all of the details for the day. As always, your co-planners can pick and choose which elements they'd like to handle or team up on, so that you're not overwhelmed with so many event-arranging details and so that they can share in the rave reviews of your stunning soiree.

Invitations

You have a world of fashion images to consider for your invitation design. Look at the fashion icon invitations at Pingg.com, and the many invite styles at Evite.com that feature illustrations of women in high-fashion clothing, shopping bags, or designer stilettos.

Choose the in color of the season, whether it's hot pink with black zebra stripes, fall's jewel-tone purple, or springtime tangerine, or even the runway showcase patterns of plaids or stripes. A big trend is to accessorize your printed invitations with glued-on rhinestones for the in-season sparkle, or even peacock feathers if that's what the designers are showing right now. We've seen buckles and DIY belts made of faux leather wrapped around an invitation as the stylish accessory, and, of course, invitations can feature the logos of top design houses or fashion magazines.

A great invitation must convey not just the look of the event, but the style of it as well. So your invitation should announce that guests will be treated to a VIP fashion show with (name of the elite boutique) closing its doors to host your private party. "After the show, all of Katie's guests will be able to shop from the collection as well as buy anything in the store for an amazing 50 percent off!" This last piece of information is crucial so that guests know to bring some spending money. It's never to be left as a surprise, or guests will feel you've left them unprepared to fully enjoy the event.

Let your guests know what will be served. A 7 pm start time, remember, can be dinnertime to some. If you print on the invitation that "Light hors d'oeuvres will be served, along with fine champagne and wine," guests know to grab dinner beforehand.

Send out your print or e-invitations at least a month in advance, especially if the party date is within the busy summer months or within a holiday weekend when everyone is in town. And set your RSVP date for at least a week before the big event, so that you have time to adjust and finalize your rental order.

I had to share this cute invitation idea: the hosts of a fashion party created their invitations on computer, and they slid each into a small (six-inch) shopping bag from the craft store. They designed square labels with the Chanel symbol on them and affixed them to the bags, stylizing the presentation of their invitations. Each shopping bag was then packed in a box for mailing to faraway guests or hand delivered to local friends and family.

Money Mastery

Check with your rental agency for its deadline on order adjustments. Since you will likely rent glasses and service ware for your guests, you'll need a reliable head count so that you're not stuck renting champagne flutes for forty guests when only twenty people can make the party. If the rental agency requests a two-weeks-prior deadline for changes, set your RSVP date for three weeks prior, and send your invitations out a week earlier. Early sends make it more likely that people will attend and protects your investments.

Menu Items

High-fashion celebrity events are most often catered with tiny bites of gourmet fare, such as blini with caviar, spoonfuls of seviche, tuna tartare, mango and shrimp bites, and barely there spinach puffs. You won't find greasy, heavy appetizers passed on those silver platters, so keep your hors d'oeuvres on the fresh side. Some items to add to your caterer's order: canapés, mini crab cakes with tartar sauce, five different kinds of sushi, spring rolls, pears with goat cheese bites, a watermelon square with feta cheese, stuffed mushrooms, mini turkey meatballs in an apricot glaze, and other light bites.

Steer clear of outfit-wrecking pastas and molten cheese-filled puffs and poppers that also create greasy fingers—not a good thing to have near new fashions and accessories at this hands-on party.

It is best to have a professional caterer or personal chef prepare the food for this event, since it would be a tremendous amount of work for you and your co-planners to prepare and heat foods on-site. Another factor is the lack of kitchen facilities at a store—the microwave doesn't count and is indeed a terrible idea for party fare—so order delicious cold appetizers for your guests to enjoy during the cocktail

Style Savvy

Since you won't have dining tables, arrange for all appetizers to be finger foods, with none requiring utensils.

hour. And bring along several packs of GladWare or other take-home containers to divide leftovers among the hosts and important guests. That's way easier than trying to ship home the big aluminum pans each food item arrived in.

Cake and Dessert

In keeping with the stand-up, no-utensils party style, serve easy-to-pop petit fours, mini cupcakes, small-sized pastry, even cookies shaped and iced to look like dresses, handbags, or shoes. And fruits speared three to a toothpick are also a welcome bite at cocktail parties, so mix up your grapes, pineapple, and cantaloupe for a pastel-colored fruit dessert, or offer sizeable strawberries, also on toothpicks to keep those hands clean.

Drinks

Champagne is the drink of the hour for the celebrity-inspired, high-fashion party, so visit WineSpectator.com to learn about new vintages of champagnes that can please your guests without spending a fortune. It can be quite surprising that excellent champagnes exist on the market for under $20 a bottle, and a discount liquor store will often give you an added discount for your purchase of a case of bubbly. Whatever's left over after the party gets divided among the hosts.

Another top drink at fashion parties is the stylish martini, so experiment ahead of time with new martini recipes at Cocktail.com, and be sure to rent at least three martini glasses per guest. At just a few dollars apiece, it's not a jaw-dropping expense, and having real glassware at the party—rather than party store plastic martini glasses—reflects well on your style and taste as a host.

Décor

The boutique's design is all the décor needed, and you won't need to bring in floral arrangements like they do at fashion week fetes. One nice touch, though, is wrapping each chair back with a length of colorful tulle, and tying on a bow at the back to make the seating area stand out with just the easiest of décor touches.

The store will appreciate your incorporating its logo in any way possible, so put a vase of flowers inside one of its vellum-style shopping bags if you would like to do one inexpensive floral focal point at the entrance or on the bar. The bag becomes the vase, and the flowers extend out the top.

Theme Gifts for the Bride

The bride may need to assemble her trousseau, so if all of the hosts chip in, they can get her a gift card to the boutique for her selection of a great fashion item or fun accessories for her getaway. Or, as host, you can keep an eye on her browsing, see that lovely scarf she keeps going back to, and then slip away with it to buy it from the shop owner, pop it into a gift bag, and present it to her after the party as her big surprise and the perfect finishing touch to her celebration.

Another surprise you can give the bride after the event, not in front of the store owner, is a wrapped item from her favorite fashion designer's collection. You might not be able to afford those Louboutins, but perhaps you can group-gift her a pair of Ralph Lauren gloves or Vera Wang's newest fragrance.

Money Mastery

Stock up on $4.99 bunches of daisies and filler such as Queen Anne's Lace at the supermarket floral section or in discount meccas Costco or Sam's Club to create that one big floral piece that might sit behind a DIY sign announcing the bride's fashion show event—a décor piece that becomes a keepsake for the bride, especially if all of her guests sign it before departing.

Favors

Create swag bags just like those given out at fashion events, filling each with items from the $3-and-under bins at the beauty supply store—lip glosses, fabric tape (a must for any fashionista!), no-static sprays, petal-shaped stickers to put inside high heels for nonsliding comfort, and inexpensive, stylish silver jewelry such as hoop earrings or bangles from Target. Allow the boutique to slip in its brochures or coupons as well as the caterer's card and be the only two advertisers in the bag, which is a vast improvement over the kinds of goodie bags that brides take home from expos.

And, of course, edible treats are always fantastic favors, so those dress-shaped cookies may make for better take-home treats than dessert offerings.

Entertainment

The runway show, at just fifteen minutes in length with great music that you've mixed, is the highlight event of the party. After the show, guests mingle and browse through the boutique and step to the side for chatting and champagne-sipping time. The less structured the event, the better, since we all adore time to talk with friends we don't see as often as we'd like.

The store is likely wired for sound and probably has a great music system with a subscription to satellite stations, so you can request a certain type of music as your party's soundtrack. At celebrity-packed fashion parties, the music ranges from remixes of current hits to softer mood-setting artists like Michael Bublé to 1960s songs that coordinate with the current fashion trends in throwback 60s styles. Visit with the shop owner to check out her music offerings and see if you can bring in your own iPod dock and personally created playlists featuring the bride's favorite songs—the tunes that will bring her back to so many girls' getaways and high school and college memories. Then pop a copy of the party's playlist into the bride's swag bag with a card signed by all of her fashionable friends.

Special Additional Touches

If you have enough co-planners to split the cost comfortably for a two-to three-hour limo package, rent a stretch limousine to take you all from a starting point such as your home (where parking is free and easy) to the fashion boutique. When your limo pulls up outside the store, all eyes will be on you, the celebrities headed to a private VIP fashion show.

CHAPTER 16

Five-Star Parties

These parties take your group out on the town but not on a drink-fueled club hop. We're dialing up the five-star factor for these classy girls' nights out, and this chapter will provide inspired planning details for each of the six most popular styles of VIP parties.

Limousines and Cocktail Dresses

For all but the last party, transportation is likely to be a stylish requirement, since it will make the night more fabulous when you arrive at a notable restaurant in a stretch limousine, stepping out in your finest cocktail party dresses and high heels. So revisit the chapter on transportation, Chapter 5, to help you choose and book the perfect stylish ride for your bride and her guests.

Speaking of cocktail dresses and heels, these parties—with the exception of the winery tour—give everyone the chance to dress to impress, perhaps even to get that second or third wear out of a prior bridesmaid dress. Be sure to give all party guests notification that this is a dress-up evening, and the ladies are hitting the town in their fashionable best. Some hosts ask all of the guests to wear a little black dress so that the bride can stand out in her white, or hot-pink, dress, which gives her the star treatment at your location and creates fabulous group photos.

No More Drama

There's one in every group. I'm talking about the guest who doesn't want to wear a dress and heels, and writes you to say she'll be coming from the office and wearing her pants and a sweater. If she's not amenable to your suggestion of bringing a dress to the office that day, it's not worth a fight. If she wants to be underdressed at the party, so be it. This is one of those things you can't control, unfortunately.

Steal My Party Idea

"We knew the bride always wanted to go to the celebrity-favorite restaurant 21 in New York City, but we knew it was expensive. So we checked the website and found out about their lower prices during the earlier dining hours. If we made a reservation for 5 pm, we could get a prix fixe menu that was affordable and still give the bride her dream dinner." —Ainsley, bridesmaid

Dinner at a Five-Star Restaurant

There's a four-month wait at the hottest restaurant in town, that chic eatery that everyone wants to dine at for status value. If this is the restaurant you want to surprise the bride with, make that call way ahead of time to book your VIP table. The bride won't believe it when the limousine pulls up in front of *that* restaurant, her dream restaurant, and realizes that her party is taking place *there*.

Not all fine restaurants have that kind of elite, exclusive status, and you might not even want to dine at one that does. After all, some of the top upper-crust restaurants are insanely expensive for two people to dine there, let alone twenty-two. If the bride isn't a fan of status restaurants with their tiny portions and astronomical prices, it's far better to choose a fine restaurant based on its style, menu, atmosphere, and your group's happy dining experiences there.

Does the bride have a favorite fine restaurant that would feel like "coming home" to her? A place where she's known and gets the VIP treatment when she arrives? That could be your ideal restaurant choice. Does the bride have a dream restaurant that's local she'd love to choose? Or someplace not so local, perhaps one that requires a longer limo ride into the city? It's quite common for bachelorette party groups to take a forty-minute ride into the city to arrive at a five-star restaurant, enjoying champagne and drinks during their travels.

Invitations

Invitations to a fine dinner party are most often designed similarly to wedding invitations. They're printed on top-quality card stock, using fancy, formal script, in rich, jewel-tone print such as deep burgundies, greens, reds, and other striking colors. Think about menus you've seen in fine restaurants—

the colors, the textures, the decorative fonts. Dinner party invitations draw from the same inspirations, conveying the same feel that you're about to enjoy the meal of a lifetime.

You can also draw from the type of cuisine featured at your chosen restaurant, such as an Asian motif for a Japanese fusion restaurant in rich reds and parchment colors, with pearlized borders. Or for a Creole restaurant, the rich jewel tones of purple, green, red, and gold, just as you'd see at Mardi Gras—with the lettering.

A popular trend right now for this style of party is to design the invitation as a single-paneled card in the same style as a menu card that the bride might design for her guest tables at the reception. A menu card-inspired invitation may have a monogram letter at the top of the card—for a bachelorette party, you'd

Style Savvy

For color combination and pattern inspiration, look at the websites of famous formal restaurants to see the color palettes they use, the size and swirl of script, any icons such as a palm tree or a domed silver plate. Then use those same colors and motifs in the design of your invitation.

use the first letter of the bride's name—and it can creatively outline the party's essentials of date, time, and place in the same gorgeous script that might be used on a wedding menu card or even invitation. That script conveys the formality of the event you've planned.

An elegant invitation tells guests the style and tone of the party as well as its five-star status, so that guests know what to expect of the evening. As a considerate touch, add a line describing the dress code: ". . . a dressed-up evening out at Spago" or a bottom-of-the-invitation note to "Put on that little black dress!"

A fun insert or link for an e-invitation is a rave review the restaurant has gotten, that little something extra to get guests excited about celebrating there.

Menu Items

It's most common— and financially wise—to arrange a prix fixe menu at the restaurant. You'll go there ahead of time, sit down with the chef or manager, and select items that will be offered as a package to the party guests. That controls the expense, since you won't have to worry about guests going wild with their orders, racking up hundreds of dollars per person when they choose the $40 house special in addition to those pricy wines and cocktails.

When you set up a prix fixe menu, you'll most often get to choose three or four different appetizer platters for the table, the guests' selections between three different entrées, a salad course, and coffee and dessert. You can, of course, add additional items if the mood strikes or if the bride wishes to try a separate dish. You do have the freedom to customize once you've set the menu parameters.

As you're making prix fixe menu choices, be sure to include two indulgent entrées such as a salmon and a beef dish, and one lighter, perhaps vegetarian entrée to suit all of the guests' dietary preferences.

If the restaurant does not offer a prix fixe menu and cannot accommodate your smart request to create one, then you'll have to take control of the menu. A wise and stylish way to do this is to preprint menu cards showing the parameters of the meal. It might look like this:

MENU
Appetizers: Six appetizers for the table
Entrée: Chicken marsala, salmon with ginger sauce, fettucine primavera
Salad: Mixed greens with pine nuts, carrots, cranberries, and cranberry vinaigrette
Coffee and three desserts for the table

You've set the foundation for the menu, and guests know that the group will be asked to select those six wonderful appetizers for all to share. Each appetizer plate, on average, feeds three to four guests, and it's smart to have at least four different appetizers available for guests' enjoyment. Six is the most you will need for a twenty-person group.

If the restaurant serves family-style dishes, such as a big platter of lobster ravioli or a moo shu chicken dish, you may need only three or four of these platters to serve your twenty-person group.

Money Mastery

If your party will head to your home, or the bride's home, after the dinner, it's okay to request leftovers to be packaged and brought home for the bride to take with her to share with her groom. If you're headed out on the town after dinner, it's best not to bring home leftovers.

Many restaurants have a signature dish or dessert that has made the news, that famous offering that provides the ultimate experience of the meal. If it's a wildly expensive dish, as some signature dishes are, just get one or two for the table to split, and take photos of the bride and your group with that famous dish before you all dig into it.

Cake and Dessert

It's your choice—you can have desserts at the restaurant, go somewhere else for dessert, or head back to your place after that amazing meal to enjoy your bought or made cake and coffee, cappuccino, or espresso.

Some restaurants are known for their dessert lists, and it just wouldn't seem right to depart without ordering the white chocolate cheesecake or the crème brûlée. In prix fixe style, you may choose to prearrange a choice of three desserts for each of your guests. Everyone gets to choose her dessert—that cheesecake, the crème brûlée, a trio of gelatos, or other indulgent end to the meal.

You can also arrange to get four or five desserts for the guests to share, and if you have a group of twelve or more, it's considerate for guests' reach and access to the desserts to order two of each type and have them placed on the separate ends of the table.

Some of the more elegant desserts to consider:

➤ A custom-designed cake made by the restaurant's dessert chef

➤ Chocolate mousse in martini glasses with a raspberry sauce drizzle

➤ Crème brûlée, classic, chocolate, or pumpkin during the fall months

➤ Molten chocolate cake with fresh vanilla bean ice cream

➤ Cheesecakes in different flavors per slice assembled as a whole cheesecake

➤ Red velvet cake with white chocolate filling and frosting

➤ Rum cake with vanilla bean ice cream

➤ Green tea ice cream

➤ Bananas Foster

There's no rule saying you have to remain at the restaurant for dessert. A great many party groups continue on via limo to the next stop: a gelato place with outdoor seating, a cupcake bakery for gourmet flavors of the popular treat, a Godiva store for everyone to pick out their choices of truffles, even a retro ice cream shop for cones and sundaes.

And of course, if you do go back to your place for dessert, you have any dessert items as your choices. In addition to the stylish customized theme cake that you select for the bride (in the shape of a Tiffany box, or topped with a chocolate Louboutin, or any design that suits the bride's style), you can create a fabulous dessert bar filled with pastries, fruit-topped tarts, chocolate-dipped strawberries, tropical fruit slices, cookies, and more. Buy them premade, or DIY them as a group in advance of the party and serve them with an array of fantastic dessert wines, champagne, cappuccino, or espresso to finish off the indulgent evening in a relaxed atmosphere where everyone can kick off their high heels.

Drinks

When you're at a restaurant, the wine and cocktail lists can be quite enticing—and pricy. You do, of course, want the bride and her guests to enjoy fabulous drinks, but it's a budget danger—unless you've earmarked a very generous amount of cash for this event—to skip the essential step of arranging a set drinks menu.

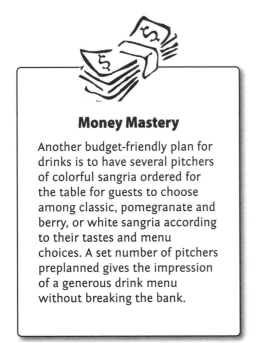

Money Mastery

Another budget-friendly plan for drinks is to have several pitchers of colorful sangria ordered for the table for guests to choose among classic, pomegranate and berry, or white sangria according to their tastes and menu choices. A set number of pitchers preplanned gives the impression of a generous drink menu without breaking the bank.

When you stop in to arrange the prix fixe menu, also arrange a drinks plan. For instance, even at the most upscale of restaurants, you can ask to have a certain number of wine bottles purchased for table service. I love the drink calculators at ThatstheSpirit.com and Evite.com—two free tools that ask you for your number of guests, the duration of the party, and the guests' low or high drinking capacity, and then tell you approximately how many bottles of wine you'll need to provide. Speak with the restaurant manager to arrange for, say, ten bottles of wine included in your preset price package. If the group should speed through that collection, a server is to subtly let you know that you have two bottles left on your order. You can then decide to purchase another bottle, if needed.

The drinks issue often presents an etiquette challenge, especially when you don't know some of the people on the guest list and find them to be in the partying mind-set, able to down drink after drink in a far speedier pace than any drink calculator would have predicted. Some hosts decide to limit their own alcohol consumption to make room for those guests' orders and still remain within budget limits. And other hosts feel comfortable mentioning to a circle of close friends that there are only eight bottles of wine on the menu, and everyone is free to go to the bar to order any mixed drinks or

No More Drama

The bride should be told about the limited drink menu and your plan to have guests purchase their own mixed drinks at the bar just so that she's not surprised or offended when that scene plays out in the middle of the restaurant. Most brides appreciate knowing what the drink rules will be, and since they know all of their guests so well, they know if they should let certain guests know ahead of time to bring extra drink money along since only wine will be included with this meal. It may seem strange to you that drinks would become the center of a guest drama, but it has happened, so pre-empt it with an honest discussion with the bride and if she requests, an e-mail to the guests letting them know about the drink rules and sending them a link to the drinks menu at the restaurant. This smart move lets guests see what the cocktail prices are, in many instances, so that they can plan ahead.

different kinds of wines they prefer. Should they be told to put their drinks on your tab? No. If they need to order extra drinks, or strong drinks such as Long Island Iced Teas, it's up to them to pay for their own choices.

Décor

No extra décor is needed at this style of party. The restaurant's own décor becomes the setting for the dinner party, and its tables set with candles and fresh florals provide essentially free centerpieces. A fine restaurant is no place for balloons or signs, so those can be skipped as well or reserved for surprise décor back at your place for that desserts after-party.

Theme Gifts for the Bride

No gifts are needed for the bride, either, since it's her present to enjoy this fabulous meal with her closest friends, sisters, and cousins. But if you do wish to give her a group gift, consider a gift card to the restaurant you'll be at, so that she can take her groom for a romantic night out before or after the wedding.

Favors

Match the favors to the theme of the restaurant. At a Creole restaurant, for instance, give out pretty little packets of Creole spices (an easy DIY project!). At an Italian restaurant, give out packets of garlic knot rolls or baggies of Italian cookies or biscotti, or pick up those small, round olive oil-dipping plates and wrap them for guests to take home.

Favors are not necessary at this party, since guests will be enjoying a wonderful meal and dessert, but it's a nice touch to have a little take-home treat for them to share with their significant others or families.

Entertainment

The restaurant may feature entertainment, such as a live pianist, or the night's musical act, such as the big-name jazz ensemble at the jazz club restaurant. At the very least, fine restaurants pipe in the night's soundtrack via their sound system, to set the ambiance for patrons.

If your dinner party will take place in a restaurant's private room, as many establishments arrange for groups of twenty or more guests, ask if they can pipe in the same music that is playing in the main dining room. Most restaurants will be glad to do so. And ask if the featured singer or guitarist would be willing to pop into your party room to perform a song or two for the bride for an added charge or your generous tip for the command performance.

A fine restaurant is obviously not the place to have a male dancer or other racy entertainment, and it's also not the place to bring in your own musicians unless you get prior approval from the site's manager. It would be quite unfair to the party in the next room if your musician's volume is up too high, and unsettling for restaurant patrons to hear your performer blended with the main dining room music. Some restaurants won't allow outside entertainers for this reason, and some don't allow performers due to legal reasons and insurance, so always ask first before you spend a moment searching for performers.

Special Additional Touches

Ask for that special honored moment when the chef comes out of the kitchen to greet your party group. At many restaurants, the chef is quite well known, perhaps a James Beard Award-winner, and upon your request he or she may be willing to step out of the kitchen, accept your accolades for the fabulous meal, and wish the bride the best. Foodies live for this kind of special attention from the chef, who in the world of gourmet cuisine is like a rock star.

Set on your table or tables several one-time-use cameras to capture the excitement and indulgence of your dinner party. Kodak has a new bachelorette party design single-use camera that you can place within guests' reach so that they can take a wonderful collection of images from the party, such as photos of the bride sharing a sinful dessert with her maid of honor, or everyone lifting their champagne glasses in a toast to the bride. In this latter shot, some might photograph the glasses clinking, and some might photograph the bride's radiant face, captured in the soft glow of the table's candle centerpiece.

Concerts and Shows

The bride's big night out could center around the hottest ticket of the year. It might be her favorite artist on the biggest concert tour of the year, or a Tony-winning play or musical— whatever the bride loves. Perhaps you want to arrange this concert event as a surprise to her, allowing her to think she's headed to a dinner party. But when the limousine approaches the concert hall or stadium, she'll be thrilled beyond words that you've planned such a fabulous surprise event for her. Especially if she's never seen her favorite artist in concert before and you have great seats.

Invitations

A square invitation can be designed to feature the artist's latest CD, then open to reveal the details of the party: "We're going to see Carrie Underwood in concert for Melanie's

Shop Here!

When you're searching for concert tickets, don't limit yourself to the big venues such as stadiums. A great many local community theaters now attract fabulous acts from present-day Grammy winners to retro performers such as groups that were hot in the 1970s and 1980s. These theaters are heavily underwritten by big corporations, and top stars say they love performing in the smaller spaces for a more intimate show experience, so they book dates between their big concert tours. Check the websites of your nearby community theaters to get great seats at discounted group prices. You may be able to use a co-planner's theater membership to snag better seats at better prices—plus a visit backstage to meet the artists.

bachelorette bash!" Another popular DIY invitation design trend is creating a Photoshop collage of the artist's images—just six to eight photos for a small invitation card will do—and again putting the party details inside.

Another creative twist on the concert party invitation is to make or order a round invitation with the design style of a CD or a vinyl album. Taylor Swift, for instance, loves and collects vinyl albums, so if the bride's party group is headed to a Taylor Swift concert, the vinyl album is a superfan's true invitation design.

Sticking with the CD theme, creative party hosts are burning video invitations onto DVD, opening with the artist's new video, and then expertly transitioning into the party host's spoken (or titled) party invitation. If you're the star of this video invite, put on your favorite star's concert T-shirt, play that artist's song in the background, and make this very brief video a well-produced one that shares all the essential party information and provides the URL of your party's web page (again, check out the free event page templates at WeddingMapper.com—no wedding required!)

For a play, design the invitation to look like a playbill, using the same dimensions and the same glossy cover, even if the invitation is just a greeting card-style fold and not a booklet with many pages. Use your home computer's graphic design tool to place images of the playbill logo and the performance's icons on the invitation cover, and print the party details inside using the same or a coordinating font as seen on the invitation's front cover. Get creative with the wording inside, as well. Consider these ideas for a play-centric party:

➤ "The play's the thing! Join us for a night at the theater in honor of Jasmine's bachelorette celebration!"

➤ "Get your rock on for Jasmine's bachelorette party, we're all going to see *Rock of Ages*!"

➤ "Denzel's on Broadway, and we're taking Jasmine to see his latest dramatic tour de force! Join us as we celebrate Jasmine—and Denzel!!"

So which comes first? The tickets or the RSVPs? It's tricky when you're creating invitations, since some show tickets can be wildly difficult to get. A smart strategy is to send out invitations way in advance, as far in advance as possible, explaining that RSVPs determine how many tickets the hosts will purchase. Those who reply by (date) will have a ticket purchased for them. Those who don't reply won't be in the block of fantastic seats and may miss the show altogether. Those RSVPs will speed in.

Money Mastery

Who pays for each ticket? Is this something the hosts pick up? That can be quite pricy, especially since some concert tickets can cost over $100 apiece for quality seats. Many party hosts worry about obligating guests to pay for their own tickets, but when you land a discount group fee, it's quite exciting for guests to know that they can see this phenomenal act or play for so little money. Think about destination bachelorette party guests. They pay for their own airfare and lodging, so this expense will almost certainly amount to far less than that. So don't worry about asking guests to pay in advance for the tickets you'll buy, and require prepayment from them so that you can buy that block of tickets without having to spend weeks hounding guests to pay up.

Menu Items

Choose a nearby restaurant—although not too close to the theater because you'll get stuck in a crowd of theater-goers rushing to eat—or have a preparty at your place before you pile in the limo to catch the show. The at-home preparty allows you to self-cater on a budget, serving anything from platter sandwiches and salads to family-style lasagna, meatballs, salad, and garlic bread. Set up a buffet of appetizers, and set out disposable themed party plates and clear utensils so that co-planners can help you clean up before it's time to go to the show.

Cake and Dessert

After the show everyone can come back to your place—as the limousine ride may require anyway—for cake and coffee. A big trend in parties like these is to order a cake that features the artist's likeness or CD or the program cover. These are quite easy for many bakers to create—you give them the image you want on disk, and they run it through their equipment to create an edible decal sheet that they lay right on top of the cake frosting. The effect is spectacular and surprisingly inexpensive. With any cake, you're paying for labor. So when a baker just has to print out an edible decal sheet, it takes far less time (and costs you far less money) than if the baker had to spend twenty hours hand-making sugar paste anemones, tulips, roses and other florals, or stilettos made from rolled fondant.

Another big trend for postshow party desserts is a tray or tiered display of cupcakes. Choose classic designs in an array of flavors from standard vanilla to red velvet, even cocktail-infused cupcakes, for your guests to enjoy with after-dinner drinks and coffee.

Drinks

Any drink menu will do, and your wine collection should include both reds and whites, since some guests have not just a preference but may have health issues such as celiac disease that make red wines intolerable.

For the dessert portion of the evening, pair those cupcakes or that cake, mousses, and fruits with dessert wines that are sweeter and fruitier than standard wines. Check out WineSpectator.com for more information on, and the newest award-winning vintages of, dessert wines. And finally, serve a fabulous brand of coffee in regular and flavored varieties. A French vanilla or hazelnut coffee may be the perfect pairing to a nutty-flavored cupcake.

Décor

No special décor is needed for this pre- or post-party at your place. If you wish, a low-set cluster of fresh flowers at a focal point is a lovely touch. And avoid candles, since you'll all be leaving the house in a flurry of activity and preparations; you don't want any hazards in your home while you're out if you should forget to blow out a candle somewhere.

Theme Gifts for the Bride

Of course, a concert T-shirt makes a great keepsake for the bride, and a second one purchased that all the party guests sign lets her wear one and treasure the other. The same goes for a theater production's T-shirt, or a theme-matching T-shirt from CafePress.com that you give her after the show.

Favors

No favors are necessary at this party, but if guests spent a lot on their concert or show tickets, it is a nice touch to give everyone an edible favor such as a chocolate-covered brownie in a wrapper, a trio of gourmet cookies, or some other treat that they get to take home after the after-party.

Big-City Sprees

In this high-style, *Sex and the City*-inspired celebration, the bride and her girls take a limousine into the nearest big city for a fashionable day of VIP shopping. You're looking for such amazing iconic shopping meccas as Fifth Avenue in New York, Rodeo Drive in Beverly Hills, or the Magnificent Mile in Chicago; or it could be an elite stretch of designer showrooms in any metropolitan area. You'll map out your stops—from Bloomingdales to celebrity-favorite boutiques—and shop-hop for that socialite experience. You might drop in at Stuart Weitzman to try on sky-high, gem-encrusted heels, or you might take a stroll through Tiffany's to try on jaw-dropping jewelry.

So which big cities are the best for shopping sprees? *Travel and Leisure* magazine puts out its World's Best list every year, naming the hottest shopping cities. Here are the results of a recent survey:

1. New York City
2. Chicago
3. San Francisco
4. Houston
5. Los Angeles
6. Charleston
7. Boston
8. New Orleans
9. Miami
10. Sante Fe

Be sure to check out its annual awards for shopping, dining, hotels, and more at TravelandLeisure.com.

When you choose your ideal big city for shopping, go in top fashion. Dress for the occasion in your most stylish ensemble, and get ready to turn heads as your gorgeous group emerges from a top-name boutique, shopping bags in hand, ducking into your limousine to return to your awaiting champagne. The paparazzi will appear out of nowhere. You have to be famous to look that good, after all.

Invitations

Choose an invitation featuring a sophisticated illustration of modern ladies in colorful dresses toting shopping bags, presumably enjoying the same big-city shopping excursion you're planning. The invitations at Pingg.com and PSAEssentials.com are just two of the collections that feature this type of image, and more. Illustrated images give a stylish, modern kick to both print and e-invitations, and the new class of fashion-inspired images makes this the best time ever for designing an invitation.

Another option for conveying the excitement of a big-city shopping spree is showing the icons of top-flight stores and designer brands, or that luxury brand of the light blue Tiffany shopping bag.

Sample wording for your invitation includes:

➤ "It's style in the city at Tabitha's bachelorette shopping spree!"

➤ "Look out, Rodeo Drive! Tabitha and Co. are headed your way for a day of shopping, strutting, and champagne along the way!"

➤ "Come join us as Tabitha gets the *Pretty Woman* treatment at the city's top designer showrooms!"

A 3-D design could be the creation of an actual mini shopping bag, perhaps in Tiffany blue, with faux plastic credit cards (make them platinum or black cards) included as props along with your printed-out invitation to a day in the big city for lunch and dream designer shopping.

Menu Items

Eat at a quintessential big-city restaurant for lunch or brunch. You might go to the Plaza or to the Ivy, even for a round of appetizers if that's all your budget can manage. And take plenty of pictures of the bride and her stylish girls having an ultra-special meal along your shopping path.

Cake and Dessert

Dessert may be enjoyed at a fabulous restaurant—yes, you can just order drinks and desserts at the fanciest of places—or you might stop in at the city's notable bakery or cupcake shop where everyone can enjoy their choice of sweets. In New York City, one of the iconic dessert stops, Serendipity, is best known for its frozen hot chocolates and sinful sundaes. If the bride loves the movie *Serendipity*, stopping in here can be a dream-come-true surprise.

Every major city has its celebrity-favorite dessert locale. In Los Angeles, it's Hansen's Cakes. It makes the designer cakes for Tori Spelling's and the Kardashians' parties, so grabbing a treat

Style Savvy

Not sure where the iconic restaurants are? Check Zagats.com and especially DailyCandy.com for their mentions, suggestions, and reviews of the must-go eateries. And check out the columns in *OK!* and *Us Weekly* that mention where the stars were spotted lunching in the city. That builds your list of possible high-style restaurant options.

from here gives your VIP shopping spree a celebrity flavor at the end. So take lots of pictures of yourselves in front of and inside the shop.

If you'd rather enjoy dessert at home, have a cake designed to look like a Tiffany box, or a designer shopping bag, a pile of big-name shoe boxes, or stilettos with red soles à la Christian Louboutin. Chocolate shops now make a range of stylish stiletto chocolates in real-life sizes that can be placed on top of or next to your choice of color-matched cake. And, of course, cupcakes can be topped with fashion-forward patterned sugar disks in such styles as zebra-stripe, houndstooth, or the shiny effect of silk.

Shop Here!

Check out TravelandLeisure.com's new app for your iPad for the latest award-winning restaurants and big-city musts.

Drinks

Of course, champagne served in the limousine always makes for a classy toast in celebrity style, and for your pre- or post-party—or at a cocktails stop during your day in the city—consider theme-fitting cosmopolitans or bright red drinks to carry that Louboutin red sole motif throughout the celebration. In some big cities, it's legendary to have a drink at restaurants like Sardi's or 21 in New York City, or Azul in Miami Beach. Again, check TravelandLeisure.com to help you plan your drink-stop locations.

Theme Gifts for the Bride

While you're out on the town, keep an eye on what the bride is perusing. Is she longingly touching that Burberry scarf? Checking out the sexy stockings at Donna Karan? When she's in another part of the store or otherwise distracted, secretly purchase the longed-for item and present it to her at the end of the party.

Favors

Most bachelorette party groups don't have the budget to get everyone a Burberry scarf, so have the group stop at a sidewalk vendor table to choose small, touristy items as their keepsake for the day. They might be snow globes, tote bags, $2 bracelets, or any number of other affordable items.

Entertainment

Shopping doesn't have to last the entire day when you're in a big city. In fact, it can get quite tiring after the first three or so hours. So plan a secondary event for the group to enjoy, something that fits with the big-city theme. For instance, when you prepurchase group-rate tickets, it's quite affordable to bring everyone to the city's most notable museum and walk through its breathtaking butterfly habitat, where live butterflies encircle you and land on your shoulders. Have your cameras ready for this wondrous experience, a lovely breather in the middle of your shopping spree day.

Special Additional Touches

Big cities are often locations where movies and television shows are being filmed. Your group might just be in town to see your favorite stars at work! Check out LocationVacations.com to see where upcoming shoots will take place, and if the bride's favorite show will be in action at your location. This would be a terrific surprise for her!

Steal My Party Idea

"We were in New York City on a big shopping spree—and having fun just trying on amazing designer clothing and shoes—and we stopped in at the big M&Ms store just for fun. While we were there, we had everyone custom blend their own baggies of M&Ms from the wall of amazing dispensers, and those were their party favors!"—Amy, maid of honor

Winery Tours

For so many people, wineries are a dream destination. Several areas of the country are home to the top wineries and vineyards in the world, and they're open for tours and tastings. Imagine taking your bride and her party group to such a gorgeous locale, with winery after winery nestled in some of the most beautiful, natural scenery. You'll ride bikes or take a limousine from winery to winery, tasting the diverse vintages and even lunching in a private garden where groups are hosted for special occasions.

These alfresco luncheons put you out in the middle of perfectly manicured gardens, or out in the midst of the vineyard beneath arbors and arching trees, with personal servers bringing you course after gourmet course, plus a steady stream of fine wines. On a perfect day, this picture-perfect lunch at a vineyard will be a highlight of the bride's entire tenure as The Bride. And to share it with her favorite women? That's priceless.

When you book a weekend stay at a local bed and breakfast, you can take in the entirety of what a winery region has to offer, from vineyard tours to hot air balloon rides, antiquing in town, to fine dining, and even early morning hikes and bike rides as a group. This is the type of location that many brides and grooms book for their destination weddings, so if that was a style the bride originally considered—but couldn't arrange for her wedding—making this her five-star bachelorette party style is making her dreams come true.

Invitations

Your invitations can be designed with the image of a vast vineyard nature scene, or you can focus on the bottle itself, showing a fine vintage placed by a tray of breads and grapes and cheeses. Showing edibles, the tastes of the event, shares with party guests what they can expect to experience in artistic style.

At established invitation sites such as Pingg.com and Vistaprint.com, you'll see their collection of wine-centric images and invitation designs to choose from, and Evite.com also has winery-themed designs for your free invitation sends.

You can also use an image of your own, a styled shot that you take with your digital camera, as the graphic for your invitation. Play stylist with your arranged shot, such as placing several bottles of wine that you own on a sunlit table next to a vase of fresh, vibrant flowers or even next to a wedding tiara to show guests that this will be a wine-themed party to celebrate the bride. You'll then upload your best shot onto an invitation-making site, and you have a custom invitation design.

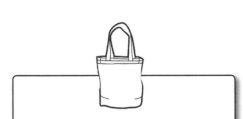

Shop Here!

Browse the most amazing top-name wineries in a region through several top websites: WineSpectator.com, FoodandWine.com, Gourmet.com, TravelChannel.com and TravelandLeisure.com are just some of the best-known and most-respected resources. Look for TravelandLeisure.com's World's Best awards, and, of course, the Travel Channel frequently posts reviews of wineries that make its best-of lists each year.

Since a winery tour party can be held on one day or planned as a weekend getaway, you of course have to include all of the pertinent information in your invitation. For an e-mailed invite, a link to the bed-and-breakfast, as well as links to the wineries you'll visit, allows guests to envision the excitement to come and book their rooms on their own, if necessary.

Menu Items

When you work with the winery events manager to plan that special luncheon for the bride, whether it's to be served outdoors or in the winery's private tasting room, be sure to include the local tastes of the region on your menu. Ask for a list of locally grown produce, artisanal cheeses, signature breads and appetizers for an authentic collection of dishes, and not the same-old lunch that you could have anywhere.

Add lots of fresh, healthy dishes to keep the natural theme of your all-natural surroundings, including fresh salads, antipasto, tapenades for your still-warm breads, and family-style platters of the luncheon's entrée. The community table is a staple in many of the world's top wine regions, such as France, Italy, Spain, South Africa, and New Zealand, and a big, beautifully decorated table set here for the bride gives her that same beautiful scene that's often created in movies to depict the blissful, happy ending to the main character's wonderful journey in an idyllic setting.

Cake and Dessert

Cake and desserts may be served at your vineyard table, or you may venture onward to a specialty dessert shop for indulgent baked masterpieces. A fabulous trend in desserts is serving wine-infused cupcakes, such as cabernet cupcakes, or a cake topped with a wine-infused frosting; or you could style your cake design to feature grape clusters made from sugar paste atop a rich buttercream-frosted cake.

For further cake flavor inspiration, look at the flavor notes on fine bottles of wine. You might read about blackberries included in a vintage, so choose a blackberry-infused filling, or a buttercream and blackberry filling with juicy bits of blackberry for a tart accent to the sweet frosting. Some wines have apple tastes, or raspberry, even nutty bouquets, so perhaps a hazelnut buttercream frosting on a cake to pair with a wine featuring just the slightest touch of hazelnut in the mix. A bottle of wine can inspire your cake baker, especially one who's located in wine country and very much accustomed to pairing desserts with wines.

At the end of the day, fresh strawberries and other fruits with fresh whipped cream or chocolate-dipped fruits provide the perfect additional dessert offering. For a creamier indulgent dessert, think about crème brûlée, Chantilly cream fruit tarts, white chocolate mousse, gelato, tiramisu, or hazelnut mousse served in shot glasses with a Pirouline cookie standing up in it.

Theme Gifts for the Bride

The perfect gift for the bride is a fabulous bottle of the best wine you discovered during your adventure, tied with a ribbon and bow, and paired with a note encouraging her to share this bottle of wine with her groom now or upon their return from their honeymoon.

Favors

In keeping with the wine theme of the celebration, one of the smartest favors to give to guests is wine bottle stoppers. I gave out the silver heart-topped ones from KateAspen.com at my wedding, and we still use ours to this day. Wine bottle stoppers come in so many different designs, from simple silver shapes to blown glass mini globes in bright colors and starburst effects inside. They're among the most inexpensive, most impressive favors to give out, and a winning idea for this party theme.

Style Savvy

Arrange for the bride and groom's wineglasses to be delivered to her home while she's away on this winery jaunt with her girls. This group gift from all of you will surprise her when she returns and fulfill her wish for a stylish collection of stemware.

During your travels on this trip, you'll find gift shop after gift shop as wonderful resources for small bags of wine-infused chocolates, chocolate drink stirring spoons, and other treats under $5 that you can give to party guests as a thank-you for sharing this trip for the bride. On a larger budget, you can buy a case of a crowd-favorite vintage, and give each guest a bottle of her own to take home, sharing with her sweetheart or celebrating her own life's best moments.

Special Additional Touches

Plan an hour within your travels to stop off at a beautiful scenic overlook, perhaps during vibrant fall foliage season, for a photo session. You'll take fun group pictures to commemorate your trip, and also snap lots of solo photos that each guest can use as her gorgeous online dating profile image or as her new Facebook profile photo. It's quite thrilling whenever you get a fabulous photo of yourself, so this magazine-worthy setting is ideal for capturing gorgeous images of everyone in the group. The bride will likely be the most excited, since she gets wonderful pictures of herself with friends who may have traveled from afar to attend her special getaway party.

Additional Party Themes

What says *five-star* to the bride? Ask her! She may envy the girls' get-togethers she reads about in *Us Weekly*, in which celebrities host ladies' night parties in hotel penthouses in Vegas, or other this-is-the-life fêtes. Her if-only ideas could spark a wonderful, doable plan for her VIP bachelorette party. Here are a few of the leading trends in celebrity-worthy party themes:

➤ A day at an ultra-private, elite country club, arranged by a friend who is a member, and featuring a private lunch and hours at poolside

➤ VIP tickets to an elite sporting event, such as the bride's dream access to the U.S. Open to see her favorite celebrity tennis players

➤ Celeb-favorite at-home cooking class, taught by a private chef. Ivanka Trump recently said that she was planning an at-home Thai cooking class for herself and her girlfriends, and this VIP-style party provides the perfect classy interaction, plus a great meal served by the chef and plenty of fabulous wine!

➤ A mingle with the stars party at one of the Madame Tussauds Wax Museum (MadameTussauds.com) locations across the country, where your party guests enter rooms with different themes, such as nightclubs or Rachael Ray's kitchen, to take fun and funny photos next to (if not kissing) fabulous wax figures of actors, singers, sports stars, politicians, reality stars, and royalty. The two-hour tour through the museum results in hilarious poses and great photo keepsakes for the bride.

CHAPTER 17

Charity Event Parties

In This Chapter

➤ Choosing a cause

➤ Choosing an event style

➤ Party details

The giving-minded bride looks for ways to involve charitable giving into her wedding these days, so she may be very interested in taking the occasion of her bachelorette party and turning it into an event that gives back. In this chapter, you'll learn the ins and outs of planning a charity event party that begins with your group participating in a charitable event such as a 5K or a walk, then gathering after the race for a celebration.

You must take one important step first: clear this idea with the bride. While you may be sure that she would love to have her party give back in this way, she might have cause for concern that the topic would be upsetting to her guests. For instance, if the groom has recently lost his grandmother to breast cancer, it might be too soon for his mother and sisters to participate in a breast cancer walk. Yes, the cause is a great one, but for some people, just seeing that pink ribbon trips their grief. It is too soon.

Some brides also worry that the fundraising aspect of a charity walk or run might not sit well with certain guests. You might know that they can walk without raising money, but the bride might worry that her busy friends and relatives would feel obligated to raise funds or be embarrassed by an online fundraising page that shows a small amount of money raised. They might not want to ask their friends and family to contribute. These may be the bride's fears, and fears are not the stuff of a great celebration. So make sure the bride is completely enthusiastic about having a charitable event party before you take (no pun intended) another step.

Choosing a Cause the Bride Believes In

It's always smartest to consult with the bride so that she may choose the cause that her party will support. This is a highly personal decision, and it's never wise to assume you know the bride's most treasured charity just because of her recent Facebook posts. Given the opportunity to choose the cause for this celebration, she may have a different one in mind.

Here are the top types of causes that brides and grooms choose for their charitable wedding registries, according to the IDoFoundation.org:

1. Children's health charities
2. Cancer research charities
3. Environmental charities
4. Education and literacy charities
5. Animal charities
6. Hunger charities
7. Clean water charities

This last one is newest on the scene, with many couples finding that their guests universally support making clean water available to the world's population. Not that they're against children's health charities. Some people have strong feelings about the politics of certain charitable groups, and they may prefer a cause that is less polarizing than any organization that's been in the news for questionable asset allocation or support of political parties.

The bride may wish to steer clear of any conflict, particularly if she knows that politics are a hot button with her future in-laws. One bride recently confided to me that her mother-in-law believes that most eco-friendly charities are scams designed to make money. The bride had witnessed her groom's mother's ire at a family party, and she didn't want to invite her future mother-in-law's wrath or disapproval by planning an event that benefitted that sector of charities. The bride, herself, would continue to support that particular group, but for this party she would stick with a less-loaded cause: benefitting the local animal shelter that often conducts rescues from natural disaster areas. Everyone, she said, could get behind that.

Choosing an Event Style that Guests Will Enjoy

Next, you'll decide on the type of charitable event. Will it be a 5K or a walk? Most guests of all fitness levels can handle a walk, and they can walk the 5K like the thousands of others who will be doing the same, moving at their own pace. Mention to the bride that a 5K or walk can be enjoyed in two ways by party participants: those who wish to race can race, and others can sign on as volunteers, handing out water bottles or being designated cheering sections along the route.

The next style of charitable event is a fundraising barbecue or other low ticket price event. For under $20 per person, your group can attend a charity's lunch in the park. This option is far more affordable than some groups' elite fundraising dinners at $200 per person, and some say their casual nature is far more enjoyable than a stuffy, dress-up dinner filled with speeches, awards, and auctions. To find events of this nature, check your community events calendar as well as the websites of your church, the local Junior League, and men's clubs like the Elks. The latter often runs charitable breakfasts and fish fries to raise money for local families with children fighting illnesses.

A charitable event may include getting down and dirty in an entirely different way than the traditional racy bachelorette party. Your group may join a horticultural group to plant beds of pansies, zinnias, daisies, and other pretty flowers all through the center of your town or as a beautification event for a school or library. If your guests love to garden and wouldn't mind a rewarding afternoon in the dirt, this could be your ideal party plan, stage one, with a celebration after cleanup at your place.

Style Savvy

Check also with local boutiques and gift shops that often plan charitable shopping days to benefit different local groups such as scout troops, high school bands, and sports clubs. Your group shops, and a percentage of your purchases go to the cause. Even the Gap is in on this one. Its recent Gap Give & Get campaign raised over half a million dollars for the Leukemia & Lymphoma Society.

Style Savvy

"We asked everyone to bring items that we'd send to our military troops overseas. We called our local recruiting station to ask if they run a donation drive, and they do. We got the list of what the troops need—toiletries, magazines, phone cards, and so on—and our party guests stocked up! We had a really big collection of great stuff for them!" —Carrie, bridesmaid

Always be sure to donate through a sanctioned group suggested by your local recruiter's office.

Find these events through your favorite charities' websites as well as on their Facebook pages and tweets, and visit VolunteerMatch.org—one of my favorite sites for upcoming 5Ks, fundraising lunches, and donation drives.

Speaking of donation drives, your charitable party doesn't have to involve running shoes or shovels. You can simply ask party guests to bring canned goods, clothing, jackets, kids' books and other commonly collected items to benefit local charities.

Party Details

Here is where you'll create your charitable events party from start to finish.

Invitations

E-mailed invitations are ideal for this party style, since they can include the URL of the charity or specific charitable event the party will be benefitting. Guests want to be sure they're getting involved with a legitimate cause, and they want additional details on what's involved with the event, such as the course route if the event is a 5K. It's easiest if you just send them to the official event webpage where they may even be able to join the group you've set up, such as Dana's Bridesmaids Running Wild or other fun name your team dreams up. Most charitable races allow you to organize your fundraising pages within your group, and payments are automatically and safely received and tallied using PayPal or another secure tool.

So that's the link to the charitable event. Your invitations—whether online with a link or in print with the charity race URL shown—can feature cute illustrations of the charitable event, such as:

➤ Women running a race in colorful running outfits and brightly toned shoes

➤ A woman riding her bike through the mountains with woodland creatures looking on, and her contest number is the date of the party

➤ A beautiful arching flower for a gardening event

Photos also make your invitation design job easier, so get out your camera or look through your collections for pictures of the bride and her friends participating in charitable events. You might have pictures from the last time you all ran a 5K, crossing the finish line together, or you might have access to a picture of the bride warming up for her run. For the latter, your wording might call to the photo's composition, saying "Dana's warming up for her bachelorette party! Put on your running shoes and help us raise money for cancer research" or "You've heard of the Running of the Brides? Dana's *our* bride who's going to be running the Susan G. Komen 5K, and we're running with her as her bachelorette bash! So forget the stilettos, it's Nike time!"

You can also take fresh, new theme-appropriate photos, such as a photo of the bride's running shoes shown under the hem of her wedding dress (but don't show the wedding dress! That has to stay a surprise for the big day!) or a shot of the bride running through a race-win ribbon with her arms raised in the air.

The invitation has to include vital information for the party, including the event's start time and location, rain date information, and fundraising guide, and it must include a second invitation within: the one to the after-party. When everyone's crossed the finish line, it's common for the charity to serve food and drinks to the participants, and you may stop by for a quick bite. But the overwhelming trend is to have everyone on your guest list come to your house or to a co-planner's house for a post-run party, so you get to design a second invitation for that phase 2 of the event.

Style Savvy

Create an invitation packet, such as a DIY pocket folder in a 5 x 5-inch square, holding the two invitations—one for the run, and a separate brightly colored one for the after-party. Make sure the party invitation has all of the essential information on the party's location and your phone number or e-mail as the host, plus RSVP information with the reply-by date set for two weeks prior to the party.

For a charitable event that involves training, such as a 5K or mini marathon, send out your invitations four to six months in advance so that guests have time to limber up and build their stamina. For less intensive charitable events such as planting flowers in the town square, three weeks' notice is fine for the sending of your invitations. Since both involve similar after-parties, set the RSVP date for at least two weeks prior to the event.

And for parties that focus on donation drives in which you ask guests to bring items, include a detailed printed sheet of what's accepted in the drive, plus a list of what the charity does not accept. For instance, you might want to bake cookies for the troops, but those are often on the Don't Send list.

Menu Items

If you'll be gathering at your place before heading to the race site, set out a platter of bagels and fruit so that guests can fuel up for the run or ride. Morning buffet items can include those bagels and light spreads, a fruit platter, muffins, and water served in bottles you've affixed with custom labels. Skip the sugary donuts and other energy sappers.

For your race's after-party, create your buffet from preassembled party platters of sandwiches that you can get inexpensively at warehouse stores like Costco or Sam's Club. A three-foot sub can feed your guests easily, as well. Additional buffet choices include fresh salads with lots of healthy vegetables and an array of dressings, a variety of sandwich wraps, hummus and pita triangles, focaccia topped with cheeses or tomatoes—dishes that are easy to just pull out of the fridge and serve on a buffet table. After a run or the exertion of gardening on a hot day, you won't want to deal with heating up chafing dishes in the oven, timing dishes for readiness to serve, or other kitchen work. Cold platters, including ultra-popular bowls of red grapes and trays of veggie crudités and onion or artichoke dip fill out your buffet bounty and reward your guests with an amazing meal to share with the bride in this part 2 of your party.

Style Savvy

On a fall day with a bit of a chill in the air, your buffet may be inside and ideally served with hot platters that will be heated up in the oven—pastas and meatballs, lemon chicken, shrimp scampi, and other party fare. Here's a secret that keeps those entrée pans from bubbling and spilling over, filling your house with smoke and burned food smell: just have those containers filled halfway rather than to the top. Your caterer or DIY cooks can be told about this requirement for your reheating needs, and you'll get all the food you ordered in friendlier-to-heat batches, preventing atmosphere-wrecking oven disasters.

Cake and Dessert

Create a cake with a fresh buttercream filling and icing, which is not only less expensive than fondant toppings but can be blended with fruit flavors for a refreshing cake taste. A vanilla-frosted cake with raspberry buttercream inside and the sweet taste of fresh berries blended in works so perfectly in a sheet cake or round cake.

Believe it or not, you can match your desserts to the cause you just ran for. A dark chocolate-frosted cake calls to the health-improving aspects of dark chocolate. Fruits topping Chantilly cream tarts also showcase a lifestyle that improves health. And a pink cake with pink frosting pays tribute to the breast cancer charity you just supported, with the white chocolate-dipped strawberries on it making it extra pretty for the bride.

Color matching can also be done with cupcakes and frosted cookies, and brownies and cookies can be cut into heart shapes to honor the heart disease charity the bride supports.

Drinks

Any drinks are ideal for this post-party, but they need to be served in addition to still-needed hydrating water from pitchers filled with lemon and lime slices. The exerted body needs to replenish its water supply, and your pretty offering of water in glass pitchers turns that H_2O into a stylized bar feature.

Shop Here!

Bethenny Frankel has made the Skinny Girl margarita a stylish sip at ladies-only parties, so shop at Bethenny.com to provide your party guests with this celebrity-favorite flavor.

Additional stylized bar features include fruit-filled sangria in colors ranging from rich cranberry red to pink to pear-flavored pale green. Check out the sangria recipes at FoodNetwork.com and have plenty of juices and wines available to mix these crowd pleasers. Green tea wine spritzers are also a huge trend in healthy cocktails.

What about energy drinks? Not everyone is used to them or enjoys them, so you can save up your money and leave these off your celebration menu. A small cooler bucket with Gatorade in a festive color such as orange is a welcome item to those who may have dehydration headaches or cramps, so add those to your shopping list.

And do have regular and decaf coffee on hand for those who wish to partake, even if you'd never touch java after running several miles. Those who volunteered and didn't run say they like it when party hosts prepare for their end-of-party caffeine fix.

Décor

Borrow from the style of decorations shown at charitable walks and runs. That means lots of colorful balloons that you can use in bunches of six to eight as table centerpieces, or have the balloon company make a balloon arch to feature in your backyard—the perfect spot for taking lots of fun pictures with the bride.

Stock up at the party supply store on inexpensive solid-colored party tablecloths to cover each of your guest tables and the buffet table, giving your party space a unified style and color scheme. You don't have to go with the color of the charity. If the bride loves purple, choose a range of purple tablecloths and purple floral high-quality picnic plates and plastic cups.

Don't forget that your favors can work double-duty as table décor. Place pretty $3 potted flowers in front of each guest's place setting, leaving the center of the table open for pitchers of sangria and iced tea, and you've just essentially spent nothing on tabletop décor if the cost of the potted blooms is in your favor budget.

Money Mastery

Ask all of your party planners and the moms to keep an eye out for coupons to the local party supply store. You may land a fabulous 20 percent off everything coupon that allows you to get all of your table settings and balloons at a comfortable price. If coupons can't be combined, bring a few co-planners with you to the store to make good use of multiple 10 percent or $5-off coupons that you've found. This shopping spree can add up mightily without the help of coupons, so check RetailMeNot.com and Coupons.com to boost your coupon collection.

And skip the confetti or other sprinkle-type décor on each guest table. They may not cost a lot, but they make a minimal impression on guests, and they make vacuuming after the party a big hassle. A simpler clean tabletop is far smarter.

Steal My Party Idea

"We went to the website for the children's charity the bride selected, and we found a great list of what $200 provides: books, crayons, craft supplies, and healthy lunches. The bride, and all the guests, loved seeing our printout of that, which we tucked in with the printed announcement that we donated $200 to that cause." —Melinda, cousin of the bride

Theme Gifts for the Bride

Make a surprise donation to the bride's favorite charity. If she's ultra-dedicated to her cause, she'll get teary-eyed when you tell her that everyone in attendance—plus friends and family far away who couldn't attend the party—joined forces to give $500 to her chosen charity. She'll love that far better than any item you could buy off of her housewares registry, and it's quite easy to arrange a safe donation through the bride and groom's charitable registry. If she doesn't have a charitable registry, you can wrap the donation check in a pretty box with a satin bow for her to open in front of everyone.

Favors

If you wish to give out favors, keep in mind those little potted flowers that you can get at the supermarket floral section or at your local nursery at under $5 apiece. You can also order from a bakery or specialty cookie chef a design for decorating cookies such as a sneaker with bright pink stripes, iced and delicious and packaged as take-home favors.

M&Ms has packages of pink and white candies with a percentage of your purchase going to a breast cancer charity (MMs.com), and if you shop in September and October for a fall or winter party, you'll find additional candy bars and candies packaged with the pink-and-white motif for that particular cause.

Special Additional Touches

If your group is the type to enjoy attention in a crowd, think about having matching T-shirts made in a bright color, decorated with "Dana's Girls' Day Out" or "We're Celebrating Dana's Bachelorette Party!" or your choice of any G-rated saying. Check CafePress.com for cute T-shirts that could unite your group, or design your own icon and saying on your home computer and use easy iron-on transfers to custom-make your group's shirts.

Shop Here!

Go to the official websites of the charity you've chosen and click on its Store icon to reach a collection of low-priced icon-stamped items such as key rings, coasters, drink cozies, and T-shirts, with a percentage of your purchase—if not all of it!—benefitting the cause. Just be sure to shop only through secure websites from official charities that you've checked out through Give.org or the Better Business Bureau (BBB.org).

The bride can run or walk the race wearing a cute tiara and veil—the same kind bachelorette brides wear out to the bars on racier pub crawls. Check the bachelorette party supply sites listed in the resources section of this book to find a fantastic style of tiara and veil, or just shop at a teen accessory store at the mall. Stores like Claire's always have fun tiaras in candy colors that the bride can wear during the race.

Finally, make a lovely toast to the bride, sharing your stories of her giving nature, her empathy, how she is a bright light in this world, and thank her for letting all of you share in this exciting and rewarding event. It's the words that make the party, so a short and sweet toast from you and the other co-planners puts the perfect finishing touch on this celebration.

CHAPTER 18

 **Sporting Party**

In This Chapter

➤ Choosing the activity

➤ Choosing the location

➤ Planning the details for the sporting celebration

The bride may have been feted so many times by now—at engagement parties, showers, bridesmaid luncheons—that she wants to do something entirely different, something befitting her active and adventurous personality, something that calls to mind the sporting element of her way-back single days. For instance, the bride may love playing tennis, and it's been years since she and her friends kept their usual Sunday morning tennis date. Life's gotten busy for all, so a return to this "date" with her girls makes for the perfect bachelorette party.

The bride who wants to give her girls an unforgettable adventure that transports them into fabulous scenery will happily climb into a raft to share a white-water expedition with her closest friends, or hop onto a majestic horse for a guide-led ride through the woods to the beach. Everyone shows off their jeans and hiking boots rather than their little black dresses and stilettos, and photos and video of your adventure show your group laughing your way through your active adventure.

A sporting party doesn't have to be out in the wild or at the mercy of the waters. A big new trend in active bachelorette parties is a private yoga class by the pool or on a co-host's or mom's gorgeous backyard lawn—the kind of private yoga class that celebrities plan on their own grounds with their own private trainer. Your private trainer leads your group through a yoga class tailored to your group's skill level, out in the open air, and you celebrate afterward by the pool or on the terrace.

In this chapter, you'll plan the perfect sporting celebration for the bride to love and for guests to rave about to everyone they know.

Style Savvy

This is definitely a party style that requires the bride's input. Since it involves a sporting activity, the sport in question has to be a passion of hers and not something that will make her feel uncomfortable (such as if she never really enjoyed those tennis outings with the girls years ago, always losing in the first round.) Many brides with an active lifestyle love the idea of doing something different and experiencing an adventure with their friends, but some have dreamed of the traditional wild night out with champagne toasts in the limo. Get the bride's wish list before you book those courts, horses, rafts, or snowmobiles.

Finding Nearby Sporting Activities

If you don't know the local sporting establishments like some party-minded people know the happy hour schedules at every bar, you'll need to explore the opportunities. I've found my local REI store to be a goldmine of information, including brochures and their sales staff's personal recommendations for the best beginner-level rafting expeditions in the area. I've been warned against substandard rafting companies and encouraged to have guests bring a pair of dry socks and shoes and keep them in the car for changing after the ride. REI is an outdoor sports store chain that you can find at REI.com, and when you go for info searching, you can also stock up on favors for the party guests, plus a gift card for the sport-loving bride's surprise gift.

The park service is another fabulous source for outing information. Visit the site for the National Park Service (NPR.gov), and you'll find a fabulous find-it tool that links you right to your state parks and allows you to search by the activity you have in mind, such as horseback riding, or biking. Many state parks run their own tours, and you'll get full essential details such as fees, permit requirements, and park hours.

I also like to check the regional magazines for their Best-Of lists and reader-voted awards, which point out the fabulous revelation that an award-winning horseback-riding establishment is just a half hour away, or that a certain kayaking expedition company won by a landslide, with kayak enthusiasts proclaiming this the best ride in the state.

And, of course, first-hand experience will be your best guide. Ask your co-planners if they happen to belong to a fabulous tennis club that can be the site of the party, or if they regularly bike through county park trails in the area. If your bride loves the idea of the celebrity-inspired private yoga class, does the bride or any of the co-planners have a favorite yoga instructor who offers private classes on-site? The bride herself may be the point person for connecting you to an instructor she loves, and the event may be extra-special to her if her own yogini is leading her group.

Invitations

You'll find full invitations planning details in Chapter 6, and here you'll find creative twists on your invitations to suit the party's theme. In this category, though, you'll need to let guests know what to expect as far as exertion level, so include in your E-vites a link to the park system's website, showing the path you'll be taking and sharing the skill level that the park itself sets (beginner, intermediate, advanced).

Shop Here!

Check Yelp.com, where you may find fantastic reviews of tennis centers, yoga centers, and other fitness-oriented establishments that could be home to your fabulous party.

As a good rule of thumb, always choose the beginner-level path. Guests who don't hike regularly, for instance, may find those hills and rocky paths, the tree trunks to hop over and the leaf-covered walkways enough of a challenge, particularly on a hot day. No one needs the workout of their lives at this gathering, so the easier the better. Guests say they'd rather take in the scenery of overlooks and leaf colors on the trees than have to look at their feet the whole time, stepping over root systems and avoiding mud puddles.

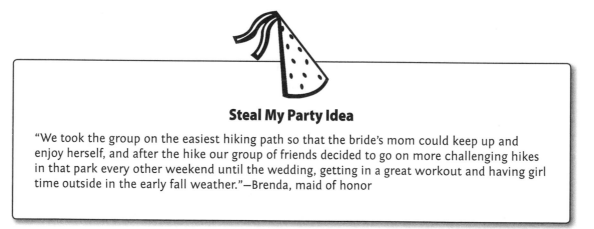

Steal My Party Idea

"We took the group on the easiest hiking path so that the bride's mom could keep up and enjoy herself, and after the hike our group of friends decided to go on more challenging hikes in that park every other weekend until the wedding, getting in a great workout and having girl time outside in the early fall weather."—Brenda, maid of honor

Your invitations have to convey the exertion level and let guests know what to wear and what to bring. One water bottle isn't going to be enough on a three-hour hike in peak summer, so tell guests to bring two to three water bottles to supplement the case the hosts will bring for the start of the hike. Let them know that you're providing lunch at a scenic stop along the path, and what the rain date is. And guests appreciate knowing that mosquito spray would be a great idea.

Invitation Images

Functionality aside, you get to design pretty invitations on your own printer or through a free online invitations site like Evite.com or Hallmark.com. Choose from these image inspirations:

➤ A cute illustration of a stylish woman playing tennis

➤ A cute illustration of a woman in lotus position, with soft sage colors announcing your yoga party

➤ A photo that you take of a tennis ball in a martini glass, or a hiking sneaker next to a lineup of sky-high stilettos

➤ An image provided by the active adventure company, such as a group of women in a cluster of kayaks, with stunning scenery behind them

➤ A photo that you've had for a long time showing the bride and her girls during a years-ago biking trip, or a photo of the bride in her tennis whites, or as a little girl riding a white horse as a sentimental image

Create a few versions of the invitation just like magazine editors do with the covers of magazines they're styling. Try different backgrounds, different fonts and decide on the winning style with just the bride's input. Experience has shown that when you send an invitation style to ten co-planners, everyone may have too much input, requesting changes and different images. Everyone may have good intentions at heart, but some may want to put their own stamps on this style element of the party. So keep your review team small and your winning design can take its place as the final version.

Invitation Messages

Get creative with your themed invitation messages. Guests get excited when your playful wording announces that this party will be fun as well as completely different from other bachelorette bashes they've attended. Here are some wording inspirations:

➤ "Come play with us! It's Hannah's bachelorette party, so put on your tennis whites (or hot pinks!) and join us for a day of overhead smashes and net jumping at the exclusive Oak Grove Country Club!"

➤ "We're getting wild in the white-water rapids for Claire's bachelorette bash! Join us for a rafting trip you'll never forget!"

➤ "It's Downward Dog instead of Dirty Martinis at Elizabeth's poolside yoga party! We have celebrity yoga instructor Marcella coming to Liz's house to lead us in a VIP private yoga class followed by champagne and a fabulous brunch!"

➤ "Let's ride! Sarah loves horseback riding, so we're joining her on a sunset trail ride to celebrate her upcoming wedding. (And we hear the trail guides are *hot!*) So come join us, pick your pony, and saddle up for Sarah's celebration!"

➤ "We're taking the mountain! Dianna's bachelorette party will take us all to new heights as we climb to the top of a mountain and toast to her happiness overlooking the valley at sunset."

➤ "We're going to shake it up for Cindy's bachelorette party! No, not martinis—we're taking a belly dancing class at the elite Sage Day Spa!" (A party host wrote in to share the story of how the bride loves the singer Shakira, so she added a banner with the phrase "Your hips don't lie!" as a personalized touch to the invitation.)

RSVP Details

Sites, pros, and tour times have to be booked in advance, so send out those invitations at least a month before the party, two months to be on the safe side—especially during the summer when families with kids take up the morning and afternoon kayak and raft slots. If you'll ask co-planners and perhaps hosts to send in their share of the money, advance notice is essential, as is an early pay-by date. You don't want to get stuck paying for the twenty-five people you promised to the tour company when only ten people show up.

Menu Items

For tours and outings, everyone gets a packed picnic lunch in cute little lunch totes, ideally a thermal-protected tote with a tiny ice pack inside to keep food fresh and drinks refreshing during a hot day. Some ideas for your packed lunch: sandwich wraps, veggie sandwiches on round rolls, little containers of pasta and veggie salad, a baggie of three or four chocolate chip cookies, and an icy cold bottle of water.

For a class that takes place at your home—such as that yoga class or the belly dancing class set for your private poolside area or your living room—an enticing buffet might include cold appetizers such as salmon mousse on endive leaves, hummus and pita bread triangles, veggie-packed pasta salad, lush leafy green salads with a unique dressing such as pomegranate vinaigrette and goat cheese, spinach puffs, and other light foods that are pleasing to the stomach after a fitness class. Add in lots of fresh fruit slices and fruit square kebobs with flavored yogurt dips, and multigrain nacho chips with fresh guacamole and mango salsa. No creamy, heavy foods, no hot chafing dishes, nothing fried or greasy. Just light taste treats.

Style Savvy

For healthy menu items, cruise the recipe collections at CookingLight.com, FoodNetwork.com, MixingBowl.com and AllRecipes.com. You can make any lighter dish look extra-special with easy garnishing: full leafy greens laid on the plate below those canapés, grape tomatoes, julienned zucchini strips mixed with julienned carrot strips as a platter garnish, bright lemon and orange slices fanned out, and dips placed in small square appetizer bowls bought on the cheap at Pier 1 or Crate & Barrel.

Cake and Dessert

Yes, cake is allowed after an active party! That dose of sugar comes guilt-free after you've burned off calories during that hike or multiple tennis matches. The cake doesn't have to have a sporting image on it, since it's not necessary to carry the activity's theme into every aspect of the party. A simple, pink-iced sheet cake with bright pink flowers and pretty green icing leaves piped on top, or a bridal-white round with iridescent white icing pearls piped on it is perfect for this and any style of bachelorette party.

As long as it tastes good as well as looks good, your dessert is a smash success (no tennis pun intended).

In addition to cake, load up your dessert buffet with mini gourmet cupcakes in red velvet or pink lemonade flavors, among others. A platter of homemade cookies is always a big draw for party guests whose diets keep them from baking whole batches at home, and, again, fresh fruits are always a winning choice for your party. Make it a multi-fruit mix, or go gourmet with grilled slices of pineapple topped with a dab of feta, or honor the bride's southern background with an authentic ambrosia.

Drinks

Drinks provided during the activity need to be hydrating—water and sports drinks leading the way. As much as you enjoy a cola, that sugar is going to deplete your energy and dehydrate you. Party hosts should bring along a case or two of small water bottles for each guest to take in addition to the drinks they've been instructed to bring (and your supply provides for those who have forgotten.)

At the after-party, drinks can get sweeter. Fill your bar with flavored iced teas, fresh fruit smoothies, colorful colas such as orange soda, black cherry and birch beer, and fruit punches with that fruit-filled ice ring and a generous dollop of sherbet on top.

Alcoholic drinks may be chosen to fit the style of the post-party. If you're hosting that celebrity-style yoga class by the pool, then platters of champagne and mimosas or Bellinis fit your theme well. And, of course, a selection of wines and martinis are always a welcome sight to those who are ready to toast the bride.

Style Savvy

Check out Cocktail.com to explore creative, new martini and margarita flavor blends to make your drink list stand out, and perhaps even include the party's theme. For instance, in keeping with the horseback-riding theme, perhaps you'll serve perfectly made mint juleps as a nod to the Kentucky Derby.

Décor

With the exception of parties held at your home, such as the celebrity-style yoga party, the environment is all the décor you'll need. That stunning sunset. The cabernet-colored leaves on the trees during your fall season hike. The view of the ocean from atop a hill.

For your at-home party, keep décor minimal yet befitting your theme. For the outside yoga class, manicure your existing landscaping—get rid of weeds, trim down uneven flowering bushes, deadhead your rose bushes so all that remains are fresh, pink, in-bloom roses. Set a pretty floral arrangement on the buffet table—matching the colors and types of flowers to any that may be growing in your yard for a uniform, coordinated look. And set each guest table with low-set bunches of flowers in small glass bowls filled with water. Add some tiny tea light votives, and your minimalist elegant scene is set.

Of course, if you have the budget to glam up your outdoor area, you can copy celebrity event planner style and create curtains of white or pink fabric that dance in the breeze, set rented white couches around the pool, and change patio chair cushions to match the color scheme. Those weather-beaten green-and-white-striped cushions have to go!

An excursion-type activity such as hiking, rafting, or horseback riding can reach its destination where your post-party is already set up by party volunteers who preferred not to participate in the activity. These nonsporty types, including moms and pregnant bridesmaids, can decorate a scenic spot they've booked through the park system. It may be a gazebo or tented party area, a scenic overlook picnic area, or other suitable surprise gathering spot for an open-air lunch.

The party scene that your group hikes to appears when you round a corner, and the bride will delight at the sight of gauzy white curtains hanging from tents or trees, strings of white lights glowing in the dimming daylight

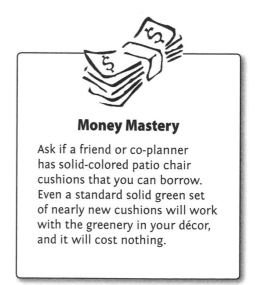

Money Mastery

Ask if a friend or co-planner has solid-colored patio chair cushions that you can borrow. Even a standard solid green set of nearly new cushions will work with the greenery in your décor, and it will cost nothing.

hours, and a lavish buffet set up for your group's enjoyment. Again, no need to go overboard with décor items, especially pricy floral arrangements. The scene itself will be lovely for its surrounding views.

Theme Gifts for the Bride

As always, no gift is necessary for the bride, especially when the party itself is an event. If your group does wish to surprise the bride with a little something special, a top trend for this type of party is a gift card to REI.com or a sporty item the couple has registered for. Photos taken during this sporting bachelorette party can be made into a photo book at KodakGallery.com, Shutterfly.com, or any other photo-to-gift site and given or sent to the bride at a later date so that she can relive the wonderful party you planned.

Favors

Colorful water bottles are a top favor choice for this style of party, with guests choosing their own from a collection of three or four different designs. And socks are another top favor choice, with cute colors, stripes, or images on them.

Entertainment

The activity itself provides all the entertainment one could ever want, especially when your group spots amazing wildlife like turtles and a family of ducks and ducklings, fawn and does, and a heron on the shoreline as your boat goes gliding by.

At the after-party, your entertainment is fulfilled when you set up your iPod dock and play your specially created playlist for the party. Ask your co-planners to suggest songs, and burn the collection for the bride to keep after her celebration.

Style Savvy

Another top trend is giving out single-use cameras such as the colorful ones and the waterproof ones (perfect for that raft ride) at Kodak.com, so that guests don't need to risk their pricy digital cameras. These high-quality cameras deliver ultra-sharp images and the eco-minded bride and guests will like knowing that these cameras are made mostly of recycled materials.

CHAPTER 19

Subdued Parties

> **In This Chapter**
>
> ➤ Dinner party at home
>
> ➤ Relaxed movie night at home
>
> ➤ Party in your pj's

Everyone might have had more than enough of party planning after the fabulous shower you put together, and the bride too may prefer a completely relaxing at-home get-together with her girls. You might all be on limited budgets—especially if that shower cost a pretty penny—so if everyone agrees, the Subdued Party could be the perfect plan for your group.

No reservations. No limousine timing. No high heels. No hassles.

The subdued party is a growing trend among bachelorette party planners, since the best gift they can give to a harried, over-scheduled, over-stressed bride is a laid-back gathering with just her closest of friends and sisters, which is why more brides request this style of party these days.

The top types of subdued parties are the dinner at home, movie night, and the old-fashioned slumber party—all of which you'll explore in this chapter. Remember that the key is that it's subdued, so in most cases don't bother with games and activities, thinking that structured play is what makes you a good host. On the contrary, many guests would find you annoying if you kept announcing games and activities. Everyone is stressed and overdoing it these days, and they don't want to be told they have to do something you've planned. They just want to drink their wine and kick back. Conversation naturally flows, and this less is more party style adds up to so much more than you might imagine.

Read on and discover the details of your bride's choice in subdued parties. She may choose the style, but you can still surprise and delight her with some additional party elements.

At-Home Dinner

Forget the fine china that has to be fished out from the breakfront, washed, and the table set with sparkling silverware and stemware. Leave that for the rehearsal dinner, and instead plan a casual sit-down dinner at your dining room table that's been set with your colorful stoneware, basic flatware, and wine and water goblets. This family-style dinner with friends doesn't have to be upscale to impress.

Invitations

Dinner party invitations don't have to cost a thing. Since the theme is *ease,* send E-vites in a pretty design and let the party guests RSVP on the site for all to see. How to word your invitation? Consider these wording examples:

> ➤ "It's dinner for twelve at Katie's place! Join us for Sherry's laid-back dinner party."

> ➤ "No stockings, no stress, so schedule . . . Sherry wants a laid-back dinner party for her bachelorette bash, and who are we to say no?! Come join us for lasagna and laughter."

> ➤ "Fine wine, good food, good friends. That's what Sherry wants for her bachelorette party, so dinner's on us at Katie's place!"

With no fuss to be made about the plans, and no pros to book, it's fine to send out invitations a month in advance, with the RSVP date set for just two weeks before the party.

Menu Items

Part of the allure of the at-home dinner party is working together as a group in the kitchen to prepare the courses and the meal, complete and heat up any platters you and other co-planners have made at your place, and, of course, open a bottle of wine to enjoy during your group efforts. The bride too may want to spend this prep hour with her nearest and dearest, so pour her a glass as well.

The most common dishes served at this type of dinner party include:

> ➤ A lush salad of mixed greens, veggies, goat cheese or gorgonzola, and an array of fabulous organic dressings

Style Savvy

Use this occasion as a reason to buy a $20 set of matching modern wine glasses from Bed Bath & Beyond or Crate & Barrel. A casual table needs to have a unifying element, and it would look a little too casual if your wine glasses didn't match—that's how college students adorn a dinner table. So take this opportunity to refresh your entertaining wares now.

➤ Easy pastas, such as ravioli stuffed with mushrooms or standard cheeses

➤ Lasagna

➤ Enchiladas

➤ Fajitas, with family-style access to the toppings on a lazy Susan at the center of the table

➤ Chicken marsala with lots of mushrooms and onions

➤ Pizza—standard pepperoni or gourmet pizzas with asparagus and ricotta, or pineapple ham pizza, Sicilian squares, and a range of indulgences that when served with a big, beautiful salad are fine to enjoy in small portions

Cake and Dessert

Cake is a must at this party, so have fun with its flavors and shape. You might choose a fun polka-dotted circular cake or go dark chocolate with a rich chocolate mousse-filled cake, smoothly iced and topped with a dark chocolate buttercream rose. Ice cream cake is also a possibility for this party if it's the bride's preference, and she can choose the flavors of ice cream for the layers. We're beyond the days of vanilla and chocolate only, so encourage the bride to place her order to include her beloved moose tracks and caramel flavors, with an espresso chocolate sauce on the side.

Cupcakes are always a top dessert for laid-back events, so make your own if you're on a budget (and ice them high like the pros do!) or visit a cupcake shop to select from several creative flavor mixes in addition to standards like vanilla on vanilla or chocolate on chocolate, red velvet, and key lime.

Steal My Party Idea

"We know the bride is a huge *Top Chef* fan, so we bought the *Top Chef* cookbook and made several of the dishes from it for her party, including her favorite chefs' dishes. We made little signs to announce Hung's dish and Casey's dish and so on, and she *loved* it. We then gave her the cookbook as a gift."—Kelly, bridesmaid

Other dessert options are creamy pies such as a pumpkin cheesecake during a fall dinner party, or a New York-style cheesecake with cherries on top. Individual chocolate mousses served in cereal bowls take the formality level way down but still give everyone creamy delight. And, of course, this laid-back party shines when you set up a make-your-own sundae bar with three flavors of ice cream, several different sauces and toppings, and whipped cream.

Style Savvy

For guests who can't eat dairy or who have food restrictions, ask them for their favorite brand of frozen treats, then pick up a soy ice cream for them so that they can partake in the fun. A great host works to please every guest!

Drinks

Any type of drinks are appropriate for this dinner party and the hours after dinner, so ask your co-hosts to each bring a bottle of wine that corresponds with the dinner menu. For wine selection advice, tell them to explore FoodandWine.com, a fabulous resource with an archive of daily food and wine pairings and menu inspirations. Cocktails, too, are a welcome match to any dinner menu, and again the FoodandWine.com site will help you create a complementary drinks list. Be sure to provide plenty of soft drink options from seltzer with lime to colas to iced teas and water.

Décor

A simple centerpiece on the dining room table may be all the décor you'll need, and even that—for a sit-down dinner—should be small and low-set so that guests can converse across the table. A trio of small flower clusters, each in round or square 3- to 4-inch vases, creates a lovely sit-down dinner centerpiece, especially when arranged with three to six votive candles in a coordinating color.

The same low flower grouping in a single vase paired with two or three votives in the same colors as the dinner table centerpieces create fabulous décor touches on a coffee table or end table, or on your bar surface. These inexpensive décor groupings, when placed around the room, add up to a big visual impact.

Theme Gifts for the Bride

Since the event centers around the culinary arts and entertaining, gift the bride with a collection of bestselling cookbooks and entertaining books from her favorite celebrity experts.

Favors

Gourmet favors are always a welcome take-home from a dinner party, and DIY foodie favors will be friendly to your budget. Some of the most popular ideas are:

➤ Flavored oils

➤ Flavored vinegars

➤ Tropical salsas

➤ Exotic spice mixes

➤ Tapenade

➤ Chutney

➤ Garlic or rosemary bread knots

➤ Baked desserts, such as a trio of cookies, a generous brownie square, or rugelach

➤ A themed bite, such as fortune cookies if your party's menu has an Asian flair

If the bride is a fan of celebrity chefs, shop from the Food Network store and even at your own supermarket to get foodie favor items from the chef's line. At your supermarket, you'll find Barefoot Contessa brownies and Emeril Lagasse pasta sauces, for instance. Martha Stewart has many lines of products that would create fantastic foodie favors, and Rachael Ray's cookware line also offers up colorful favor ideas.

Steal My Party Idea

"Since I knew the bride *loves* Rachael Ray, I signed up for an alert from three nearby Barnes and Noble stores so that I'd know when Rachael would be signing her newest book. I found out about her signing at one of them, stood in line, and got Rachael to sign a book *to the bride.* That was our big gift to her, and she loved it!"–Emily, bridesmaid

Sign up for booksigning alerts through BN.com and Borders.com to catch your bride's favorite authors on their booksigning tours, and you might even bring the bride to that author's signing event, too!

Style Savvy

Create a unified look and theme to your favors and the bride's gift by shopping from the same collection for both. For instance, the bride might get a collection of Barefoot Contessa cookbooks while the guests each get a packet of Barefoot Contessa brownie mix.

Entertainment

Your iPod playlist provides easy and budget-friendly entertainment, and your co-planners can bring their own iPods along for additional music. Again, there's no need for games, or paid entertainment, but many dinner party groups do combine this party with the at-home movie night party to create a dinner-and-a-movie plan. Your On Demand channel may have newer movies that your group wishes to watch, so the entertainment may cost under $5 for all of you with just one movie order.

At-Home Movie Night

With or without the dinner party before it, your relaxed movie night party at home might be just what the bride has been craving—together time with her friends, watching a chick flick or musical on the big-screen TV. Whichever co-planner has the best setup—big-screen TV, comfy couches, entertaining area with a bar—hosts this event in her home for everyone's enjoyment. This type of party requires lots of seating space, so make that your number one priority in choosing your location.

Invitations

An easy e-vite can feature a retro container of popcorn or a 1950s-era photo of a convertible at a drive-in theater, or you can design your own invitations to resemble a movie theater ticket but with the party information listed as the showing time.

If your bride has told you which movies she wants to watch with her girls—*Breakfast at Tiffany's* perhaps—you can use a still from that movie (the iconic photo of Audrey Hepburn in tiara and gloves, for instance) to convey the night's theme.

Compose the invitation to let guests know that they will be watching a movie—some will skip the skirt and wear jeans for better comfort on the couch—and what the movie theme night will be. Here are some examples:

➤ "Tomorrow is another day, but we're all watching *Gone With the Wind* at Tania's place for Steph's bachelorette party next Friday! And no, there won't be a Rhett Butler lookalike stripper ☺ "

➤ "Cosmopolitans are on us! Come watch *Sex and the City* with the girls for Steph's bachelorette party movie night!"

Two weeks' notice is all you need for this type of party, with the RSVP date set for a few days prior since there's not a lot of prep work involved.

Steal My Party Idea

"We did the *Breakfast at Tiffany's* theme for our bride's party, and we played the soundtrack from the movie during the hour when everyone was arriving and snacking on hors d'oeuvres."— Diane, bridesmaid

Menu Items

Think of typical movie snacks like popcorn and nachos and raise them up a few levels, going gourmet with your flavorings. Popcorn can then be white cheddar or cinnamon kettle corn. Serve pumpkin seeds and healthy almond bites in your

DIY party snack mix, and check out recipes at FoodNetwork.com and MixingBowl.com to create sensational snack blends that match the theme of the movie. For that *Sex and the City 2* movie night, add some Middle Eastern flair to your snack mix with cumin, nutmeg, caraway, or baharat.

Steal My Party Idea

"We rented an authentic popcorn-making cart from the rental agency as our splurge for the movie party, and the place smelled *amazing* when guests arrived!"—Kate, mother of the bride

For your nachos, set up a make-your-own bar with two different types of nacho chips—one being whole grain—grilled chicken, chili, refried beans, three types of shredded cheese, jalapenos, diced tomatoes, diced onions, salsas mild and hot, and sour cream.

And of course, you can go ultra-casual and just order in a few pizzas. Mix up your order with different toppings, and ask that your Sicilian pie be cut into party squares. Another favorite is a style of pizza called Grandma's Pizza with fresh diced tomatoes and basil. And serve a lush salad on the side for those who don't want too many carbs and fat grams.

Cake and Dessert

Decorate your cake with an image of the movie poster. Just bring a digital image to your baker, and he or she can scan it onto an edible print that goes right on top of your frosted cake. Cupcakes in a range of colors and tastes make for a great movie viewing party platter, as do homemade cookies. And since movie theaters offer Dove and Häagen-Dazs bars, stock up on a few boxes of each for your guests' choices, along with Good Humor bars and ice cream sandwiches.

Drinks

You might not be able to drink liquor in a movie theater, but you can at this party! So serve wine and cocktails, and fire up that frozen margarita maker you've had in your cabinet all year.

Colas and iced teas are also welcome at this party so that everyone can pace themselves, or use as drink mixers.

Shop Here!

Some fabulous sources of contemporary and retro movie posters are:

➤ AllPosters.com
➤ Art.com
➤ MoviePoster.com
➤ MoviePosterShop.com

Décor

Hang movie posters in your house, just like you'd see at the movie theater. If you and your co-planners don't have a supply of posters to hang, check eBay.com to snag a few budget-priced prints.

Set up film theme vignettes around your party area. For that *Breakfast at Tiffany's* party, arrange some faux pearl strands on a countertop along with an iconic blue Tiffany shopping bag (ask if a friend has one, or buy a plain blue bag from Target or a craft store.) For the *Sex and the City* party, decorate your place with shoe boxes and shopping bags, and set out a pitcher of cosmopolitans with two martini glasses as décor. For *Under the Tuscan Sun*, set out plates of red grapes everywhere, with wine bottles beside them to give that Tuscan feel, and, of course, those bright sunflowers from the movie poster are a perfect idea for your floral décor touches on the buffet table and all around the room. You'll be able to create vignettes to match any movie's theme.

Theme Gifts for the Bride

Tiffany has a new charm designed to look like a Tiffany bag that's a popular gift for bridesmaids to present to the bride. Shop at Tiffany.com for this charm and for Tiffany key chains and other affordable indulgence gifts.

For the bride who's a big fan of a particular movie, give her the collector's edition DVD with the added movie memento like a copy of the movie's script in the collector's box.

Give the bride and groom the gift of date nights: give her a sizeable gift card to her local movie theater as a present from all of you.

Favors

Packs of candies or gourmet popcorn bags are the number one favor for this style of party, keeping costs low and party guests snacking on their way home.

Entertainment

In addition to watching the movie, take time for a brief game of Scene It? in any topic the bride loves, such as the Twilight Scene It? game.

You can also conduct a movie quotes contest, getting your material from MovieQuotes.com, and giving a prize to the person who correctly identifies who spoke those words in a movie or finishes the second half of the quote. Another fun party idea is researching movie trivia on IMDB.com and quizzing the crowd.

Special Additional Touches

Have the groom surprise the bride by walking into the darkened movie room holding a flashlight, wearing black pants and a white shirt, and telling everyone to keep it down. He can then grab a piece of pizza—and a kiss from the bride—before he leaves.

Steal My Party Idea

"I went on MovieMistakes.com and printed out some of the mistakes and flubs from the movie we'd be watching, and everyone got the cards before we watched the movie. It was a lot of fun catching the missing bracelet and the fact that the cat changed colors in the scene."—Gina, bridesmaid

Pajama Party

Invite your party guests to put on their cutest pajamas and join the girls for a night of movies, dancing, snacking, and silly fun like making prank phone calls to the groom.

All of the menu and dessert ideas from this chapter work well for this party, and your entertainment can be your own dance contest to current hit songs or to songs from when you were preteens. Now, the new pajama party entertainment includes video games, so fire up that Wii or PlayStation and play in your pj's, holding a tournament or rocking out to Rock Band, taking great video and photos the whole night.

The beauty of the new pajama party is that not everyone has to sleep over. Most adults would rather not spend the night in a sleeping bag on the floor, not when they have a comfy big bed at home. So if some guests choose not to snooze at your place, the ones who wish to stay can claim a couch or a corner of the floor for an all-night party and a breakfast buffet served with plenty of top-notch coffee.

CHAPTER 20

Getaway Parties

In This Chapter

➤ The ten best getaway party destinations

➤ Party detail basics

➤ Arranging for surprises

If you'd like to take your tame party on the road for a girls' getaway, this chapter shares the top ten most popular types of destinations as well as some insider secrets on how to get VIP service for your group, and surprises to plan for the bride. In Chapter 4, you explored the ins and outs of travel planning, booking discounts for groups, orchestrating room-sharing, and other essential details for everyone's attendance at the party. The same advice applies here.

As a reminder, party guests need to devote their vacation funds and time to this party since everyone's so busy and often crunched for cash. So as a good host, you'll tap into the many new bachelorette party packages that offer jaw-droppingly good prices, group perks, freebies, and special surprises for the bride. If the getaway bachelorette bash is a new idea for your circle of the bride's guests, you'll need to convey to them the budget friendliness of the plan right at the outset so that the bride's closest friends and family don't immediately reject the notion. If it's the norm for brides in a circle to plan a getaway, you'll get much less resistance, but you still need to convey the perks to any guests who are new to the circle, untraveled with the group, and uninitiated to the clique's penchant for girls' getaways.

We'll start with the top ten getaway types list for your bride's inspiration—since it's most often the bride's joyful task to choose the party's style. True, there are some groups who tell the bride to pack a few bathing suits and a few little black dresses since the destination is a surprise—and that may work if your bride is the type to appreciate a mystery. But keep in mind that the bride may be frazzled at this point in the planning and quite unable to handle another unknown in her world. Many party planners say they didn't expect the bride to get angry when they told her to pack for a surprise vacation. So don't risk a shocking overreaction. Let the bride know this is the style of party you have in mind for her, the other guests are ready to go somewhere fabulous, and she gets to decide where everyone will go.

Some brides say they had so little decision-making power in so many parts of the wedding their parents were paying for, that it was a highlight and a sanity saver to get to make the big decision for this event and plan a girls' escape that's truly *her* style.

The Top Ten Types of Getaway Parties

Here, you'll consider the most popular types of girls' vacation parties and research the near and far possibilities that could be home to your bride's big celebration. You might choose to fly across the country or to an island, or just to drive fifteen minutes away to the cutest bed-and-breakfast in wine country.

Money Mastery

Just because you live near a tourist mecca doesn't mean you should count it out. Yes, you may have taken friends and out-of-town visitors on tours of the area's hot spots, but many people who live near a vacation hot spot say they haven't really taken the opportunity to truly explore the best of what that attraction has to offer. "Locals just don't do that" is a limiting belief system, so practice great money mastery by being open to the vacation heaven right nearby.

The Tourism Offices Worldwide Directory will provide you with a wealth of free information on local attractions, tours, festivals, and coupons and two-for-one discount deals, as well as have goodie bags filled with freebies for your group. This site connects you with the tourism boards in all manner of states, cities, towns and islands, so you will find your local board through it. If your destination is small and sublime, the local town hall may direct you to the town library for the same welcome packet. And state tourism websites also quicken your information search and give you coupons, reviews, links, and other essential tourist information to guide you in your itinerary planning.

Wine Country

Wine country is not just in Napa, California. If you explore the articles in *Food and Wine* and on WineSpectator.com, as well as TravelandLeisure.com, you'll find travel stories about a wide range of wine regions all over the country. Any one of these offers a constellation of fantastic hotels and resorts, charming bed-and-breakfasts, and the kinds of winery tours you saw in the movie *Sideways*. Some regions allow you to bike from vineyard to vineyard, tour the wineries themselves, or enjoy lunch in their private dining rooms or out in the open air. Some will offer you Tuscan-type wooden tables and benches situated beneath grape arbors, and some will have a wine expert attend to your group for a private wine tasting, paired with fruits and cheeses.

When you're not traveling from winery to winery, the area offers amazing dining establishments that your hotel will recommend to you, with the concierge's expert tastes applied to the Must Visit list. Your ladies' dinner, then, may be in a four-star restaurant owned by a celebrity chef, since many own dining establishments in wine country.

The surrounding town may offer a morning's worth of shopping at adorable gift shops, antique stores, and, of course, the requisite fudge stores and ice cream shoppes.

Bike trails may take you through the lush landscape, past scenic mountainous vistas, even to brooks and lakes where you can take photos as a group, with all of you standing on the flat rock edges. A misty morning may have you walking as a group through these trails, with hot coffee in hand and those cameras clicking the beauty of nature all around you.

Beach House

If your group of friends has a history of sharing a shore house for a week, whether it's recent history or long-ago memories, renting a little place by the ocean gives you that beachy getaway to share with the larger circle of ladies. For many brides, it's a blissful return to the ocean waves, the fine sandy beach, the boardwalk rides and people-watching, and lobster dinner at their favorite seafood restaurant, with drinks and toasts and suntanned shoulders looking great in everyone's going-out clothes at night.

You can enjoy a slow pace or plan for visits to nearby aquariums, lighthouse climbs, biking at sunset, even free concerts at the shore town's gazebo that attracts fun cover bands.

Beach towns often have fantastic shopping, as well as fun, kitschy shopping on the boardwalk, so everyone can pick up a zany pair of sunglasses or a funny T-shirt and walk as a group, hitting the funnel cake and ice cream stands along the boardwalk. Stop and play games to win the bride stuffed animals, and those who have the stomach for it can hop on the most adrenaline-pumping rides.

Steal My Party Idea

"We took a ride over the bridge to a touristy town that had trolley ghost tours led by the author of a book on local haunting. The bride loves ghost stories as much as she loves the beach, and I knew that was something she always wanted to do when we all went to the beach in our younger years. So we made it happen for her now!"
—Eliza, bridesmaid

If your shore house is a lake house, the nicely appointed cabin can be your home for a quiet weekend in nature, making s'mores by an actual roaring fire, kayaking and canoeing, hiking, reliving your golden childhood summer camp days.

Ski Resort

For the bride who loves the atmosphere of a ski resort, whether or not she actually skis, taking the group to a snowy ski resort town makes the most of winter wedding timing. In many areas of the country, ski resort towns are just a short drive away—often less than two hours—so your group might not have to fly anywhere.

Some of the most enjoyable activities at a ski resort include not just schussing down the slopes, but group horse-drawn sleigh rides, open-air hot-tubbing, enjoying cocktails by an enormous fireplace at the hotel lounge, and in some ski towns celebrities are often spotted on vacation. Check Festivals.com to see if any fun winter festivities will be scheduled during your group's visit and talk with the resort's booking agents to see if bridal groups qualify for extra discounts and freebies.

Las Vegas

The girls' getaway to Las Vegas has long been *the* destination of choice, with so many entertainment possibilities. Sin City doesn't have to be so sinful if your group is on the tame side. Instead of drinking and clubbing, visit the many celebrity chef-owned restaurants, shop at the upscale boutiques, take in some of the many shows and concerts. Bachelorette party groups are often given discount or free tickets to a range of activities and shows, so don't be shy about mentioning to the reservations agent that you are a bachelorette party group. Many resorts have special bachelorette party packages that are friendly on the wallet and can get you VIP access to clubs, poolside parties, private cabanas during the day, and even special treatment at the concierge desk.

Casino Resort

Don't forget that Las Vegas is not the only casino resort area in the country. To name just a few, Atlantic City has the Borgata and the Water Club, as well as the new incarnation of

Caesars that is attracting a steady stream of celebrities who surprise-deejay at their nightclub and for their poolside parties. Here are just a few of the casino resorts spread across the country:

California

> ➤ Palm Springs: Monrongo Casino Resort and Spa

Connecticut

> ➤ Foxwoods: Foxwoods Resort & Casino
>
> ➤ Uncasville: Mohegan Sun Hotel Casino

Florida

> ➤ Everglades: Miccosukee Indian Reservation; Miccosukee Resort and Casino
>
> ➤ Hollywood: Seminole Reservation, Seminole Hard Rock Hotel & Casino
>
> ➤ Miami, Everglades: Miccosukee Resort & Gaming
>
> ➤ Tampa: Hard Rock Hotel & Casino Tampa

Indiana

> ➤ French Lick: French Lick Resort & Casino

Louisiana

> ➤ New Orleans: Harrah's Casino & Hotel

Michigan

> ➤ Detroit: MGM Grand Detroit Casino
>
> ➤ Mount Pleasant: Soaring Eagle Casino & Resort

Mississippi

> ➤ Biloxi: Beau Rivage Resort & Casino
>
> ➤ Isle of Capri Casino Resort
>
> ➤ Tunica: Grand Casino Hotel Tunica

Nevada

> ➤ Lake Tahoe: Mont Blue Resort Casino & Spa

New Jersey

> ➤ Atlantic City: Borgata Hotel Casino & Spa; Caesars Atlantic City Casino Hotel;

Harrah's Hotel & Casino, Atlantic City; Trump Marina Hotel Casino; Trump Plaza Casino Resort

New York

> ➤ Niagara Falls: Holiday Inn Niagara Falls at the Falls

> ➤ Verona: Turning Stone Resort Casino & Spa

Each of these resorts offers a mecca of fine dining, shopping, and gambling, and you can time your visit to coincide with the bride's favorite performer appearing at the resort.

Shop Here!

For more casino resorts and easy access to all of the resorts' websites, visit ResortsOnline. com.

Festival Destination

Speaking of coinciding, you can plan this getaway celebration for the very same weekend when a big-name festival will take place at the destination. It might be the bride's lifelong dream to attend events at the *Food and Wine* festival in Aspen, Colorado, as she's seen featured as one of the big prizes on *Top Chef*. If she's a music fanatic, perhaps the South by Southwest festival in Austin Texas—with its lineup of notable and indie acts—would be a thrilling vacation to share with her best friends. There's the Sundance Film Festival, always heavily attended by countless movie stars and other celebrities, and in New York there's the Tribeca Film Festival, also celebrity studded.

Check Festivals.com for schedules of large and small festivals taking place all over the country, all through the year.

And while it's not a festival, per se, if you can get your fashionista bride tickets to a runway show or two during New York City's Fashion Week, as well as entry into some of the glitterati parties that take place that week, you've done a masterful job of planning a dream-come-true bachelorette party weekend.

On a smaller and noncelebrity scale, you may discover a unique festival such as a tulip festival (the bride's favorite flower!), including live music and auctions, taking place in a charming touristy town with lots of cute gift shops. Or a crawfish festival taking place at a fabulous restaurant overlooking the bay, strung with lights in the evening and offering live entertainment. During the winter months, you might discover holiday festivals complete with guided tours of gorgeous Victorian mansions—some of them said to be haunted—ice sculpture contests, carolers, and hot toddies.

Grab a room at a charming inn or bed-and-breakfast (BnBFinder.com), and you have a home base right near all the action with a roaring fireplace of your own to enjoy, plus a gourmet breakfast included.

Desert Spa

This trip often requires a flight, and your group gets that amazing blast of warm air when they step off the plane or out of the airport. You've arrived in hot-weather country, and a shuttle or limo is there to whisk you to one of the grandest spas in the country. Desert regions are home of some of the world's most elite spas, such as the Golden Door, and the scenery is a breathtaking vista in all directions, including upward. The clear night sky full of stars is a sight to behold in the desert, since the smogless environment allows for a stunning display above. The purple sunset over the mountains too is a gorgeous view and the perfect backdrop for group photos.

Steal My Party Idea

"The bride requested something that her mom and grandmother, also her groom's mom and grandmother, would be able to share with us all, and she didn't want to do the dinner first and partiers go out second thing. So I proposed that we go to a Christmas festival at a nearby shore town where her family always spent their summers. She said the holiday festival is something she and her mom always wanted to do, so it was extra-special that we made her bachelorette getaway such a fabulous plan!" —Eleanor, maid of honor

At the spa resort, your bride and fellow partiers can sign on for group classes from the resort's group itinerary. Imagine sunrise yoga in the cool morning air or a hike through desert canyons or horseback riding in the mountains. You can arrange for several group classes to be included in your package and allow your guests to book and pay for any additional treatments they'd like.

Theme Park

We're talking Disneyworld, Disneyland, Universal Studios—those not-just-for-kids parks that are now becoming wildly popular for getaway bachelorette parties. It may have been years since the bride vacationed at a Disney park with her family, and if she's a Disney girl and her groom prefers tropical islands, your trip makes her dreams come true. She can now go to her favorite "happiest place on earth" without any guilt or potentially pouting fiancé. Her girls are equally excited to be there, squealing with joy over a sighting of Tigger or a taste of Butterbeer at the new Harry Potter theme park.

The top parks—especially Disney—have fabulous wedding party packages in their special

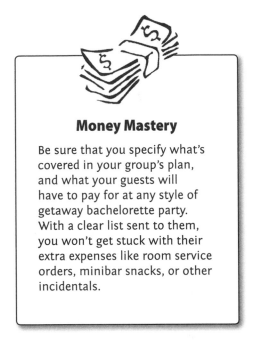

Money Mastery

Be sure that you specify what's covered in your group's plan, and what your guests will have to pay for at any style of getaway bachelorette party. With a clear list sent to them, you won't get stuck with their extra expenses like room service orders, minibar snacks, or other incidentals.

events plans, and dedicated events managers at the ready to create a fabulous and fun itinerary for your group. Disney has a masterful organization designed for planning lavish family celebrations of all kinds from weddings to vow renewals, anniversary parties, birthday parties, and your bachelorette weekend can be planned by its team of expert celebration designers. They'll present you with fun itineraries, design beautiful upscale brunches for you, arrange for spa treatments, dinner reservations, VIP access to the rides, and special Disney-themed gifts presented by Disney characters who greet you in the park. You may even be able to stay in the Cinderella castle.

Take the magic of the theme park and create special moments for the bride. Ask her to share her most unforgettable memories when she came to the park as a child. Ask her family members—if they're not in attendance—to write out their favorite memories of her at the theme park, such as the time Goofy threw her into the men's room, and her Dad went in to rescue her, then got in Goofy's face to tell him to keep his hands off his daughter.

At Disney's Epcot park, you can take your bachelorette party group "around the world" with drinks and eats at each country's pavilion, then stay to see the water and light show. And there's always the late-night club scene that bridal groups love to frequent for drinks and dancing.

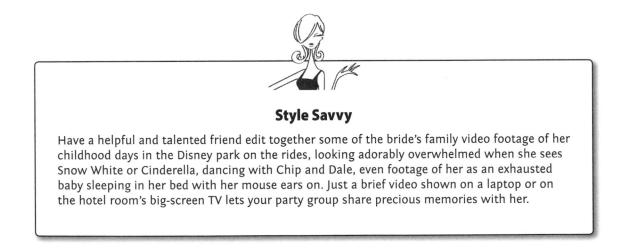

Style Savvy

Have a helpful and talented friend edit together some of the bride's family video footage of her childhood days in the Disney park on the rides, looking adorably overwhelmed when she sees Snow White or Cinderella, dancing with Chip and Dale, even footage of her as an exhausted baby sleeping in her bed with her mouse ears on. Just a brief video shown on a laptop or on the hotel room's big-screen TV lets your party group share precious memories with her.

Explore the many theme parks, large and small, that your group can visit. Visit ParkInfo2Go. com for an impressive list of amusement parks with ride reviews and links to park websites for group rate and discount information.

Island Resort

This is the big one, the one that transports your group to an island resort the way a destination wedding would require guests to pay a sizeable amount for their travel and lodging, all for the experience of sharing a monumental event. Your getaway island resort party can be that monumental event.

Before you panic about expenses totaling thousands of dollars per guest—which would offend the bride's friends and lead to certain regrets when it comes to RSVPs—be aware that many resorts have very affordable weekend packages for everyday travelers, plus additional discounts and freebies for wedding groups.

Caneel Bay in the U.S. Virgin Islands is one of my favorite destinations and also the home of my honeymoon and first anniversary return trip. So I can with all authority report that this is one upscale, pricy resort that offers a jaw-droppingly fabulous four-day, three-night weekend package. With two girls staying comfortably in each room, the price is easily affordable. This example shows that you don't have to rule out big-name resorts and look only at budget hotels, because the tourism industry learned in these past years that it will attract bridal groups through discounted packages. So the Westin, the Hilton, Rosewood Resorts, and all other top name hotels will show discount weekend rates that make this trip doable.

The bride's wedding coordinator may be a priceless ally in your search for the perfect getaway plan for the bride. At the time of this writing, the Association of Bridal Consultants (ABC) offers a special discount rate to Sandals resorts for members' clientele. That means the bride's wedding planner could lead you to a sizeable discount for your group's three days at a Sandals all-inclusive resort.

Money Mastery

Bachelorette party groups qualify for bridal-type discounts and special packages. While the label *bridal* may mean elevated prices in the wedding world, the label *bridal group* most often means discounted packages and opportunities in the travel and tourism world. You have to ask for it, though. Never think that the packages you see on a resort's website are all it has to offer—I've found that 70 percent of the time the resort has additional packages that haven't been posted on the site yet.

Without a wedding coordinator's help, tell everyone involved in booking your trip that you are a bachelorette party group. Travel agents, hotel booking agents, transportation companies (for the limo ride to the airport for all of you), and others will often offer you a special package rate or throw in a discount to treat your group like stars. In return, you each may hire them when it's time to plan your wedding, additional bachelorette parties, or future celebrations.

Now that the business of booking is over, and you've refreshed your familiarity with the travel and lodging advice in Chapter 4, think about the fabulous time your group would have at an amazing island resort lying on the beach under massive umbrellas as golden-bronzed waiters bring frozen margaritas to you; dancing under the stars at a beach concert by a local reggae band that's every bit as impressive as MTV acts; swimming with dolphins and sea turtles; taking a sunset champagne cruise with the girls as a steel drum band plays on board; duty-free shopping in the port city where jewelry, clothing, shoes, and designer sunglasses are available for ridiculously low prices; getting massages on the beach as you look out over impossibly clear waters of the ocean (is this the same planet?!); dining on the freshest of seafood and tropical fruits; hopping over to a neighboring island to sample the culture, food, and attractions there. In four days of "pre-honeymooning" with the girls, you will all enjoy the kinds of activities and conversation that just may not happen if your respective men were in attendance.

Steal My Party Idea

"We were able to get tickets for the bride and six of us to get bleacher seats at the People's Choice Awards red carpet area. So we camped out there, claimed our spots close to the front, screamed our heads off, and saw some amazing celebrities. We worked for almost six months to get the tickets and bring this plan together—including the trip to LA—but it was so worth it!"—Christa, bridesmaid

While you and the bride may each have been avid spring breakers while in your early twenties, perhaps acting wilder than you can believe now, this tropical island getaway with the girls allows you to enjoy a tropical paradise in a far different way. And most bachelorette party groups at tropical resorts say they enjoy the infinity pool, the near-private beach, the same VIP treatment that the resort's celebrity guests enjoy. I personally just missed Brad Pitt and Angelina Jolie at Caneel Bay, and bridal groups say they've spotted Megan Fox and Orlando Bloom at the Hawaiian beach on their tropical getaway. If this getaway is where the stars choose to spend a weekend, imagine the thrill and the thanks you'd get as the planner who chose this VIP-magnet resort for your bride's own bachelorette weekend.

Planning the Details

Now that you've been inspired by the styles of getaway girls' weekends for the bachelorette party—and also for girls' getaways in the future!—now it's time to look at the finer creative details of your party plans. Here, you'll start imagining and assigning the many elements, crafts, and tasks your group will use to make every part of this party impressive.

Invitations

The invitation conveys the location and style of the getaway. It may be the iconic Vegas sign, the logo for the *Food and Wine* festival in Aspen, an image of the island resort's pristine beach, the New York City skyline, or any other transporting image. When guests see the invitation, they immediately know they're headed to this particular locale.

If you'll be creating your own printed cards, your wording helps tell the tale: "It's Girls' Getaway Time for Sarah's Bachelorette Party!" or "We're taking Sarah to Vegas!" or "Come Away With Us to Celebrate Sarah!" Or you might use the phrase that you and the girls have always e-mailed or said to each other: "Road Trip!" And, of course, there's the famous, "We're going to Disneyland!"

Style Savvy

Some resorts, casinos, and hotels have their own collection of invitation e-cards that you can send to your guests. They've thought of everything, and their ready-to-go e-cards are a fabulous, stylish way to get guests excited about the party. So ask if they have a collection you can review. Be warned, though, that they may offer packs of printed cards that may be a bit pricy. Include those in your research, and don't just buy them on impulse because your free e-card sent from a different site could be your saving grace.

Your invitation needs to convey a great many more details than the average traditional invitation. Guests will need to know the when and where, but the invitation is where you share the special discounts you snagged for the group and the lineup of amazing activities you'll enjoy. So the invitation sent via e-mail will include a link to the resort itself, so that everyone can see where they're headed.

Since additional planning will almost surely need to be done as you collect RSVPs and book rooms and room-shares for guests, a vital line on the invitation is "More info to come." This calms those guests who may be likely to call you in a fluster, wanting additional information about what this trip will cost, what's included, what's not included, and a flurry of additional concerns. Some guests even send over their meal restrictions and requirements on day one. Calm those fired-up guests by promising more details as soon as you have them.

Menu Items

The big issue here is whether or not food and drink are included in an all-inclusive package that you arrange, or if you'll pay as you go with every meal and every round of drinks. It takes some investigation, including looking at the resort's restaurant menus and bar list, and thinking about your group's likelihood to indulge, so that you can do the math and figure out if each person will use the $100 or so per day that the all-inclusive or meal plan rates provide. When you add up estimated meals, snacks, and drinks via the menus, you may find that a good estimate per person is $200 per day, so that all-inclusive or meal plan would be a savings.

Whichever plan you take, talk with the group events planner at your resort to arrange for private breakfasts, brunches, or dinners on a prix fixe plan, also keeping expenses down while still providing an impressive array of gourmet treats.

No More Drama

Rather than schedule and cater every meal during the getaway, leave some lunches and dinners unplanned. Then as a group you can hit the town to discover inexpensive eateries that the locals love or that your hotel's concierge recommends. Concierges don't get offended if you say you'd like to dine off the resort property, and they know where the best deals are. They also have packets of coupons to hand out at select eateries, so they're a smart resource and your guests will appreciate that you're taking smart steps to save them money. Of course, if you're on an all-inclusive plan, you might just stay with those unlimited menus at your resort and all drama is avoided.

Cake and Dessert

At your destination, talk with the events manager to arrange for a special dessert surprise for the bride on one night of your visit, usually at the main celebration dinner. You might have an artistic cake designed by the resort's team of award-winning cake masters, or select an array of dessert bites as a sampler platter for your party group. From little crème brûlées to chocolate mousse bites to sinful molten chocolate cake, your choices create an indulgent celebratory dessert for the bride.

If you'll be staying in a shore house or ski house, not in a hotel environment, then it's up to you to get a fabulous celebratory cake and desserts from a local bakery. Don't try to drive hours with a cake in your back seat. Research area bakeries to find a fantastic one, and pick up a cake from its display case to bring right over the house. You'll serve it as part of your first night celebration, then everyone gets to snack on it throughout the duration of your stay.

During your daily and nightly adventures and touring, stop in at local flavor spots like gelato bars or fudge shops to grab mini dessert bites along your path. Some of the most delectable dessert discoveries happen by chance, by turning a corner and stumbling onto the most amazing dessert crêpe place or ice cream shoppe with servers in 1950s outfits and sock hop music blaring.

Drinks

Be adventurous. Check out the local drink specials and vintages as you absorb the flavor of the location you've chosen. If you're preparing your own drinks, such as at a beach house, collect fabulous drink recipes at Cocktail.com and whip up creative drinks with a theme for each night of your stay.

And since your task as a host is to fulfill the guests' needs during all hours of the day and night, be sure you're supplied with plenty of coffees, teas, milk (2%, 1%, skim, and soy for the best buffet), sugars, and cups for all. Even if hotel rooms will have complimentary coffees, it's smart to provide small bags of known-brand coffees and some herbal teas so that guests have at hand tastes they know they enjoy.

Favors

The goodie bags that you have placed in each guest's room count as favors, to be enjoyed all through their stay. Choose iconic local items, such as fudge squares at the beach, fluffy spa socks and lotions, packets of hot chocolate for a winter getaway (make it Godiva hot chocolate to treat your guests well!), wine bottle stoppers for their use on that bottle of cabernet they have in their room, wine-flavored truffles, and, of course, bottles of water and soda as freebies they won't have to get from the gift shop. Mix pampering items with edibles, and the goodie/favor bag is a welcome treat.

Entertainment

Rarely will a destination bachelorette party group need to book entertainment. After all, when you're in Vegas, you can go to nightclubs

Money Mastery

Overshop at your local discount liquor store, getting perhaps a case of wine for your group's enjoyment during the weekend. If you bring more than you'll need, you won't find yourself overspending at the resort town's local liquor store where prices are increased. And bring plenty of mixers, as well: sodas, juices, tonic water, Tom Collins mix, and other extras that can be divided among all of you if any leftovers remain at the end of the weekend.

and to an all-male revue if the bride wants her moment with male dancers. On a tropical island, steel drum music plays at the restaurants and terrace bars. A beach resort may have free cover band concerts or musicians playing by the pool. The amusement park is nothing but entertainment. The opportunities are endless no matter where you go, and the attention you get as a bachelorette party group attracts even more festive frolicking and freebies.

Special Additional Touches

Since not every close friend of the bride will be able to attend a getaway bachelorette party—due to budget or work schedule, pregnancy, another wedding on the calendar, or other life obligation—it's a smart idea to include those missing out by taking lots of fun photos including one with a big sign saying, We Miss Claire (with Claire, of course, being the friend who couldn't make it.) Pick up some touristy keepsakes for those close friends of the bride such as nice T-shirts to let them know you were thinking of them. The bride will love this gesture for her faraway friends.

Special Surprises and Events

One of the biggest thrills a bride can get is when a faraway friend makes a surprise appearance at her getaway bachelorette party. If the bride has been active in planning the party, some element should be a surprise so why not the gift of a long-distance friend's attendance at the celebration? With a wink to you, the long-distance friend, sister, or cousin sends her RSVP with regrets marked, but you've secretly arranged for her room to be booked in your group, a ride available for her at the airport or train station, and, of course, a grand entrance.

The surprise friend might pop into the bride's suite during your group's first night cocktail party before you go out to dinner. Cameras flash, the bride is thrilled beyond words, and the party's the hit of her lifetime from the very start.

Or, the surprise friend might be sitting on the porch of the bed-and-breakfast when your group drives up. She can prearrange for champagne and glasses to be on the porch table so that you all can toast to the overwhelmed bride's happiness and the start of a fabulous weekend.

Other surprises to arrange for the bride:

➤ Serenades by singers or musicians at an outdoor concert or in a restaurant

➤ Having her participate in a comedian's act (you've tipped off the manager beforehand that you have a bride with your group)

➤ The hotel's VIP bride welcome basket, with a spa robe, chocolates, pampering items, and more, awaiting her in her room

➤ A floral arrangement awaiting her in her hotel room

➤ A card from the groom left on her pillow in her room

➤ Video greetings from friends who couldn't attend the party

➤ Tickets to a show or concert that's taking place while you're in town

➤ A surprise-a-day plan in which the bride receives a little something fun each day of your stay. It could be that note from the groom, a kitschy present from the gift shop, or that bracelet you saw her admiring in a shop during the day's travels (someone went back and bought it for her!)

One of the big surprises that bachelorette party groups arrange is a limousine awaiting them at the airport, ready to take them to the hotel. Forget that crowded shuttle or cabs; you can book an inexpensive ride in style with the help of the hotel's or resort's concierge so that the party starts the moment you arrive at your destination.

 # Games

In This Chapter

➤ Variations on the standards

➤ Telling games

➤ Stripper-centric game options

➤ Games to match your theme

➤ Racy and tame prizes

You might wish to plan games to add to the party's excitement. I say *might* because some party hosts and guests hate it when they're summoned to participate in organized group fun. They don't see these friends very often, so they'd rather have time to talk at a fabulous gathering rather than spend a half hour listing what's in their purse or pinning the manhood on the man. Some brides don't want racy games planned for a party that includes their mothers or future in-laws, and some are just not game enthusiasts. As a great host, you must consult with the bride as to whether or not she wants games planned for her party.

If she's excited about having games but doesn't want the same-old cliché games that everyone's played at every other bachelorette party and bridal shower, this chapter will help you give classic games a fresh, new twist, and will also help you plan unique games tailored to the party's theme.

Before you start, consider which games to play, keeping in mind that brief game sessions are most welcome to party guests. Again, guests want to chat, enjoy the food and drinks, toast to the bride, and they can't do so if they're falling asleep while a lengthy game drags on. So choose games that provide quick thrills and laughs, then allow everyone to return to unstructured social time.

Twist the Standard Games

Party guests don't want to play the same games they've played a dozen times at other brides' parties, and party hosts don't want to be thought of as unimaginative. Many classic traditional bachelorette party games can be given a twist of originality.

Pin the Macho on the Man

The first game that probably comes to mind when you think bachelorette party is Pin the Macho on the Man, which has blindfolded guests being spun around a few times, then sent teetering toward a poster of a hot naked or nearly naked man with a penis-shaped card in her hands. She presses it onto the poster to see how close she is to where that penis should be. The one who gets theirs closest or right on target wins. Other guests cheer her on or shout out directions.

Keeping it racy, but a bit less X-rated, a twist on this can be Pin the G-String on the Man, with the players approaching the poster holding out a G-String-shaped card to cover the area. As a creative angle, guests can choose from a variety of G-string or Speedo designs such as leopard print; hot pink, black with a glittery silver initial, or other wild motifs.

If you have a poster of a fireman, you could play Pin the Hose on the Fireman. A baseball player presents the chance to Pin the Bat on the Ballplayer, with the intention being to get it in his hands, and the ones that land further south elicit laughs and cheers.

If the bride is a fan of an actor or movie character, his poster can go up on the wall with your choice of stick-it-on-him items ranging from X-rated to tame such as heart-shaped photos of the bride.

How Well Do You Know the Bride?

This game can sometimes cause uncomfortable moments if the groom's invited family doesn't know the bride as well as her friends. That circle of newer guests is at a clear disadvantage, and it's never fun to feel like the least knowledgeable person in the room. So twist this game to make it a memory game instead. At one point in the party, have the bride leave the room. Then give everyone a game card asking them to describe what the bride is wearing, what color nail polish she has on, if she has a right-hand ring on, etc. It then becomes a game of observation, which puts everyone on the same playing level.

Pass the Vibrator

In this traditional racy game, everyone stands in a circle and passes from person to person either an actual vibrator (new) or a toy vibrator designed for just this game (some models light up when time is up). With music playing, everyone passes the toy around. When the music stops, the person holding the toy is out.

If you like the idea of the game, but not the vibrator, change it to pass the cucumber or pass the panties, using lacy, racy panties you've purchased new as a party prop.

Hot Word

This one is played at so many parties that some guests fear the appearance of clothespins or other props that mean they're going to have something clipped to their shirt and ripped off of them aggressively if they happen to say a certain word that's been chosen as the hot word of the party. It may be the bride's name, the word *wedding*, the groom's name, curse words, or—most annoyingly, the word *like* that some people say in their regular speech patterns (as in, "I was so, like, excited to see that!" and "I was like, Um, *yeah!*")

Ask the bride about this style of game, since she may have strong feelings about not having her guests afraid to speak, or chastised by others for being so forgetful about the hot word. If she's game for it, twist the hot word style to remove those clothespins or other items from people's bodies, and have them keep a pile of poker chips by them. When they utter the hot word, they lose a chip. That's far less annoying than giving people grains of rice for others to take from them, which was suggested on a top bridal website recently.

In the classic version, the winner is the one who winds up with the most chips, but that's just likely to be the person who hovered over everyone, listening to their conversations, waiting for that forbidden word, yelling *Aha!* and grabbing that clothespin off of shirts. That's a party wrecker. In your new version, you might reward the person who said the bride's name the most, since she's all about the bride's happiness. Or the person who said the most curse words, as a surprise to all.

Keep this game brief, since guests won't want to be on guard about their speech for more than a half hour, tops.

Style Savvy

Some games are considered out of style, and even if they were classics years ago, they're not finding a place at today's parties. These include Word Search and Word Scramble games, What's In Your Purse? (in which the person with the purse that has the largest collection of items from a list wins), 'What's in the Bride's Purse?' (which can be embarrassing if she doesn't know the game is planned, and she has prescriptions or other personal items in there).

Confessions and Advice

When you get guests talking, especially if they've been drinking and your party has a racy tone to it, the games get wild and the guests get loud. In this section, you'll consider (and perhaps twist to your liking) some of the most popular guest input games.

I Never

You may have played it at slumber parties when you were a tween, with the questions having to do with whether or not you kissed a boy. Now, the questions get racier, and this one can turn into a drinking game if you'd like. In your game of I Never, you create a list of sexy situations and read them out loud. Anyone who hasn't done that particular sex act or had that sexy experience either takes a drink or loses a poker chip. Again, the winner can be the one who winds up with the most poker chips, or the most innocent person can be the winner and gets the prize: a book on spicing up your love life, a sexy toy, or a T-shirt saying I was the Pure One at Stacy's Bachelorette Party.

Some suggestions for your I Never game card include:

➤ I Never…had sex on a first date

➤ I Never…made out with an ex's friend

➤ I Never…had sex in a car

➤ I Never…laughed during sex

➤ I Never…told a small guy he was the biggest I'd ever seen

And so on. Be creative and making up these questions with your co-planners will be almost as much fun as playing the actual game.

Guess Whose Sexual Fantasy

On hot-pink index cards, have each guest write down her wildest sexual fantasy, with full details. The bride then has to guess which guest has which fantasy. Her guesses, wrong and right, make the party hysterical fun, especially if she finds out the wildest one is from her future mother-in-law.

Another twist on this game is having guests write down the wildest place they've ever made love, and the bride guesses who was on the D train, and who was in the back of a limo.

A to Z

On a sheet of paper, list to the left all of the letters from A to Z, and guests have to write down words or phrases starting with each letter. This game has infinite variations, from naming the bride's exes (but only if there are no groom relatives there!) to naming sexual acts and sexy items, or items to use on the wedding night. You can also do this one as a tame game, with guests asked to write down words related to the bride's personality and life. The person with the most entries wins the prize.

Sex Life Advice

Each guest writes down on an index card her best advice for keeping the spice in the bride and groom's marriage. The bride then has to guess which guest contributed which nugget of wisdom.

Stripper Games

If you'll have a male dancer perform at the party, you can base a game on him. After he does his act and leaves, that is. You don't want to make him uncomfortable with a game he's not aware is going on, such as giving guests points for touching him on different body parts or handing him dollar bills in different sexy ways.

Instead, have guests take a fun quiz about the stripper and his act. If he'd performed multiple songs, have each guest write down the names of the songs he danced to.

Another twist on the Stripper Game is having guests fill out a questionnaire that tests their powers of observation. You can ask:

> ➤ What color were the dancer's eyes?

Steal My Party Idea

"We wanted a quick game, so we had everyone write down their guesses as to which color bra the bride was wearing. Once everyone wrote down and submitted their guesses, we had the bride flash her bra to the room. Everyone who was right got a prize—a chocolate bra!" — Emily, bridesmaid

➤ How many tattoos did the dancer have on his arms?

➤ What was the word the dancer had tattooed on his bicep?

➤ What color was his G-string?

➤ What was the dancer's name?

➤ Who was the second person to give the dancer a dollar bill?

➤ What was the first thing the dancer did to the bride?

And so on. This game keeps the energy the dancer brought to the party going full tilt.

As a fun activity, have party guests write down on a sheet of paper the songs they suggest for the groom to strip to for the bride. Everyone gets a laugh, and the groom is given the list for his use.

Theme Games

For tame parties and classy nights out, you don't need to schedule games at all, since your theme may provide all the entertainment and enjoyment needed. A spa party, for instance, has guests visiting pampering stations like a foot massage area or a mani/pedi table, and the relaxed atmosphere doesn't welcome the energy level of a wild game, or any game for that matter.

But you might wish to plan a theme-centered game for the ending hours of the party, after everyone has unwound, when treatments are over and champagne sipped for the better part of the afternoon. A tame game for this particular style of party involves having the bride and guests smell different aromatherapy lotions and write down the scent for each unlabeled vial. They may get vanilla or sandalwood, or they may need to tell the difference between orange and tangerine. This scent challenge leads to the prize of a basket of aromatherapy lotions.

For a charity-themed party, prior to which everyone ran or walked a 5K, or worked on a charity home build, a game might center on trivia about the bride and groom, and the winner gets a theme-matched prize such as a pink headband for a breast cancer walk, or a pink mini flashlight to match the theme of that house build. If your charity centered on gardening, the winner might get a gift card to a gardening catalog or a garden center.

If your party's destination is a fine restaurant where yell-out-the-answers games would not be tolerated, you can still conduct a game, such as by distributing cards for guests to write down their best honeymoon, sex life, or marriage advice, and the bride can read the tamer ones out loud, keeping the rest as a memento of the party.

Prizes

Racy games call for racy prizes, such as chocolate body paint, edible panties, and edible body glitter. I just stopped by LingerieDiva. com, and I found a fabulous collection of inexpensive body paints—from chocolate to glow-in-the-dark—as well as a trio of chocolate paints in three different chocolate flavors, which would make a fantastic prize that's sexy and stylish. Heart-shaped boxes of body paints also remove the sleaze factor that you might not like in more X-rated prizes found on bachelorette party websites.

For tamer bachelorette parties, prizes can be tied to the theme. For the spa party, the game prize can be a luxurious basket of aromatherapy lotions or a gift card to a local flower shop with a note explaining that this prize allows the winner to pick out a bouquet of roses in her color choice, with the petals to be used in setting a romantic and sexy scene for her man or to indulge herself with a petal-filled bath.

Style Savvy

For a destination party, be sure that your gift purchase is something stylish and usable, not the cliché shell necklaces that are found in the gift shop. If you're at an island resort, local artisans often sell their wares on the beach or in tiny little gift booths in the main city.

For parties with a food theme, a prize can be an autographed celebrity cookbook—bought in person or on eBay—or a collection of hot, new cookbooks in a basket. Foodies love exotic spices, so the prize may be a collection of those little bottles of menu enhancers.

If you're away at a destination bachelorette party, that shopping outing your group takes can be your perfect opportunity to pick up a dazzling $15 bracelet made of island sea glass and present it later as the game prize. Any local treasure will do.

Presentation is key when you're giving out the prizes, so be sure that each item is wrapped prettily, with obvious effort put into it. You could certainly buy $1 gift bags at the craft store, but it impresses guests far more when you create a display presentation such as items set in a pretty woven wood basket, propped up for all to see, perhaps sitting on metallic tinsel filler rather than on crumpled tissue paper. It's these tiny accents that make a big impression.

WORKSHEETS

Use the following worksheets to keep yourself and your co-planners ultra-organized as you plan the bride's big celebration.

As you know, being organized cuts down planning stress, and it can also save you money. Keeping track of who's buying what means no one is buying an extra set of unneeded decorations or invitations and then expecting the group to split the cost. Keeping track of your budget with this worksheet helps you avoid extra spending in any category.

So use these worksheets here in this book for the fastest, easiest, and most efficient way to keep all of your info in one place.

Planning Timeline

Six months before the party:

_____ Talk with the bride to find out her desired party style, location, size, and other preferences

_____ Get the bride's guest list from her, along with each guest's addresses or e-mails

_____ Get the bride's wished-for party dates that work best in her busy schedule

_____ Contact the bridesmaids or other co-planners to begin organizing your party tasks

Five months before the party:

_____ Team of planners starts scouting locations for the party

_____ Team of planners starts researching caterers and other essential experts for the party

_____ Team of planners starts researching possible entertainers for the party, asking friends for referrals to who they've hired, etc.

Four months before the party:

_____ If this will be a destination/getaway party, decide on the location and arrange a group travel discount

_____ Send all destination/getaway party guests an e-mail detailing the travel and lodging plans for the party, and ask them to book their trips

_____ If the party will take place during a busy party or holiday season, send out save-the-date cards now

_____ Decide on and book the party's location

_____ Decide on and book the caterer

_____ Decide on and book the menu

_____ Talk with your caterer about any extra rental needs he or she requires you to cover

_____ Arrange for your rentals order, and pay the deposit

_____ If your party takes place during busy prom or wedding season, book your limousine or party bus now

_____ Let your co-planners know how much money they owe you (or others) at this point, and request their payments

Three months before the party:

_____ If you haven't already, book your limos or other transportation

_____ Decide on and book your entertainers

_____ Decide on and book your experts

_____ Send your co-planner reminders about any payments due

Two months before the party:

_____ Send out invitations

_____ Order decorations

One month before the party:

_____ Confirm with your co-planners who is working on which remaining tasks, and how they're coming along.

_____ Begin any DIY projects

_____ Decide on games that will be played during the party, and get supplies

_____ Create your party playlist and load your iPod with party soundtrack songs

_____ Confirm your location reservation

_____ Confirm your bookings with your experts

_____ Confirm your booking with your entertainers

_____ Confirm your rentals order

_____ Confirm your transportation order

_____ Confirm your travel plans and lodging

_____ Decide on your cake's style and flavors, and order the cake

_____ Order any additional desserts

Two weeks before the party:

_____ Find something cute to wear to the party and buy all accessories as well

_____ Finish any DIY projects for the party, wrap and label favors, and set aside

One week before the party:

_____ Send out reminder e-mails to guests, giving them the details on where to arrive, limo rides, how to dress, and more essential information

_____ Confirm the delivery details of any rented items that will be delivered to your party site

_____ Create your last-minute shopping list (ice, etc.) and assign shopping tasks to your team

_____ Remind any co-planners about outstanding payments required

One to two days before the party:

_____ Shop for food, snacks, desserts, drinks, ice, and other supplies

_____ Pick up single-use cameras for everyone to use during the party

_____ Prep menu items like slicing lemons and limes, etc.

_____ Put your china, crystal, dishes, glasses, and serving platters through the dishwasher

_____ Clean the house where the party will take place

_____ Have your car washed, if you will be driving friends to and from the party

_____ Decorate the party space

_____ Stock items for the morning after the party—breakfast foods, extra coffee, aspirin, etc.

_____ Assemble your emergency bag to bring along to the party

_____ Charge your cell phone

_____ Hit the ATM to get cash

_____ Pick up any friends who are coming into town for the big party

_____ Arrange a pickup plan with the other co-planners—who's picking up the cake, décor items, and other items

_____ Get a mani/pedi before the party day

_____ Confirm with entertainer, experts, limo company, and more so that everything's likely to go extremely smoothly

_____ Make and arrange any game props or game areas for the party

_____ Arrange all of the bride's props like her tiara and veil or T-shirt, plus wrapped gag gifts, and set them on a table for her discovery

Day of the party:

_____ Check to be sure you have all of the food and drink items you need, plus lots of ice

_____ Complete cleaning and decorating

_____ Welcome the bride and her guests to the party!

_____ Have an amazing time!

After the party:

_____ Send thank-you notes to everyone who helped plan the party and to all of your experts

_____ Send co-planners a reminder of any money they owe to you or to another co-planner

_____ Develop or share online the photos from the party

Guest List

Name	E-mail	RSVP Received √	Attending √

Shopping List

Item	Type/Style/Color	How Many Needed	Where to Buy	Who's Buying

Budget Chart

Item	$ Budgeted	Actual Cost	Person to Reimburse	Paid √
Invitations				
Catering				
Cake				
Desserts				
Drinks: alcohol				
Drinks: mixers				
Ice				
Rental items				
Décor				
Craft items				
Entertainment				
Experts (spa & beauty, massage, etc.)				
Transportation: rides				
Transportation: lodging				
Transportation: other				
Games				
Photography				
Other:				

Itinerary—Rides

If you'll book a limo or other type of transportation, your driver will need to know where to be, who to pick up, when, and where you'll all go next. So use this driving itinerary to organize everyone, and you'll all get where you need to be without expensive waiting or not-fun confusion.

Pickup #1:
Picking up:
Location:
Contact phone number:
Pickup #2:
Picking up:
Location:
Contact phone number:
Location #1:
Name:
Location:
Pickup time:
Location #2:
Name:
Location:
Pickup time:
Location #3:
Name:
Location:
Pickup time:
Drop-off #1:
Dropping off:
Location:
Drop-off #2:
Dropping off:
Location:
Drop-off #3:
Dropping off:
Location:

IMPORTANT!! Phone number of the limo company dispatch line, for when you need to call your driver to pick you up and take you to the next place:

RESOURCES

The following websites are listed here for your research purposes. We don't endorse any particular sites, and we encourage you to practice smart online shopping at all times!

Invitations

Evite.com

Hallmark.com

MountainCow.com

PapyrusOnline.com

Pingg.com

PSAEssentials.com

Shindigz.com

Shutterfly.com

WeddingMapper.com

Crafts and DIY Items

BellaCupcakeCouture.com (cupcake wrappers!)

Michaels.com

Target.com

Walmart.com

Wilton.com (cake and cupcakes supplies)

Bachelorette Party Décor, Props, Games and Prizes

Bachelorette.com

BacheloretteParties.com

BachelorettePartyDepot.com

BachelorettePartyStore.com

BacheloretteSuperstore.com

BridalGuide.com

Brides.com

TheHouseofBachelorette.com

TheKnot.com

WeddingChannel.com

X-Rated Items

Available at all bachelorette party sites above, plus:

LingerieDiva.com

PajamaParties.com (X-rated toys and props parties)

Coupons and Deals

CouponCabin.com

CouponMountain.com

Coupons.com

RetailMeNot.com

SwagGrabber.com

Favors and Gifts

Amazon.com

AuraCacia.com

Bn.com

BathandBodyWorks.com

Borders.com

CafePress.com

CherylandCompany.com

CustomInk.com

eBay.com

Envirosax.com

Godiva.com

KateAspen.com

Kodak.com

Shutterfly.com

Target.com

Tiffany.com

Walmart.com

Food and Cakes

AllRecipes.com

Bethenny.com

BHG.com

CookingLight.com

FoodandWine.com

FoodNetwork.com

HansenCakes.com

MarthaStewart.com

MixingBowl.com
PaulaDeen.com
RachaelRayMag.com
Wilton.com

Drinks

Cocktails.About.com
Bethenny.com
Cocktail.com
CocktailTimes.com
DrinkJockey.com
DrinkMixer.com
Evite.com (bar stock calculator!)
FoodNetwork.com
SuperCocktails.com
ThatstheSpirit.com
TheBar.com
Webtender.com
WineSpectator.com

Restaurants

Restaurants.com
Travelandleisure.com (World's Best Awards)
Yelp.com
Zagats.com

Travel

AAA.com
BnBFinder.com
Expedia.com
Festivals.com
OnLocationVacations.com
Orbitz.com
ParkInfo2Go.com
ResortsOnline.com
Towd.com (Tourism Office Worldwide Directory)

Check the websites of the hotel chains you're considering for a destination bachelorette party. They often have group rates for special events like weddings and family reunions, and you can call to arrange the same special rates for your bachelorette party group! You *are* a group, after all!

INDEX